HEY,
IT'S
ONLY
LUCKY
ME!

HEY, IT'S ONLY LUCKY ME!

DANIEL J. MOLONEY

Parchment Global Publishing
1500 Market Street, 12th Floor, East Tower
Philadelphia, Pennsylvania, 19102
www.parchmentglobalpublishing.com

ISBN 978-1-963068-88-7 (sc)

Library of Congress Control Number: 2024927065

2025.01.15

FOREWORD

As I have often said to Daniel, "I wasn't consulted on being here, but now that I am, I'm not in a hurry to leave!" when we have been in the throes of discussing the meaning of our lives. Daniel has chosen to believe that it has all been a matter of being lucky, hence this book's title, and he maybe hopes that this delightful set of memoirs will be similarly lucky and a runaway best seller.

At the very least the book leaves a trace of Daniel's long strides across the World which is luckier than the experience and fortunes of most of us. But though the title is a modest disclaimer in the casual style of the regular Ozzie bloke, I believe that luck only comes about when you are ready for it, and have the personal attributes that make you grasp the many possibilities that 'luck' seems to bring.

So let's enumerate those attributes that make my life-long friend the remarkable young fellow I have known. First of all, he is tall and that goes a long way with the ladies, and even the blokes when reaching over the scrambling pack. He has always loved and participated in oh so many sports, and even now his beloved Sydney Swans continue to look down over the dismal scores of my beloved Carlton in our weekly phone post? mortems.

Next is his remarkable ability to maintain his many loyal friendships over the years by continual correspondence and, wherever possible, return visits. The memoirs are peppered with his reunions of more than forty years of first meeting and conversations that seem to last from dawn to dusks. Whenever he meets these friends he has the great merit of always being able to pick up on the last words of that conversation.

Ever initially flexible, he has turned his hand to rapid quick-start learning curves sometimes demanding hard physical yacka or almost delightful paradisiacal rests in charming company, but beneath the endless yearnings of the traveller who can take it as it comes, no matter how wealthy or poor the country is, from First World down to Third World and even beyond that.

He is endlessly curious on these trips and a great omnivorous reader who soaks up the history of the country he is visiting, comments on national differences with a righteous desire for egalitarian justice at the same time a love of nature and landscape that leads time and again to an ecological understanding that we must not continue to waste the World's great resources.

His temperament cannot be confused with that of the Hippy and one sees he can be entrepreneur, as a restaurateur feeding a Prime Minister, or swinging deals with Border guards with generous giftings of liquor and artefacts, or riding out in dubious company of a gambling bout over cards or casinos.

A man for all seasons, and a mate in any fight, but not a braggart and quite capable of the humorous put down of himself when it hits his ironic sense of humour.

Much of his life we have all shared or had in common, but the opening section of his travels in Ethiopia had me gob-smacked, travelling in a country that even now few Australians have ever seen. Before this I had only once had an insight in that country and that was of all places in London, when I came upon a Rastafarian in Hyde Park Corner in Speakers' Corner talking of Haile Selassie and the Queen of Sheba. Dan's writing soon disabused me of my romantic notions of that amazing and ancient country.

Come aboard then dear reader for a lifetime and delight in the amazing twists and turns in Daniel Moloney's journeys in the here and now and onwards for we hope many more eventful years. Treat him as your elder brother who will see you through thick and thin.

Peter JEFFERY OAM
Poet, literary judge, anthologist, broadcaster,
film maker and what you will
PERTH WA 2019

CONTENTS

FOREWORD v

THE WAR YEARS 1

INTERSTATE MOVE 4

FIRST SCHOOL DAYS 8

BOARDING SCHOOL... 16

CHRISTIAN BROTHERS PERTH 29

AND SO, TO WORK 34

FAREWELL AUSTRALIA 51

HELLO WORLD 54

A FEW BEERS IN MUNICH.. 61

TRAVELLING ON... 64

AND SO, TO WORK 67

TRAVELLING ON... 71

A YEAR IN GERMANY 74

BACK ACROSS 'THE DITCH' 87

AND NOW FOR A 'PROPER' JOB, AND 'HOME' 93

BACK ON THE ROAD AGAIN 100

DESTINATION JERUSALEM FOR CHRISTMAS 110

IN KUWAIT 119

BAGHDAD AND BEYOND 123

FABULOUS EGYPT 132

SUDAN AND AFRICA PROPER 137

A COUPLE OF MONTHS IN ETHIOPIA......................... 141

KENYA AND EAST AFRICA... 161

AT SEA, SEYCHELLES, BOMBAY 176

INDIA, MAINLY BY TRAIN... 178

CEYLON, OR, IF YOU LIKE, SRI LANKA 185

MOTHER INDIA AGAIN 192

LEAVING INDIA..200

BANGKOK TO BALI...201

LEAVING BALI 213

FLORES 221

FAREWELL INDONESIA, HELLO TIMOR.......................................230

BACK HOME AGAIN 234

POST TRAVEL REFLECTIONS.. 235

TENNANT CREEK 237

SYDNEY OR BUST!..240

THE OUTBACK BY AIR..248

LE ZIG ZIG 253

TELECHECK 257

THE NEXT SIX YEARS... 263

THIS SPORTING LIFE AND INDIA..264

LIVING ALONE.. 267

A MONTH IN VIETNAM... 269

BROTHER BRIAN, SISTER CAROL.. 271

ENOUGH OF WORKING, LIFE AS A "GREY NOMAD".............. 272

UKRAINE, EASTERN EUROPE AND S/E ASIA 274

OZ AGAIN 279

ELEVEN MONTHS AROUND AUSTRALIA....................................280

CANADA, AMERICA AND IRELAND 284

STOPOVER IN HERTFORDSHIRE..290

WHERE THINGS BECOME UNSTUCK 292

GERMANY, BUT NOT A GREAT HOLIDAY 294

AUSTRALIA AGAIN.. 296

CHINA 299

CARAVAN'S DEMISE, TRAVEL WITHOUT....................................301

RELIGION 304
THE DREADED 'SETTLE DOWN' PHASE 306
ANOTHER SALUTORY LESSON 309
TRAVELS IN AUSTRALIA 310
THE STATE OF THINGS, THROUGH MY JAUNDICED EYE 313

Perched precariously on the back of the truck, along with about a dozen others, we lurched though the Ethiopian rain forest. My companions, Tom from Wisconsin, an old lady with no nose, the result I am told, of a syphilitic birth, and a few local travellers. The second day of our journey to the Kenyan border. During the afternoon, we came to a large clearing, which the driver refused to cross as it was too wet and boggy, so he took a detour around the edge. Tommy and I walked across, and halfway encountered two camels and their driver. The camels were heavily loaded, and one camel decided 'enough is enough', and sat down on the job. No amount of swearing, kicking, punching, and cigarette burning would change his mind. Looking at his face I was reminded of the Arab explanation for the prayer beads having 99 beads; each bead naming one of the names of God. Only the camel knows the 100 names of Allah, hence the supercilious expression the camel displays. Having lost the battle, the driver unloaded, at which the camel lurched to his feet and took off across the clearing, driver in screaming pursuit. Eventually the truck made it to the other side of the clearing and we proceeded to the next village. Somehow, I found a bed, and realized that I had lost my 'Lucky' ring, which my friend Abdul Wahad in Baghdad had, against my protestations, insisted I have. Later it appeared on the doorstep of my room, courtesy no doubt of one of my fellow travellers; only to be lost a couple of years later in a car crash in Sydney, where I had earlier burst upon an unsuspecting world.

THE WAR YEARS

Being born obviously not something burned into my memory. Sydney 1941, my father Harold an Intelligence Officer in the RAAF, my mother Mary Lois, called Lois, a Trained Nurse, me the first born. War being war, Dad was often away from home, which was a flat on Pacific Highway, Artarmon on Sydney's North Shore, and Mum was also working in various hospitals around Sydney.

Because of the nature of my parents' lives I was sometimes farmed out to some institutions for a few weeks at a time. My only real memory of this place is when Mum brought a cake for my birthday, probably my third. Said cake was given to a staff member for me but I never got to see, or more importantly eat any of it. I am not sure if I am correct but ever since I have believed that the culprit was an Irish nurse, though what a three-year-old would know about Irish nurses is problematic to say the least. However, ever since when asked, I describe myself as half English half Irish and all Australian; Mum being C of E and Dad Catholic.

Contrary to the opinions of many I regard myself a soppy romantic and cite in evidence my love affair with the three-year-old blonde girl from down the street. I can still recall in detail a dream I had when I was probably three; the girl had been in a car accident, and I wanted to have her come and stay at our home, but parents would not allow. Over the years I have had some dreams recurring. One such had me believing I had killed someone and was afraid of being found out, another that I had stolen a motor bike and dreaded discovery. One that really scared me I had only once when I woke in a cold sweat believing I had dreamed that I was, in words I still recall, 'The Epitome of Evil'. Catholic teachings of Hell and Punishment of Bad Boys like me bearing fruit. Dreams, recurring or not, stay with me only very fleetingly; one that did recently, recently being 2017, was 'Sherlock Holmes' first job; threading 800 glass beads onto a string.' Analyse that Carl Junge!

As a child, I was an incorrigible attention seeker, which I suppose is not that unusual, however a couple of occasions come to mind. Once when we were entertaining a few people for lunch, I decided that not enough attention was being given to my scintillating three-year-old personality so decided that I would show all how a glass of milk should be drunk, placed it on the floor and lapped at it like a dog. The applause was underwhelming, but at least they looked at me, albeit a little strangely.

I was also acutely aware of my capacity to hurt people, most vividly illustrated by an unfortunate incident with Mrs Webster who lived next door and was always looking out for me with drinks and cakes. One day in her house I took a fancy to a can opener she had, so I took it. Mum saw it and told me to take it back. I did and saw she was watching through the window, so I just threw it into the garden; all she did was look a little sad and never mentioned it. Thinking of my petulance still evinces a wince.

The War was always present, although I had little idea of what it was all about. I knew Dad was in it, as were all my uncles. Dad's brother Cecil was also in the RAAF, and Mum's brothers, Bob, Alan, Paul and Benny were in the Army; all served overseas except Dad, who to his eternal frustration remained in Australia, serving as an Intelligence Officer in the Air Force, from Cooktown in North Queensland to Pearce WA, where he was demobbed in 1945. Benny was the rebel; while posted in New Guinea as a fighter pilot he buzzed the control tower in Rabaul, a feat which was evidently captured in a cartoon which was once in the Australian War Memorial in Canberra, and led to him being grounded and put on ground crew. Benny later worked for a taxi company in Sydney as a radio operator.

Alan served in Palestine, Greece & Crete, before returning to Australia and spending a lot of time in North Queensland. He was in the evacuation of both Greece and Crete and was lucky to survive bomber and fighter attacks in both places. Paul and Bob were both in New Guinea for the duration. Mum's sister Sylvia joined the Army to be close to her brothers, and was an Army Nurse in New Guinea, Palestine and Europe. Uncle Bob stayed in the Army after the War and served in the Korean War. When he returned to Australia he was welcomed in Uncle Paul's flat, next door to Sylvia's in Pacific Highway. I think this was my first attempt at musical appreciation. He had brought some records back from Japan, and while everyone was busy talking I took a fancy to Bing Crosby singing 'Walk me by the River' and thought the way to learn the words was to play the record a few times while I committed same words to memory. I must have played it six or seven times before Bob finally thought that was enough. I still remember the words. Bob survived two wars before taking up a soldier settlement in Queensland. One day he was pulling a ball and chain by tractor, clearing scrub when the chain caught on a tree and sprang back hitting him in the back. He lay in the paddock for hours with a broken back which killed him.

My contribution to the War effort came about in Sydney's Martin Place. When the Japanese midget submarines were destroyed after trying to torpedo shipping in the harbour, part of the wrecks were converted to small replicas to be sold to help the war effort, and Martin Place was decided on as the place to launch them. Mum took me into town and we got a front row position beside the Spitfire (I think) upon which Sydney's Lord Mayor stood with a dashing fighter pilot, whom I was convinced was Winston Churchill. In one of the Mayor's speeches, punctuated with the pauses for emphasis which important people deem necessary, I decided to say hello to Winnie and stood forward to do so. The mayor stopped and frowned, but the pilot gave me a cheery hello wave and said, "Hello son" back. It took some time for me to be convinced that I had not greeted the great leader.

We used to go to watch Newsreel Movies at a small cinema which just showed newsreels, cartoons and short films continuously, and at the time when watching news from the war I was convinced that the smoke on the screen was what we were getting in the cinema, rather than the cigarette smoke of the patrons. Gullible is my middle name.

Apart from getting my tonsils out and having to live on ice cream and jelly, the rest of the War passed uneventfully. I cannot even remember when it finished.

INTERSTATE MOVE

At the end of the War Dad was posted to Pearce RAAF base near Perth Western Australia, so it was decided that the family would move from Sydney to Perth, although no one asked me or brother Brian. This entailed a train trip of some six days and several different trains because of the different rail gauges in Australia, dating back to colonial times when English, Scottish, Welsh & Irish engineers imposed their own native country standards, much to the colony's cost. Anyway, first stop Albury on the NSW/Victorian border in the middle of the night, then on to Melbourne where we had a day's wait for the next train to Adelaide, another day's wait for the train for the short hop to Port Augusta where we boarded the Trans Train for the trip over the Nullarbor to Kalgoorlie. At one of the stops, I think at Forrest, aboriginal people with tin cans were asking for food, or anything. I put in a packet of chewing gum, and Mum admonished me saying they would not know what to do with it, but in my now 4-year-old wisdom assured her that they would. We became good friends with another woman on the train, whose name I cannot recall but she helped Mum keep us boys in control. One of a few vague memories of the Nullarbor was watching a mob of emus easily keeping pace with the train, and the window sills being about three inches deep with red dust. In Kalgoorlie the last change of trains, this time on the Westlander to Perth.

Our arrival in Perth is still a bitter memory. We were met by Dad in his RAAF uniform and went out to the station entrance where taxis were lined up waiting. We started at the top of the queue and were told by each cabbie in turn 'Next Cab' because all the bastards were waiting for US servicemen who obviously had more money than Australians. This was probably my first experience of being angry with a whole group of people and taxi drivers remained among my favourite disliked people for years. We finally got to the last cab in the rank who reluctantly had to take us to our first home in WA, 48 Woodsome Street Mount Lawley, a comfortable large house on a typical suburban block with a garage and gum trees.

Dad left the Air Force, and as he was a solicitor he had lined up a job with a Perth firm, the principal of which was Tom Sargent who lived in Walcott Street with his wife Molly, a large jolly woman, and a son and a daughter. I remember having many enjoyable times with the Sargents. There were a lot of other kids around and I was soon part of the 'gang'. My best mate was Rob Reilly and his brother Geoff, who lived up the road. There were several other kids from around the area and we could run virtually free, which makes me feel sorry for the kids of today who are driven to school and back and think that the iPad, MP3, computer screen, TV, Twitter etc. are what life is all about. To my mind, although we were vastly less well educated in many ways, we got a better idea of what life is all about.

Too many memories of childhood to chronicle, some good, some not so. I was always a bit of a fantasist. Once, after going to the Saturday afternoon flicks at the Astor in Mt Lawley, I decided that the hero of one of the Saturday serials, the 'Scarlet Horseman', who wore a mask and cape was cool, so I had Mum make me one up from mosquito net. On the following Sunday at the model plane flights in the bottom paddock, now a large housing estate, some kid asked his father what I was wearing, to which he replied that it was probably to keep the flies off. That was the last time I wore my mask.

The milkman used to deliver milk from his horse drawn vehicle, but always in early morning. Somehow, I got to know him, and I used to sneak out early and meet him on the corner. One morning, as he would deliver to a few houses at a time and would finish about 50 yards ahead of the horse, I thought I would do him a favour by getting the horse to go 'just a bit' up the road. Of course, the horse, thinking the boss was on board took off around the block with me hanging on to the reins. The milko was standing in the middle of the road, hands on hips. That was my last attempt at being the driver.

Brother Brian was always getting in trouble, and decided he liked lighting fires. His crowning achievement was to light a fire at the bottom of a block surrounded on three sides by high fences and with the wind blowing down the block. The fire brigade got there in time, but only just.

Being a Catholic kid was certainly an issue for some people. Once, while playing in the back yard with some local kids, the woman next door yelled for her son to come home as he was playing with a Catholic. At the time I shrugged it off, but asked my mother, who was an Anglican, what was the problem, but she just said forget it. Another time we were playing with some kids up the road in Woodsome Street, and some girls across the street looked as if they would like to join in but one of the boys said they could not as they were Jews. I thought this was pathetic, especially as their father owned a soft drink factory.

Across the road in Woodsome Street were also a family of a few girls, one of which gave me my first taste of childhood sex. A large tree in the backyard was an ideal place to sling a hammock, which played a large part in our adventure plays, and while lolling in said hammock with one of the girls, she asked, "I'll show you mine if you show me yours", an invitation which I accepted; but before much further exploration was possible a summons from mum in the kitchen intervened.

One day on that hammock the rope broke, and I found myself sitting on the ground with several of my friends yelling at me to get up. When I looked on the ground I saw what they were on about. A large Redback spider was advancing steadily towards my outstretched fingers. I moved fast. Another more serious event saw me at age of four carrying a pile of wood out of the laundry for Dad to cut into smaller pieces; he was about 30 feet away when the head of the axe flew off and hit me above my right eye, fortunately with the blunt end of the axe head. I remember waking up as he was carrying me in and saying, "I think I have killed him". Some people still notice the thin scar running down to my right eye.

At age six or seven there did not appear to have been many opportunities for more detailed excursions into the world of the opposite sex, although Rob Reilley would occasionally hold forth to an admiring audience how he regularly was able to get his willy into some girl's pussy, although I cannot recall what the name us kids used for said female bits was. Whether he was telling the truth or not is also subject to some latter-day scrutiny, but we were impressed at the time. Rob was the more aggressive of the Reilley brothers; many years later, on one of my trips to Perth I managed to look up Geoff who was the quieter of the brothers, but also features in a couple of minor memories of childhood sex. We went to see a movie, 'Adam's Rib' at the Metro in town, and as Katherine Hepburn was getting a massage from Spencer Tracey, Geoff inquired in a whisper if, when seeing such 'rude' things, did I get a little itch in my willy. Another time as we were laying in the bath, head to toe, I managed to put on a little show of my standing for the benefit of Mrs Reilley, who was not impressed, and Geoff promptly slapped me down with his foot. Such was the sex life of a seven-year-old.

Reilley senior, Syd, was an accountant. One day while at their home it filled up with gas, which us kids were not able to do anything about, so waited for Syd's return from work. As he came walking up the path with a cigarette glowing we almost crash tackled him, and therefore averted what would have been a pretty good bang. Life was generally a time of exploration and getting into trouble of one sort or another. The local swamp, Dog Swamp, resembled a small Louisiana Bayou which claimed the lives of three brothers of the aforementioned girl, their homemade canoe having overturned, but it did not seem to stop any of our exploits.

FIRST SCHOOL DAYS

On my first day at school in the local Convent my mother took me on my tricycle, and that was the last time I was ever escorted to school. On my next day, I rode my tricycle to school and presented a bemused Nun with a Holy picture which I had acquired from somewhere. I think this was my early involvement with Catholic religion. Mass was held in a room above the Convent, and one day I awoke to find Dad carrying me out, as I had fainted. Dad was, I think, not all that good at this parenting business, which sometimes led to him and I having some severe misunderstanding. On one of these occasions he became exasperated with my reticence and said I was an introvert. "You know what that is, don't you?", to which I replied, "Of course", but as soon as I could got hold of a dictionary to find out.

I did have my first brush with the Law while still in first grade. There is a park opposite the convent, and one day before school, myself and some other kids found some goods which turned out to be the discarded proceeds of a burglary, among which were some large ball bearings, which I thought would be terrific marbles. When the local detectives arrived, I was 'Grilled', but let off with a caution; the proceeds confiscated.

Life in Mt Lawley had pleasant memories; Perth was virtually a big country town, they had trams, and after the War still had rationing. Rottnest Island, 12 miles off the coast was, and is, the People's Paradise and two ferries, the Zephyr and the Emerald would take Perth holiday makers across, leaving from Perth Water, down the Swan River through Fremantle and across to 'Rotto'. One day a family outing was decided upon, and I was sent to the shop to buy butter for the sandwiches, but on arrival home discovered I had lost the Ration Coupons. Disaster! Which put something of a damper on the day's events. Losing things and getting lost have become lifetime achievements, although later in life I have found that getting lost often leads to interesting, even fun situations.

My convent education in Mt Lawley lasted two years, and I do not think I achieved any great scholastic heights. Dad had been working as a solicitor for Tom Sargent's firm in Perth but decided he wanted to go out on his own, and this meant moving to the country. The town he picked was Kellerberrin, a wheat belt town 200 kms east of Perth on the Great Eastern Highway and the Kalgoorlie Water Pipe. We all packed into the family car, which was probably something like a Ford or a Dodge, canvas top, open sides, Dad, Mum, Brian and me. Across the Darling Ranges, which are no more than hills, but mark the demarcation between the coastal flats and the inland. We had a house in Massingham Street, the main street through town, and I do not know if it was bought by Dad or rented, although I suspect the latter. Dad set himself up in an office also on the main street, and Brian and I were enrolled in the St Joseph's Convent. On reflection, I think we must have been in Kellerberrin for three years, as when we left to go to school in Forbes NSW, I would start in 6th Class, the last year of Primary School.

Kellerberrin was, and is, a wheat belt town, population probably about 1000. Our house, being on the main street, was opposite the Goldfields Pipeline, the wonderful lifeline to Kalgoorlie and all the towns between it and Mundaring Weir, some 300 odd miles west. C.Y. O'Connor was the Irish genius behind this and many other WA engineering projects, including Fremantle Harbour. Frustrated by carping criticism from politicians and press, he walked into the sea at Cottesloe, Perth's premier beach, and shot himself. Another victim of small minded Colonial values. The pipeline was my footpath to school when not riding my bike. Kellerberrin was a depot town for Hume's Pipes who maintained the line, and their yard, full of large pipes was a great playground. When we arrived in town Mum was approached by a representative from the local Farmers Co-Op for our grocery order; there are two grocery shops in town, and the arrangement is that one month the Co-Op gets the order, next month Truscott's, the other: country socialism at work.

School life has many memories. I assumed a dominant role for some reason. Academically I shared the honours with my first 'girlfriend' Betty Cawley, daughter of the National Bank Manager, Martin. Years later when I had joined the Bank I learned that Martin had become quite famous in banking circles; instead of remaining to enjoy retirement and pension he had quit and gone gold prospecting around Kalgoorlie, but I never found out if he was successful. Betty and I seemed to alternate being top of the class in the years I was there, but I was more the entrepreneur, at one stage hiring out pencils and other items to class mates who had run out or lost items. I remember at one stage demanding that any 'customers' should stand in front of my desk rather than the side when doing business.

Betty's older brother Bill was something of a gang leader with the boys, especially attempting to get other boys to explore sex plays; the Donavon boys were also pretty interested in exploring as much of it as possible. One summer's day they, myself and Betty were on the tin roof of our house and being a hot day, they decided against my protestations to rip the top off the water tank, so we could have a swim, and raced down the roof sans shorts loudly requesting Betty to check them out, which she did. I remained decent in my Tarzan loin cloth. When Dad came home and saw the destruction of the tank he blamed me and chased me around the yard while delivering many strokes with his belt. I felt wronged but can't really blame him.

The main feature in Kellerberrin is 'The Hill', which dominates. It is not that tall, but it was the principal playground for the town. The golf course goes right around it for 18 holes, (sand greens). The local lore is that it is an Aboriginal burial ground, but despite many attempts to locate same, we never could. Kellerberrin became translated as 'Killum Buryum' in local lore.

In keeping with my self-appointed role as leader I assumed many responsibilities, a lot to do with sport. Dad, being a New South Welshman was brought up on Rugby League, but I quickly fell in love with Aussie Rules. Being students in a Convent meant that the predominant sex was GIRLS, and virtually all the sporting equipment available was for them. I decided that something should be done and suggested that a fund-raising event should be held at our house to raise money for a football and cricket bats. Mum went along with the idea but said it would not be a success in our house; it should be at the school. She went to see the Nuns who said yes. Because Mum was Cof E, when the head sister announced the go ahead she said the idea had come from 'An Outsider', her words. Another little thing that has stayed in my memory over the years. Anyway, the fete was duly held and was a great success. The girls got netballs, hockey sticks, softballs. We got one football, which the Irish Priest, Father Philbin, kicked into the 'Police Paddock' across the road, followed by a whooping tribe of boys.

Cricket was the main summer sport, and during lunch and morning playtime we all escaped to the paddock at the back of the school. Three fellow students remain in memory. First a young aboriginal boy who had come in from a nearby Mission, and whom the Nuns told us we were to help in all ways. I decided to teach him to bat and bowl and he was a very quick learner, very quiet, and although he was the only aboriginal in the school everyone liked him, and I do not recall any name calling or other prejudice against him. There was an Irish boy, whose name I can't remember, but he was a good boxer, which on reflection, seeing where he came from was no surprise. Then there was Boris, a refugee from The Balkans. There were a number of European immigrants in town, many from Eastern Europe, which someone decided should be the subject of a ditty; 'The Balts are coming without their nuts'.

Boris was a strong boy and I decided I could make him a fast bowler, which he certainly became. One day he and I got into a playground fight, which was quickly broken up by one of the Nuns. She took me into the wash shed to clean up blood, and I burst into tears in frustration because I did not want to be seen as being rescued by the Nun. I have been in very few fights in my life, but that is one I will never forget.

Cricket became my passion, and Dad put up a practice net in the back yard. The local State school was much bigger than the Convent, but I decided that we should challenge them to a Cricket match. One of their teachers, Doug Tyrie, lived next door so I set about organizing the match. I wanted to make it, I think, under 12yo, with one exception, Boris, who was 2 years older and our best fast bowler. Doug was a tough negotiator who said that was too hard it would have to be under 14s, so undersized we turned up at the ground for the big match. They batted first, and thanks to Boris we confined them to a respectable score which we set about chasing. We were going along well and had victory in sight. Brother Brian was batting well when in the time-honoured tradition of wicket keepers, the sledging started. Brother Brian took exception to this and started a fight with said 'keeper'. The Umpire, being a State School teacher, thought this was a great time to call the match off, and so we convent boys left feeling cheated by those "Statees."

Doug was also involved in my first cooking lesson. I had decided to cook a cake, so got the CWA cookbook, got the list of ingredients together, placed them in the bowl, then got to the section called 'Directions'. Realizing I had made a fundamental error I had to go next door to Doug and replace some of the ingredients, so I could start again. Doug was a Good Bloke.

My brother Brian was not averse to getting into a bit of trouble and on another occasion, when ordered by one of the nuns to do some sort of penance for one of his many wrong doings, he let fly with a punch to her stomach and took off. Sister came into the class room (we had about 4 classes in the one room) and said, "Boys go after him". This being a Friday afternoon, we did so with alacrity, about 10 young 'chasers'. While we had a pretty good idea of where he would be heading, we followed, but when he came into sight I said to just keep him ahead till break up time, when we all headed home for the weekend. From memory, come Monday nothing further was said.

His next exploit however was a beauty. We had a big backyard, complete with great climbing trees and bush ideal for playing soldiers or wars, so naturally digging of trenches was also part of the program. When Dad came home one day he decided that the trenches should be put to use for burying rubbish and duly instructed Brian to get to it. Brian of course thought this was not on and promptly disappeared.

I did not know where and neither did anyone else. When Dad came home he started to organize a search. Being an afternoon, getting on to evening this was starting to be a big worry, and the whole town became involved. Because he had been known to play in the local railway yard, some thought he may have jumped a goods train, and so two men walked along the track to the next town, Tammin, 15 miles with hurricane lamps, to no avail. The next logical place was the Hill, and many people, including me, spent most of the night clambering over the hill, searching the caves, two dams, and many great hiding places there, also without success. I think I went to bed about 5am, when I think the search was adjourned till next morning.

Behind our house was a lane way, mainly for the night cart access, and behind that paddocks of wheat. I woke to see Dad running down the yard with half his face still covered with shaving cream, and a local school teacher escorting my wayward brother by the hand. I thought the old man would kill him, but to my surprise he just hugged him with relief. It turned out he had spent the night, sleeping in the seed bin of a harvester, and if that harvester had been started up in the morning, which it later did, young Brian would have been sliced up into many pieces. The memory of that always reminds me of what the people of a country town are like when it comes to helping their neighbours.

Being a student in a convent of course meant that religion had a pretty big emphasis on life and I confess that I was pretty much taken with all the teachings, to the extent that sometimes I did not think that going to Mass on Sundays was enough and I would go up to the boarders' chapel on some weekdays, till one day when leaving the pew after Mass I turned around and found myself genuflecting to the priest, much to the amusement of all the girl boarders. I was also recruited as an altar boy, but because one of my jobs on Saturdays was to take my trolley to the local ice works to collect a block of ice, I did not get to altar boy instruction that often. Not to worry, comes the time for the debut of the new altar boys, including me, I was kitted out in the regalia. I could handle most of the Latin responses but could not remember all the Confiteor. Father Philbin just told me to start with *"Confiteor*

Deo", then mumble till the middle which is *"Mea Culpa, Mea Culpa, Mea Maxima Culpa"*, and say *"Me A Cowboy, Me A Cowboy Me a Mexican Cowboy"*. Father Philbin at times seemed to lack a certain piety but was pretty good fun. When the time came for us to be Confirmed, we were all to select a Confirmation Name. When I wanted George, Sister told me I only wanted that because he killed the dragon, which I could not argue with, so was told my name would be Patrick. Now when asked by Irish people, my name remains Daniel Joseph Patrick Moloney, which gives bonus points in County Cork. Piety was something I probably had to some degree, but it did not seem to inhibit my general behaviour. On my First Communion, when in Perth, I had to have my toy pistol confiscated by the Nuns. Being the product of a Mixed Marriage was of no significance that I can recall.

Entertainment revolved around the radio, or wireless, and a huge part of the late afternoons was given to the ABC Children's Hour; a serial like Biggles, the various items revolving around the Argonauts Club, where we were all given names from the Odyssey, mine was Zetes 26, and points given for items submitted, like prose, poems, drawings, etc. My submissions petered out before any great fame was achieved. The other main entertainment was the Friday night pictures, held in the picture house, which was mainly an outdoor garden in warm weather, but if rain came everyone simply went inside. One night, Friday 6th February 1952, to be precise, just before leaving home, we listened to the wireless as Prime Minister Bob Menzies announced the King, George 6th, had died. This made us a little late getting to the pictures and I asked if they had played the National Anthem. When told yes, I said, "Well you shouldn't have, he's dead".

Another member of the family, my sister Carol Robin Ann Moloney, pleased one of Dad's friends Percy Cram who thought she was named after him. Shortly after Carol was born Mum decided to go to Sydney for a holiday and take Carol to show the relatives. Dad decided that he would not be able to look after Brian and me, so he booked us into the Preventorium, which was a boarding house run by the Nuns mainly for the children from more humid climates who suffered from asthma, and Kellerberrin being very dry was deemed to be a health 'resort'. There were about 20 boys and more girls, in adjoining dormitories, which occasioned the odd 'raid' with no serious consequences. 13 to 16-year-olds now would probably be more aware of the possibilities, but we were pretty innocent.

Life was generally OK, only a couple of incidents spring to mind. One day I tried to jump over a three- strand barbed wire fence and only made it over two. With blood pouring out of the cut foot, which still bears the scar, I approached the fat Nun who was busy talking to some of the girls. After what seemed ages she told me to run cold tap water over it. Eventually it stopped bleeding. Another example of the preferential treatment girls got from nuns. Every Friday, lunch in the refectory was a fish curry which was a bright green. After a time, I decided I would not eat this, so was called up in front of everyone, and given an ultimatum; fish curry or vegemite sandwiches. I chose vegemite, and for the rest of my stay there a great ceremony was made of me getting vegemite while everyone else had curry. I think I had the best of the deal.

When Mum and Carol were on their way home, Brian and I were released from the Prev. Mum was due to arrive in Perth and get the train up to Kellerberrin, but of course something had to go wrong. We heard that on the way up Carol and Mum were in a box compartment when two-year-old Carol, while Mum was distracted, opened the carriage door and fell out. Mum pulled the cord, but as it was only connected to the guard's van and not the engine, the guard had to go from the back of the train on the outside to get the train to stop. This was night time and they decided to back the train up to where they hoped to find Carol. After some miles and many minutes, she was found sitting beside the track eating coal. Instead of coming home to Kellerberrin she was taken to the hospital in Cunderdin, to where the men of the family headed by car. I remember asking Dad if she died would she go to Heaven, which did not thrill him. I often wonder if Carol's personality in subsequent years was affected by this trauma, but as time goes on Carol seems well adjusted to life.

BOARDING SCHOOL

About this time, it was decided that Brian and I would go to Dad's old school in Forbes NSW as I was next year in the final year of Primary school, 6th Class, while Brian was two years behind. This would mean us being boarders. My main concern was that I would qualify for long trousers rather than shorts, and I was now 5'3". I just made it. This also marked my starting a working life, selling the afternoon paper, the 'Daily News', around town, and on Wednesdays at the local sale yards. One day when I sold the paper to a young man he gave me a ten-shilling note for the 3p paper, and when I said I could not change that I was told to keep the change. He was working for the paper, and this was more money than I would have made in a month. On the strength of this window to the possibilities of more money I tried to convince the local gift shop that I would be a valuable addition to their staff, but they could not see it. I was also into petty larceny; thinking I was very cunning in knocking off a comic from the newsagent, probably about one per week. I was seriously disabused when I found the newsagent had been watching me all the time and told my father. This was on a weekend when Rob and Geoff Reilley came up from Perth for a visit, which made for a very uncomfortable time, but it had the effect of me rethinking my life of crime.

Kellerberrin life was coming to an end, it was decided that Mum would take us kids to NSW by train while Dad stayed in WA to keep working, so once again we boarded the various trains to the East. The only highlight I can recall is going to a Test Match at the Melbourne Cricket Ground, Australia vs. South Africa.

Sydney 1953, we were in school holidays and stayed in the flat in Artarmon with Mum's sister Sylvia before heading for Forbes. Brian and I were pretty much allowed to go where we liked and would get on the tram to go into the city where we would wander and explore. We would get the tram and pay a one penny fare, usually keeping enough for the return fare and maybe some gum or sweets. One day on the return trip the conductress asked where I was going for a penny, and when told Artarmon, I was informed that a penny would only get me over the Harbour Bridge, which was a problem as that was the only money I had left. She gave me a Tuppenny ticket and took only my penny and did the same for Brian. A week later she was in the paper as a winner with some other Trammies of a big Lottery, which made me very happy. All in all, a happy pre-school summer.

Mum accompanied us to Forbes on the train, called the Silver City Comet as its final destination was Broken Hill, and we changed in Parkes for the rail car trip to Forbes. Forbes is smaller town than Parkes, about 5000 people, situated on the Lachlan River, but with a rich history going back to the 1850's when gold was found, and bushrangers were aplenty, principal among them Ben Hall. Dad had friends in town, one of whom was Barry Gunn, who owned the leading menswear shop in town, and Barry fitted us out with uniforms and one day took us out in the bush where we had some shots with .22 rifles at tin cans etc, and we would sometimes go to his home on weekends.

Our destination was the Marist Brothers College in town, where we were quickly settled in, me in 6th Class, Brian in 4th, both in the downstairs Primary Dormitory, presided over by Brothers Philip and Richard, both of whom gave me plenty of hard times. In the convent, corporal punishment was fairly mild, but the good Brothers had a much tougher view of life. On one occasion when called up by Richard to get a cut of the cane I made the mistake of saying "OUCH" and being told on recall that I was not to express any verbal response to rightfully administered punishment. From then on as each cut of the cane was administered I would make various exclamations in various paths back to my bed, to be recalled for another cut. After I think about number 12, I stayed silent and said to Richard "You Win", in the deafening silence that had descended on the dormitory.

Brother Richard was a very handsome man who came from Broken Hill and was a very good Aussie Rules footballer.

A couple of years later he was transferred to West Australia, at New Norcia, and I played football against him. He was reputed to be approached by WAFL league clubs but did not play league. He was also sweet on one of the pretty Nuns from the Convent across the road and whenever the girls came across for Saturday night pictures, we all waited to see him sit next to her and share a box of chocolates. Those were the days when all the teachers in a Convent were nuns, unlike now when the shortage of nuns means most teachers are lay teachers. During one school holidays, I was sent out to their Retreat a few miles out of town to do some gardening and was hugely impressed by the young nuns in summer gear playing tennis and swimming. At the time thought 'what a waste', but they all seemed to be happy.

Brian and I were often left at school during term holidays, as Mother was a triple certificate nurse and was relieving Matron in several hospitals, which meant that there were no suitable places for us to go for some of the two or three weeks of term holidays. We would be given various jobs around the school and rewarded with sweets or other 'goodies'. On occasions Bishop Fox would come to dinner and I would be waiter. We were also allowed to go to town, movies, swimming, exploring. Sometimes Mum could have us for holidays when she had a rented house in the town she was working in. One such was Murrurundi in the New England Ranges, which enabled a lot of exploring in the hills. On one such day a sudden storm came up which was a pretty frightening experience in the hills around 'Sulphur Mountain', where someone said that if you walked up to the top the ground was so hot your shoes would be burned off.

Both Brian and I quickly settled into boarding school routine. School cadets started for me, which meant lots of marching around, route marches, rifle drill and in the next year a camp at the regular Army depot in Ingleburn on the outskirts of Sydney, which was all good fun. On 2nd June 1953, we were all assembled and marched to the centre of town to celebrate the Coronation of Queen Elizabeth, at which the Mayor announced from the Town Hall that Edmund Hillary had climbed Mt Everest as a Coronation gift. Years later when having a drink in a Forbes pub, got talking to a guy who said he was also marching that day, with the State School Cadets.

Sport played a large part in school life. In summer after school we all went to the swimming pool in the town where we stayed for a couple of hours. Coming from the WA wheat belt I had never learned to swim, but this situation was soon addressed by me being thrown in the deep end, which meant I soon learned. Boxing was also done in the first year, I had an inglorious draw in my first bout and a defeat in the next. The next year boxing was off the agenda for the school, not sure why, maybe education department pressure? Cricket and tennis were the main summer sports and I did well at both, getting to finals in tennis tournaments and bowling well in the cricket team. I did however fall foul of my nemesis Brother Phillip over the selection of captain for one of the teams. He lined up the team and said we had to walk up to him and vote for captain. After half the team had voted he called it off, saying the vote was wrong and declared Lyle Vane Tempest captain, as the vote was going to me he would not accept that. Lyle, from Condobolin was a very good cricketer and all-round sport, who later became a chemist on the NSW South Coast.

Many years later I was traveling through Condobolin and saw the Vane Tempest hardware store, so naturally called in to inquire of Lyle; got talking to his uncle who told me the history, then asked if I was related to Cecil Moloney, Dad's brother. He had worked in Condo as Secretary of the hospital, and has a ward named after him. He asked if I could confirm a family rumour. When Cecil was working as a radio announcer in Parkes, the Station's call sign was, "This is 2PK Parkes, the voice of the Golden West." Cecil got sick of this and one day announced, "This is 2PK Parkes the voice of the Dirty, Dusty West", which was the last day he worked there. I could confirm it was true. Some years later when travelling around WA and the Kimberleys, on two separate occasions I was asked about the same story and could so confirm; a family legend spanning some sixty years.

School rugby teams were made up into weight divisions, and I was in the 6-stone-7 team. We played teams from all around the district, Parkes, Cowra, Condobolin, Peak Hill etc., and although I was no great shakes at it I was usually played at fullback, as I had a pretty good dropkick, but was not very fast. In my second year a selection trial was held on Forbes Oval and everyone was invited to nominate for their favourite position. I did not have one so found myself on wing, which was a bit of a joke. My only moment of glory in Rugby was when John Tinkler, the school's champion all round athlete and scholar came charging up my wing thinking he would run straight through me. I laid a classic tackle below the knee and had the satisfaction of him messing up the pass and saying, "Sorry". Years later I called in to the school and asked to see 'Tink' who was now a priest and the school chaplain. I don't think he remembered the tackle.

Apart from sport, my interests were mainly in the class room, where I did fairly well, especially in history, geography and English. Every night we boarders would go into the main class room for Study, which could be pretty boring. I started to write a serial, I think called the 'Green Arrow', and did a chapter every night, which was passed around to everyone. If I had not written a chapter furious notes were passed around the room demanding I forget school work and get on with what was important. The older boys, in Years 11 and 12, had a smaller room separate from the main group, and usually one or more would leave to meet their girlfriends from the Convent across the road.

I was in love with the sister of my friend Rob Edmondson, who was unfortunately a couple of years older than me and probably hardly knew I existed. To get close to the convent I volunteered to do some gardening, and one day was trying to undo a particularly tough hose fitting which would not loosen. A nun came over and it came straight off. I was shocked and mortified, but she assured me I must have loosened it. I was just glad the object of my fantasy was not around to see my humiliation.

Being a Catholic school, religion obviously played a large part in life. Every morning we were up at 6am to go to Mass, and on Sunday evenings to Benediction. The boys sat in the middle row of pews and the Convent girls in the right-hand pews, while any others had the rest of the church. One night I was occupying the extreme front right-hand pew, and at the end of Benediction, turned right and headed out, to be confronted by all the girls coming in the opposite direction. No choice but to continue my lonely path. From that time on my name was Ziggy, or Zig Zag, which for some reason carried over for years. It could have been Crash as when I was serving as an altar boy one day I swung around with the alter wine and heavily bumped a large statue of the Virgin Mary, who proceeded to sway alarmingly while the whole congregation held their collective breaths. My quick prayer was answered, and she resumed her place on her pedestal. I don't think the priest even noticed, but he was the only one who did not.

My frequent clashes with Brothers Richard and Phillip led to one particularly torrid encounter. The school had a holiday, and a bush picnic was to be preceded by choir practice in the Forbes Town Hall. The choir was conducted by Phillip and accompanied on piano by a young lady. We were seated in the hall while Phillip and said lady were chatting on the stage. I had an elastic band and wad of paper which could be made into a missile, and someone urged me to have a shot at Phil to hurry him up, so we could all get to the picnic. Stupidly I took up the dare and let fly with a pellet, which fortunately missed. Goaded on to have another go and this time hit the sheet music Phil was holding. He immediately bid goodbye to the woman and demanded to know who fired the gun. On threat of the whole choir missing out on the picnic I owned up and proceeded to get the worst beating I ever had at school, so much so that back at the school where said beating was administered the school principal found me under some stairs crying in pain, which I had never done before, or since. When he inquired what was wrong I just said, "That bloody Brother Phillip". He looked a bit perplexed but just left me. I knew I had been stupid and deserved severe punishment but still think that was over the top. Naturally enough I never got to the picnic.

The Lachlan River runs through the town, and has in the past frequently flooded, but it also provides water for irrigation for a variety of crops, as well as leisure facilities for people in the district. One popular spot is Jemalong Weir, a few miles out of town, and a place where many school excursions are held. Brian one day managed to write himself another chapter. The weir was full and flowing over the top when Brian found a row boat somewhere and took off in it without any oars. The boat started heading for the weir and a pretty good drop before he was noticed, and I tried to throw him a rope attached to a stone or brick but could not make the distance. In the nick of time Brother Richard managed to lob one in the boat and we pulled him away from the weir wall. For some reason for ever after Brian told people that I had saved his life. Not true, it was my old pal Brother Richard. We all used to spend a lot of time in and on the river, which was full of 'snags'; fallen trees under the surface. One day one of the boys in my class got caught by one of those snags and drowned. The whole school marched out to the cemetery for his funeral.

The Forbes cemetery has several interesting and historic graves, including Kate Kelly, Ned's sister. When I was at school a very weathered tree stump simply said, Ben Hall, 1865. Ben Hall was the local bushranger, much in the style of Ned Kelly; Irish, popular with local settlers, and very much a 'Rob from the Rich, Help the Poor' Bushranger. Ben was shot by a Police party and his body paraded through Forbes on a horse. Now the tourist potential has been recognized and a much grander marble headstone marks the spot.

I also came upon a headstone which knocked me back a bit when I read, Daniel Joseph Moloney, before I realized this was my Grandfather, whom I had never met. My Grandfather was a solicitor, as was my father. Daniel Moloney was well known in the Western District as both a lawyer and sportsman, and in an interview with the local newspaper recounted a number of the anecdotes of his life; born at Hartley, in the Great Dividing Range, under the cliff verge, graduated as a Solicitor in Sydney in 1890, moved to Forbes after working for a well-known Sydney Law firm. His sporting and legal exploits made him a famous figure, winning many horse races and significant legal affairs; one such had him riding from Forbes to Condobolin in an evening, winning the case and riding back next day, a distance of some 100 kms each way. He was also a legendary punter, winning doubles such as a

50 shillings one which landed him 75 Pounds; more than a year's wages for many. My present day efforts pale into insignificance in comparison.

I had been told that my Great Grandfather was also in Forbes as a Policeman and may have been in the party that ambushed and shot Ben Hall. On a later visit to Forbes I looked up the details of that incident in the Forbes Museum, but when it came to be identifying the police there, only those with the rank of Sergeant had names, the others merely numbers. Many years later, through other enquiries on the family tree I discovered that, rather than an unnamed policeman, he was Andrew Moloney, Senior Sergeant in charge of the police in Grenfell, also in Central West New South Wales.

Years later when I was working for Parker Hannifin in Sydney I was talking to one of the workers who also came from Forbes, Sid Dawson, who told me that my grandfather was known in Forbes as 'Plead Guilty Moloney', because he advised many clients that pleading guilty to minor charges was much better for them than fighting these charges in court, and to cop a ten-shilling fine. When I asked Dad about this he got defensive and said this was only done in extreme cases, but he was certainly aware of the tag. Years later, when passing through Forbes I looked in on his old firm, Mathers & Williams, looking for my old school pal Domenic Williams, who had just been elected to the Bar, and had a long chat with one of the solicitors there who knew of both my father and his father, and he also knew of 'Plead Guilty Moloney'. Domenic however had moved to Sydney and I never did get in touch.

Forbes is still an attractive town, but always lives in the shadow of much larger Parkes, and a fierce rivalry persists. I pulled into a Parkes service station for petrol and when answered the query of where I was headed, said Forbes; the instant response was, "You don't want to go there, stay here". Rugby League provided the main opportunity for this rivalry to be played out and when the two teams met everything stopped; the game was broadcast on the radio and nothing else mattered. Back in the 50's a local hero was Darcy Henry who played five eight for Australia and sometimes came back to play for the old home town. Darcy

Henry at some stage became the publican of my Sydney pub in Glebe, the Toxteth, which was long before my time in Glebe, but then was certainly not the more genteel establishment that it is today, and Darcy would have had his hands full dealing with the Glebe locals.

The first Christmas holidays Brian and I could go to Sydney where Mum was staying with her sister Sylvia, who had bought a house in Military Road, Mosman, and ran a trained nurses club, which meant that nurses registered with her and she found them casual positions in hospitals to fill short term vacancies. While waiting for the holidays to start, someone brought a little puppy to school, and I decided to keep it. This presented something of a problem as I had to get it, now named Timmy, to Sydney on the train. A cardboard box was found, air holes cut in suitably discrete positions and a supply of bones placed in the box to keep Timmy happy for the long journey. We got him on the train from Parkes to Sydney, on the luggage rack and when the ticket inspector suspiciously inquired as to the contents of the box, I don't think he quite believed me when I said 'Books' but let it go. Timmy and I had a great summer together, but when the time came to return to Forbes, Timmy could not come. Somehow, he joined a pack of feral dogs on Balmoral Beach and for years later whenever I went to Balmoral, Timmy would come bounding up.

The train trip to Sydney usually provided some drama. One night train I was on I sat up all night talking to an old man, who told me lots of wonderful things, among them how to measure the distance to the moon, a formula which I must admit I no longer have. He told me how he had been shot in Gallipoli, a bullet which went through two sandbags; how he knew Les Darcy, the great boxer, all the while gliding along the track under a full moon. Probably in a similar situation today someone would assume he was a paedophile after my body. Another trip to Sydney, this time on the Daylight Express, Brian and I went to the Dining Car for some lunch. Came the time to pay and I realized that I did not have my wallet, so sent Brian back to the seat to find it. After an uncomfortable wait, he returned to say he could not find it. All our money and tickets gone missing. While looking desperate, a man asked what was up, and I told him I had lost my wallet. He promptly paid for our lunch and told the girls behind the counter that we could have anything we needed. He was a shearer from Queensland, and a true saviour. When we went back to our seats, and did not go back to the Dining Car, too embarrassed, the girls came down to collect us. The train guard called Sydney to appraise them of our situation and when we arrived in Central Station to go through the ticket barrier, they already knew and let us through. That everyone was so kind and generous always has reinforced my optimism about society generally.

After one year I was in High School, which meant going from the lower dormitory to the main Dorm upstairs, initially sleeping on the outside balcony, where one of my 'enemies', Max Gadsby, also was. One night a marble hit me in the head, and while I correctly deduced it had come from said Max, he was looking innocent, but I let him have it anyway. Unfortunately, I missed and made a neat hole in a window. Knowing that it would be discovered anyway, I decided to confess, but offered my excuse that I had been hit first, to which Max confessed, but said he had been hit too, to which no one owned up. The upshot was that the bill was shared by the whole balcony rather than just the two of us, and no one complained.

When I later moved into the main room I was cursed to be near David McKenzie, who snored like a lumberjack. I had heard somewhere that toothpaste is a cure for snoring, so one night when everyone else was away in the land of Nod I went to his kit, extracted his new and full tube of toothpaste, and waited till his mouth was completely open and pushed the whole tube down his throat. He took one gulp and then hardly missed a beat. Next morning, he was mystified as to how his toothpaste tube was now empty. I have hated snoring all my life. Later when eligible for National Service, and having been deferred twice, I was on the verge of volunteering when the thought of sharing a hut with thirty snorers kept me in the Bank. National Service was scrapped soon after.

I had an escape while in primary school. One of the visiting Brothers came to tell us all what a wonderful life as a Marist

Brother was, and at the end of his talk asked which we would rather be, a priest or a brother. Thinking this was a choice of one or the other, I put down Brother. Next thing I knew I was in the Principal's office and just about on a train to their training college somewhere in Victoria; I hastily lost my vocation.

Apart from cricket, tennis and football, we all took part in swimming, athletics, and gym. Every year a Cross country race was held around the streets and bush of Forbes. I have never been a great runner, in fact am SLOW, but tried anyway. While running in the cross country, just ahead of a few others and chatting with them over my shoulder, someone yelled, "Freeze", which I did and looked down to see a rearing King Brown snake about six feet in front of me. Another step and I would have been on top of it. We paused in our race efforts and killed the snake, which we hung on a nearby fence and measured it at over seven feet. Another time on a bush picnic I suddenly realized that I was swimming in a billabong with a diamond snake, which caused a hasty exit from the water.

Mum rented a cottage in Katoomba in the Blue Mountains for our Christmas holiday in NSW. This was 1953. In the first week, I managed to slip over on the Leura Cascades and sustained a green stick fracture of my left wrist, which meant most of the holidays in a plaster. This did not stop me playing tennis however but could only hold one ball up for serving. At the top of Katoomba Street was, and is, a big guest house, the Palais Royale, now a Christian lodge. I would go up to try to find a guest to play tennis with and found one man with whom I regularly played, despite my handicap. Across the road I somehow met a girl, Mary Bondieti, the daughter of a school inspector, and she also played tennis. She was on holiday from Sydney, and her address, in North Strathfield, somehow became embedded in my tiny brain. Many years later, when having a drink with Linda Magill, the Olympic swimmer whom I knew in Germany, Linda told me she also knew Mary. Small world.

Summer in Katoomba had its attractions, but also its dangers. One night everyone was down at Echo Point lookout watching the whole of the huge Jamieson Valley in one big bushfire. A little later the newly crowned Queen Elizabeth came to town and I managed to run alongside the Royal car trying to get Phillip to say Hello, but he didn't.

Summer is cricket season and Test Matches were being played. I managed to persuade Mum to let me go to Sydney, and get to the Sydney Cricket Ground, up in the Sheridan Stand, right behind the bowler's run- in. Ray Lindwall bowling from that end and Keith Miller from the other was one of the highlights of the summer, although I could not understand why Mum would not let me go down to Sydney on my own, after all I was 12 years old and could look after myself. Brian was also into whatever adventure was going around and caused some consternation when he took off to climb the Three Sisters, the iconic peaks below Echo Point. He made it OK, but never got home till after dark, which was a worry.

On another school holiday break, we went to Hoxton Park, near Liverpool, to Mum's brother Uncle Alan's poultry farm. He and Aunt Dot lived there, but no longer with 'chooks'. My grandfather was also there, although my memories of him are vague, but I do remember helping to harrow the next-door paddock behind the old house. Collecting the eggs was also part of the holiday, and a big, black broody hen who would fight for her eggs gave me a healthy respect for the power of hens' beaks. This was also when I met my cousins, Bob and Faye.

My mother's family, the Singletons, have been in Australia since 1793, only 5 years after the First Fleet. There were two brothers, one of whom was convicted of a minor crime and sentenced to Transportation to the Penal Colony of Botany Bay, while his brother came out to keep him company a few years later.

Evidently, they were industrious and prospered, acquiring land and property in the Hawkesbury region, starting the district's first flour mill, the remains of which still exist on the bank of the Hawkesbury River. The original mill stone is now in the Windsor Shopping Mall. One of the brothers married into the Rose Family, whose Rose Cottage, now in the Wilberforce Australiana Village, is the oldest surviving house in Australia. The brothers farmed in and around the colony. One is said to have had a farm on the Upper

Hawkesbury, and many escaping convicts on their way to China would call in seeking help and horses, only to be told that China was slightly out of their reach. Benjamin Singleton, son of one of the original settlers, became a well-respected settler and explorer in the area of the Hunter and Great Dividing Range, with the town of Singleton named in his honour.

Mum had been working as relieving Matron in several hospitals around New South Wales, and when in Sydney our home was with Sylvia at the Mosman Nurses Club, with Sylvia's friend Margot Wasley. Margot worked in the City at Amalgamated Wireless, whose building was at the time the tallest in Sydney, their Radio tower dominating. Margot arranged for us to go up to look over the city. Another highlight was the South Pylon of the Harbour Bridge, which featured among other things a big model railway and lots of White Cats. Now the Bridge Climb is the main attraction, but in the fifties, Sydney was much more easily pleased. Margot and I had many conversations, one of which had me saying that because of my Catholic piety I would never get divorced. Margot sagely informed me that I would change my mind in time. As it happened the opportunity has never arisen due to the fact that I have not married. Margot's other great claim to fame was occasioned by a tram conductor giving her a hard time about something and Margot telling, in front of all the passengers, that he was, "so low he could walk under a worm with an umbrella up", one of the great insults.

CHRISTIAN BROTHERS PERTH

Once again, we boarded trains, which had improved over the years since our first journey west. The first still needed a change at Albury, then on to Melbourne, with a day's layover, once again in time to go to the Test cricket, then on to Adelaide for another day, then a short trip to Port Augusta, then on to the Trans Train for a long hop to Kalgoorlie. Now the train was much more comfortable, pulled by a diesel engine, and therefore a lot cleaner. The final leg to Perth, then to our new home in Guildford, where Dad had bought a house. Guildford is the original settlement of West Australia, about 10 miles from the city on the Helena and Swan Rivers, between Midland Junction, a railway centre and livestock saleyards, and Bassendean, home to fertilizer works and various other industrial enterprises. Our new home was a comfortable three bedroomer between the bowling club and the Catholic Church.

School was the first item on the agenda. I was enrolled in the Christian Brothers College on Adelaide Terrace in the City. Brian with De La Salle Brothers in Midland, Carol in a convent in Perth. Christian Brothers are reputed to be much tougher than Marist, and I would certainly confirm that. Recent times have revealed many Brothers have been abusing boys in their care, as have many priests. While I have no great love for either, I must say that I have never heard of or experienced any such behaviour in the years I spent with both. The closest I can think of was one day walking around the Forbes school yard with both hands firmly in my pockets. Brother Aloysius, commonly known as 'Greasy' or 'Hawkeye', walked past and said, "You dirty little boy", much to my surprise, as I certainly was not playing Pocket Billiards. Rather than the perceived situation now, I would say that tough as they may be, they still imbued in us boys a standard of ethical behaviour and work ethics which have in most situations been lived by, notwithstanding that the actual religious beliefs are largely gone by the way-side.

I do remember the Bindoon Boys Town, north of Perth, and how the boys there were treated much differently. The notorious Brother Keaney ruled with an iron fist and the mostly British boys who had the misfortune to be sent there as orphans were basically slave labourers, also being sexually abused by Brothers. I met one later, who to my inquiry looked very angry and refused to comment. They were turned out as basically farm workers, with little of the further education they needed. Brother Keaney had a statue of him standing in front of the Bindoon building, but now the pedestal is empty; he has been erased from Bindoon's memory. While I was at CBC Perth, a bus carrying a lot of Bindoon boys hit a table top truck parked on a bridge, which basically cut off the legs of all the boys on one side of the bus. I saw Douglas Bader, the English WW2 fighter pilot known as Tin Legs, come out to pay them a visit and inspire many to overcome their tragedy.

By now I was in the second year of High School, in what was the Technical Drawing Class, as opposed to the Latin Class, for presumably smarter kids. I have never had any attraction to or interest in technical drawing but managed to pass the appropriate exams, but chemistry was something else. Could never see the point in trying to remember all the Atomic Numbers. English, History, Physics, Geography were fine. Brother Travers, nicknamed Boris because of passing resemblance to Boris Karloff, taught English, Religion and Geography which on one hand made me something of a star in English, but in 3rd Year Geography I objected to the Final Term lessons being solely coaching in past Exams, and every period homework was answers to past exam questions which I refused to do, so the daily ritual was, show homework, "Moloney, not done it", six cuts with his heavily weighted strap and expulsion from the class. I made sure that in the Final 3rd Year exam I got 100%. Brother Travers and I shared a funny relationship; while I was the star English pupil in his class, I refused to concede domination. Years later, when staying with my friend Phil Bussanich in Busselton he told me he had died, a much-respected old teacher, our clashes notwithstanding.

My entrepreneurial 'talents?' began to be developed here. I bought a film developing kit and advertised on the school notice board cheaper processing, which went alright for a while until such enterprise was forbidden. My main activity was running a weekly football tipping game on WANFL games. Players put in one shilling a week with their tips and at the end of the season the winner and place getters shared the pool. As the last period that the entries could be submitted was the Friday 12.30 Religion period, this was sometimes a hassle. One such time Boris stormed down the aisle to grab an entry form and demanded to know who was running this, and when told it was me simply said, "Well don't do it in religion period".

My other great scheme was running a book on horse races, in particular the Melbourne and Caulfield Cups. One day at school assembly, just before the Cup, Brother Collopy, the Principal, announced to the gathered 600, "It has come to my attention that a certain boy is running a book on the Melbourne Cup, IN OPPOSITION TO THE ST VINCENT DE PAUL SWEEP. This must cease". 600 pairs of eyes turned towards me and I was forced to suspend operations for a few days.

The 1956 Cups caused me a great deal of worry. I ran a Double on the two Cups, and one of the smarter boys who lived in Belmont, the home of WA racing, took the double 'Rising Fast/The Orb'. 'Rising Fast' duly won the Caulfield Cup but 'The Orb' was scratched from the Big One. Stephen Ryan persuaded me to allow him to change his bet to 'Rising Fast' in the Cup. On Melbourne Cup day, a school holiday, I was playing tennis at school and had to race over to a nearby shop to listen to the race, where 'Rising Fast' was just pipped. The amount of money I would have had to pay out was enough to have me contemplating having to do a runner across the Nullarbor. After that I decided that perhaps bookmaking on a limited budget was not my go.

School days were not unenjoyable in the main. I played football for the school as well as cricket, only 2nd teams. CBC was at the time the principal hockey school in the country, mainly because of the Pearce brothers, a family from Ceylon who provided, I think, three members of the Australian Olympic team. Brother Kenneth was the coach and for some reason tried to get me to switch from football to hockey, to which my verbatim response was, "football is hard enough, but in hockey they give you a weapon". Brother Kenneth once stormed into his Chemistry classroom where I was for some insane reason perched on the outside window ledge. Without breaking stride, he slammed the window shut and pulled the blind down. I was only released at the end of his lesson. Perching on an 18-inch ledge for 30 minutes over a 30-foot drop was even worse than the chemistry lesson. Ever ready with words of encouragement, Brother Kenneth assailed me with, "Moloney, you are a Fool to yourself, and a Burden upon others".

I continued playing tennis and cricket in summer. I played a couple of tournaments, including the State tennis championships, but did not get past the first round in under 16s. Several of us boys were waiting to play one day, and we were joined by Roy Emerson, winner of more Grand Slam titles than anyone at the time, whom we knew as Uncle Roy. I also played cricket for the West Perth under 16s, home ground the WACA, home of WA cricket. The captain of our team was Jim Hubble, who later opened the bowling for Australia in Tests in South Africa. On typical weekends, I played Junior Pennant Tennis, Senior Pennant tennis, West Perth Cricket, and Club tennis on Sunday afternoons. A busy weekend. In winter, football for either the school or Guildford Under 18s in the Swan Districts competition. My ruck partner in Guildford was Eric Gorman, who was recruited and played for Swan Districts and also for WA.

About this time, I started to develop an interest in music, mainly due to the rise of Rock and Roll. Bill Hayley, Elvis, the Platters, Little Richard became something of an obsession, much to the disgust of my father, who thought that the Andrews Sisters were the ruination of Bing Crosby, but the tide could not be turned on Rock. The film 'Blackboard Jungle' had us dancing in the aisles. TV came to Australia to coincide with the Melbourne Olympics, and with it a lot of American Sitcoms and music shows which further fed the Rock generation, although 50's singers such as

Patti Page, Jo Stafford, Dean Martin, etc. also were very popular. At one stage CBC in America would not have Rock on its labels and promoted Guy Mitchel and Rockabilly as the 'clean' alternative, with very marginal success.

School proceeded to its 3rd year conclusion, which for me was the end of my education. For whatever reason, probably very sound, Dad had decided the academic world was not for me; I also suspect that school fees were a factor. The Intermediate Exams rolled along, and I informed him that I would pass six of the eight subjects, and not pass chemistry or tech drawing. For chemistry, I put my name and number on the top of the page and got 12%, more than I could have hoped for. The day of the results publication he was waiting for the paper to be delivered and rushed in to tell me I had achieved the predicted six subjects, whereupon I said, "Told you so", and went back to sleep.

AND SO, TO WORK

Getting me a job was also a huge worry for Dad as he thought I would probably become a messenger boy for the Post Office or some such illustrious pinnacle of my ambitions. To this end I was hawked around to several prospective employers, including the Public Service. At that interview, I was asked what my particular interests were and when I said I liked to write, was told that I could perhaps do something in the Staff Journal. My main interview was with the National Bank, where Dad banked with the Midland Junction branch. My interview was with the manager, Ted Antill, who just looked at me and said that all he was interested in was to make sure I did not collect butterflies. Interview successful and my career as a 'Bank Johnny' commenced January 1957.

My only work experience prior to the bank was as a paper boy in both Kellerberrin and Perth City, so I was pretty naive, but not enough to fall for the standard trap for young players, who were shown a large pile of account books and told to 'balance the books.' First duties assigned were to take charge of the postage and balance daily the outward mail against cash paid for stamps. My first lesson in accounting. A correspondence school approached to enrol me in an accounting course, but Dad would not approve. The attitude of the Bank to further education also seemed to be negative, perhaps because they figured that this would make employees leave the bank for more lucrative employment. So, I have remained without further formal education since.

My first branch, the City Markets branch, was also under the management of Ted Antill, who approved my initial application; a bluff but easy-going man, whose secretary Carmel I once walked in on as she was typing furiously, and as I entered the office, had the page ripped out of the machine and replaced in a flash. I opened the drawer and checked out what was being typed, which was 19 verses of Eskimo Nell.

By this time, I had moved out of our Guildford home as Mum had taken up a job in a northern town, Mukinbudin, so I moved in to the Roches home as a boarder. The Roches have been part of my life ever since – their eldest son Frank, born on the same day as me 25/5/41. Mum however, approached the bank staff department to request that I be transferred to a town closer to her and the closest they could come up with was Three Springs about 200 miles away, and I was transferred there. I travelled up on the Railway bus and when I alighted in the main street felt like getting back on, but Three Springs was really the start of my adult life. That night, after booking into the hotel I was in the bar drinking my first beer, as a 16-year-old, and I was out at the salt lake under casuarina trees with two nurses and two bottles of warm beer. Sex was something read about in books, manifested in the physical discomfort of pubescent unrequited lust, sport seeming to be the outlet. I was also being recruited by the Three Springs and nearby Arrino football clubs; decided on the Three Springs team where I played as a 16-year-old skinny ruckman against some pretty solid farmers.

Three Springs was a great eye opener for me on the great world beyond school and suburban life, and several 'incidents' remain imprinted on my memory. I was installed in the only hotel as a resident, with a room on the first floor, above the bar in which I was usually to be found after work or football training, which, as noted was before my 17th birthday. I also, as a good Catholic boy, went to Mass every Sunday, and became friendly with the Priest, Father 'Micky' Moffatt, who tried to minimize my time in the pub by inviting me to the presbytery for a beer and to listen to records. He insisted that Irish tenors were the best, I insisted that Mario Lanza was at least equal. I hasten to add that Mickey was in no way a priest like the seeming perverts exposed years later in Australia and around the World. He was concerned at the drinking in the town; Three Springs had the reputation of being the biggest beer drinking town in WA after Kalgoorlie. At Sunday Mass, there was a great lack of Altar Boys, and on one memorable occasion

Father Moffatt stormed out to say Mass and when a local farmer who usually came forward to act as altar boy, Micky told him to sit down, raced through Mass, refused to have collections taken up, got to the Sermon in about 10 minutes, faced the congregation and furiously berated Three Springs. "I am sick of the drinking in this town, especially the underage drinking, fathers drinking in the pub with their underage sons. Where is the Law in this town?" At which the entire congregation instinctively turned to the rear of the Church where the local Policeman usually sat and sighed with relief when they saw he was not there. Drinking habits remained pretty much unchanged.

Shortly after arriving in town I joined the local branch of Junior Farmers, and met Maureen, daughter of a leading town farmer and politician and started going out with her until on another night I met a blonde nurse, which ended my relationship with Maureen. Years later, about 50, I was in Geraldton and my 'twin' Frank Roche told me that Maureen had never married, though I am sure that is nothing to do with me.

Country towns have a number of transients, often made up of Bank Johnnies, Post Office, Nurses, Stock Agents, and various others who often gravitate together, and the nurses' quarters are a very popular destination. I certainly did not let grass grow under my feet there, although my youthful innocence, which today would be laughable, ensured that romantic adventures were often such innocent thrills as lying under the stars on the nurses' quarters lawn marvelling at the clear skies and stars. One night the stars were augmented by a brilliant display of the Southern Aurora, all the way from Antarctica thousands of miles away across the ocean and inland. Many years later I was listening to a radio broadcast where several callers recounted that they had also seen the Southern Aurora from WA country towns.

The National Bank, where I was the fourth and junior staff member, was the only bank in town, this being one of the results of the WW2 decision by banks to have a 'raffle' in all towns in Australia to ensure that maximum man power was available for the War Effort. Years later, when technology had taken over everything, small town bank branches became of less importance to Bank management, and by year 2010 some 300 such branches were closed, further making small town living more difficult, as local businesses moved to regional centres.

There was no such thing as mechanical assistance; ledgers were hand written and calculated, Pounds, Shillings and Pence, no such thing as a calculator, by the Ledger Keeper, Ross, who really wanted to be in the Navy. The Teller was Colin Simpson, and Eric Hewitt, the Manager. One weekend Eric had to go to Perth, and for security reasons the manager's residence, which is attached to the bank had to be occupied, on this occasion by Ross. We had been in the pub with a couple of nurses, so back to the bank we went. Ross was showing off to one of the girls with one of the bank's revolvers, and I of course thought I could do likewise, got out the automatic pistol, took out the magazine, pointed it between two of the nurses and pulled the trigger. The resultant bullet imbedded itself in the stationery cupboard; I stood in open mouthed shock. Taking the magazine out and leaving a bullet in the breach is not recommended. We all hastily packed up and left. On the Monday morning when Colin arrived at work, puffing on his pipe, I pointed at the hole in the cupboard and asked him what he thought that was, to which he replied, "bullet hole." When Mr Hewitt arrived back from Perth he was equally sanguine, saying some of the bullet scarred stationery would need to be replaced with a suitably believable explanation to Head Offices as to the reason. Lesson learned. I bought there the only gun I have ever owned, a single shot .22 rifle which I had for five years, before selling it in my last week before going overseas.

Guns however, were standard issue in the Bank, one always kept in the teller's desk. The instructions were, if the teller was confronted by an armed robber, to faint, and as he was falling to grab the handy pistol. The next bit was a bit vague; if the robber poked a curious head over the counter to be confronted by said cocked pistol, the robbery would then become an abandoned enterprise; shooting said robber between the eyes was against Bank regulations. A few years later in a busy city branch of another bank, the staff at the 3 o'clock closing time headed for the staff room tea break, leaving the teller to balance his cash. The front door had been left open, an invitation taken up by an enterprising robber, who marched in, held up the teller and left with a large amount of cash. The teller, realizing that he was the only witness to the incident, thought he was vulnerable to the suggestion that this was a 'put up job', grabbed his pistol, leapt the counter and saw the robber running down an adjacent laneway. Without breaking stride, he let off a single shot which hit the runner behind the knee, effectively bringing the episode to a close; only result was he got into trouble for firing in a public place.

The Anglican Minister in town was Freddy Dawson, whose wife was extremely attractive and very friendly, especially to us local transients. On Saturday afternoons she would invite us around for tea and scones, at which half a dozen of us would lap up every word and vision. Freddy got on well with Micky Moffatt, and when either would conduct a fund-raising function the other would give great support. If only Sunnis and Shia could embrace the same philosophy the world would be a better place.

Sport plays a huge part of country life, and Three Springs was no exception. I played football for the local team, and in summer was also part of the tennis club. I was a member of the club team for the inter- town competition, and was generally performing well, to the extent that when the Finals were on we were playing off for the Title. At this stage, my underage drinking became something of an issue, and in the local paper a section of the town began campaigning to have me dropped, while the other half wanted me in. I was retained, and in the Final against a town, Salmon Gums, I played the doubles, mixed doubles, winning both, then came the final singles, when last night at the pub caught up with me, and I quickly found myself down Love 5, 15-40. I groped desperately at a shot which hit the wood of my racquet and fell over the net. Somehow, I won the match 7-5. Walking back to the club house to be told by a girl on the Salmon Gums team, whom I was trying to impress, that the other singles player had lost, and therefore so had we.

Back in town the club was to have a fund-raising gambling night at the courts, with a huge turnout everything was going swimmingly. The main attraction was a spin the wheel game of

Crown and Anchor, which a farm hand on a nearby property got stuck into, to the extent that he won a lot of money which kept the club broke, I believe for years. He was also drinking well and decided he needed to go home. A couple of his 'mates' went with him. Next morning, he woke up in a ditch, no mates, and no winnings.

Country towns always have their share of scandals; one which really shook Three Springs concerned the Secretary of the local Farmers Co-Op and a young boy working at the Post Office. One Monday morning the town awoke to discover that these two had eloped with a large portion of the Co-Op's finances, bad enough, but the sexual involvement of a large middle-aged man and a 16-year-old boy was the real shock.

Race played a significant but sometimes contradictory role in country life, both then and now. The town to the north of Three Springs is Mingenew, which had a large Aboriginal population mainly in camps outside the town. One Saturday the local police Sergeant made all of them assemble in the town, and then to 'March', which meant a 30-kilometre walk to Three Springs, which became their new home. Imagine that happening now!

During the summer months guests in the hotel usually slept on the veranda. One night I heard a commotion down below, and looked down to see a fight between Harry 'Bomber' Stevens, a local trucking contractor who had played football for South Fremantle and WA, and the only Aboriginal in town who had his 'papers', which allowed him to have a drink in the pub. He was also the leading football umpire in the district. I cannot recall his name. Harry knocked him down, he knocked Harry down, and the next time he was down he looked up at Harry; "If I get up and belt the shit out of you, you white prick, will you give me a job tomorrow?". "Of course, I will you black bastard", which then happened. Race relations *Par Excellence*!

A young aboriginal girl got a job in Perth as a trainee nurse. Her family lived in humpies on the edge of town and worked for a local farmer, who gave the girl a lift to Perth. On the way out of town he asked her if she wanted to stop and say goodbye to her family, but she declined, saying she wanted to put that part of her life completely behind her. I can only hope she survived the racism she would have found in Perth as well.

My time in Three Springs was rarely dull, always something to do, places to go to. A swim on a hot night meant a 100 kms drive to the beach at Dongara and 100 kms back. Football meant Sunday drives of up to 60 miles each way, and a fair amount of beer drinking after the game. One game in nearby Carnamah meant a night time lift back to Three Springs, with me in the back seat. I was handed a full half bottle of Corio Whiskey, a potent local poison. I proceeded to finish off the whole bottle, and by the time the trip was over I was comatose. I was dragged in to the hotel and deposited at the foot of the stairs, head down feet up. Someone managed to get me to bed. I could never stand the smell of whiskey for many years later. I was in fact a 17-year-old delinquent, and the hotel publican, who was also the Football Club president, told me one day when I was paying the rent that if there was anywhere else in town I could board, he would throw me out, to which I responded, "Well, there isn't, so you can't; and by the way the plugs in the showers need replacing".

Altogether my educational stay in Three Springs lasted about 9 months, then back to Perth for a short time, then learning my next branch would be Geraldton, 300 miles north of Perth. When told to get the bus, I refused, saying the trip would take about 18 hours, so I got my first trip on a plane, a DC3 of MMA, known locally as Mickey Mouse Airlines. Geraldton is a port for mainly wheat, some minerals, and sea food, especially crayfish.

Life in Geraldton quickly became more varied than that of Three Springs. Settled into a house owned by a Lancashire lady who had once worked in the same factory as Gracie Fields, the singer. My roommate was the teller from the bank, Keith, son of a butcher in Leonora in the Goldfields. Home was about one mile from the Bank, which meant a walk at lunchtime taking up a fair portion of the break. One of the young staff members, John, had a Vespa scooter which he said I and my other fellow roommate, Phil, could borrow for the trip. Neither of us had a Licence. No Problem; got it started, took off down Marine Terrace, going well, were passed by a Traffic Cop who gave us not a glance. Came to the first corner, tried to change down, something went wrong, motor going 10,000 revs to the second, took the corner at 35mph, ran up a bank and down again and took off up the road. Got home safely for lunch then decided to go for a ride to get used to the bike. On the road to the Back Beach passed another Traffic Cop but he was not interested either so on we went, hitting 50mph on the straight stretches, headed back to the Bank, missed a head on with a Holden ute by inches, but not my fault. Next day back for lunch, turned into our driveway put on the hand brake, no effect, went careering into neighbour's fence, putting one of his posts out of alignment, denting the front guard of the bike and giving me six cuts to a shin. Back on the bike to the Bank, once again brakes did not work, finished up in a clump of Sunflowers, narrowly missing a concrete drain. Told John we had bit of an accident and had dented his mudguard; he thought it was a great joke. When I told him that his brakes did not work I found out that there was a foot brake, which is Deadly! If only I had known! The damage amounted to 30 shillings, which I accepted on behalf of the Dan Moloney Insurance Company.

Joined a local cricket team, Moonoonooka, which is a hamlet near town. Opened the bowling with some success, was picked in a representative team to play Northampton, a rural town about 30 miles out. This gave me one very memorable 'on field' incident. I was fielding at 'very silly mid-on', about three feet in front of a very burley, very belligerent opposing batsman, who took exception to my close proximity and threatened to kill me. He took three wild swings at the bowling as I edged closer, and on the fourth, just managed to clip the ball into the air, where I took an easy catch, clapping him off as I waited for the ball to descend. As the next batsman came in I moved away from this 'death spot'. That was the last time I indulged in the great Australian Sledge.

Social life in Geraldton took a big upswing, mainly because of the vastly improved number and variety of local girls. One of my duties in the bank was to conduct the daily 'exchange' of the various banks' cheques, where most of the other banks were represented by members of the fairer sex. My steady was Marg, whose father was once the CFO of a State Government

Department but resigned because of the discrimination against Catholics in the WA Public Service. Marg also gave me an introduction to Greek Mythology, naming her pet budgie Telemachis, the son of Odysseus and Penelope. Another girl in the exchange group was more inclined to linger in the sand hills for 'romantic' dalliances.

My knowledge of Pop Music now became useful, as the local radio station were conducting competitions. They would play a few bars of a song and first call in wins a prize. I won a few times, till they barred me by specifying that only out of town calls could win. Before this happened, one girl I was going out with was the daughter of the Anglican Bishop, who worked in the telephone exchange and offered to hold the line open for me till I had the answer; I declined. Classical music also became attractive mainly because of the movie 'A Song to Remember' about Chopin; always remember the scene of Chopin playing piano with his consumptive blood on the keys.

Life in Geraldton was busy and enjoyable. The Geraldton Hotel was just across the road from the bank and I became a regular even though I was still only 17, much below the legal drinking age of 21. One day one of the bank's 'naughty' customers came in and got a cheque book and proceeded to cash cheques in nearly every pub in town. The bank's accountant, Trevor, started chasing him, and finally caught up in the local. When he told the publican that the cheque would not be honoured, said customer gave back the book with a sigh, having had his sport. Soon after this, myself and a mate began chasing a couple of girls who were staying in the hotel, in a first-floor room with balcony. Romeo style we stood below and serenaded with 'It was Fascination', cut short by a shower of cold water, to which we swung in with 'Splish splash, I was taking a Bath', but our Juliets remained in their tower.

Although most weekends were usually occupied with swimming, shooting, dancing, drinking, cricket, tennis, sometimes I would get a lift and go to Perth for the weekend. Usually my lift was with the teller from the Commonwealth Bank, but one weekend, at the last minute was offered a lift with the teller from 'my' bank, which I accepted; this enabled the other teller to give a lift to someone else. Half way down to Perth we came across the other car. It was going around a bend and smashed into a truck parked on the wrong side of the road. Both driver and passenger were killed outright, the passenger who took my place; just another occasion where I seem to have had the benefit of an undeserved charmed life.

My tenure in Geraldton came to its usual nine months, and off to several Perth Metropolitan branches, which meant re-establishing sporting and social circles, particularly in Guildford. One of these branches, East Victoria Park, left a few memories, particularly of one customer whom I always felt sorry for as I presented the Manager with the list of her cheques we would dishonour; Mrs Ratto ran a local grocery store; some months earlier her stupid husband became convinced that the World was to end on a certain weekend, and with a number of his equally stupid mates took practically all the store's stock and spent days on a hill in the bush consuming the food, waiting for the cataclysm. I called it Mrs Ratto's Tragedy.

A highlight was provided by a ticket which Mum bought for 'The Taming of the Shrew' at the Her Majesty's Theatre with Katherine Hepburn and Robert Helpmann, my first taste of live Shakespeare and seeing Katherine Hepburn 'live' after all the movies she has been in remains a treasured memory. Audrey Hepburn starred in another influential 'cultural' awakening; the party in 'Breakfast in Tiffany's' which provoked the comment, "They don't have parties in Perth like that", and sparked my oversea travel aspirations. Another cultural highlight; my football team, Swan Districts, had been last for the previous three years, but with a new Coach and a couple of imported players, next year won the Grand Final! I was at the game and celebrated into the night, when I then tried to catch a bus home to Guildford, last bus gone. Hailed a taxi and asked for 10 shillings worth towards Guildford. The driver turned the meter off at 10 shillings and took me home. I was able to give him a cheque for the balance.

City branches of the Bank provided many a good time, but few of the lasting influences that subsequent country postings provided. Harvey, a town about 100 miles south of Perth, was largely built on dairy and cattle farms. It was said to be populated 64% Italians, largely because of being a POW camp during the War, at which conclusion many of the released prisoners decided to stay and prospered. I arrived as Ledger Keeper and set up residence in the Harvey Hotel. The publican told me one day that during the War he was stationed at one time in Melbourne, and wanted to confirm my father's name, Harold Moloney. Duly confirmed, he told me his memory of my father, on Spencer Street Station, taking bets on local horse races from Servicemen waiting for trains. My father was a keen horse man and could recite the winners and place getters of every Melbourne Cup from the very first race.

About this time my 18th birthday arrived. One Saturday morning, myself and Ian Smart, working in the Bank of New South Wales, went shopping for washing powder, and on the way, passed a used car yard, in which stood an old car, which we bought instead of said powder. The car we bought for 50 Pounds was a 1926 Morris Cowley. That night we loaded it up with a few other local lads and headed for Bunbury, about 50 miles south. The over enthusiastic driver pushed the old girl too hard, but fortunately when he heard a loud bang, pushed the clutch, probably saving the engine from complete disaster. We parked the car in someone's yard and proceeded to the Bunbury Yacht Club dance. Next morning retrieved the car, and towed it back to Harvey, where the damage was diagnosed as a 'Big End' which would require re-metalling and tooling. Ian now came good; his father worked for General Motors in Fremantle. The piston rod sent to Fremantle, work done, returned, total cost two shillings and sixpence for split pins, placed back in engine; my first lesson on how cars work.

Having become the part owner of a car, I thought it prudent to acquire a Driver's License, which my age now made me eligible for. The local Police Station was manned by a Relieving Sergeant, who was staying in the Hotel. I arranged to take a driving test with him and drove the Morris there. He took one look at it and said, "I am not getting in that. Drive it around the block". On the conclusion of my only driving test or lesson, proceeded to fill out the paperwork. Where the age question was answered, me being three years under the legal drinking age, he swore. I just told him not to worry, and I would buy him a Gin and Tonic that night. No further words needed.

The Morris became something of a celebrity around town and featured in many excursions to beach and party. Some 50 years later I was watching an episode of Doctor Who on TV. The episode was about the Doctor going back to the year Agatha Christie went missing for a few days. The year, 1926. Two cars featured prominently, 1926 Morris Cowley. In the 'making of' part of the show, David Tennent, The Doctor, was not allowed to drive the cars because they were TOO VALUABLE.

The Cricket season proceeded uneventfully apart from a game organized by the Local Member against State politicians in Perth. Several locals became interested in basketball, and in a short time a competition was organized. I joined a team of mainly itinerants, bank, teachers etc., called the Alley Cats, and we were the pace setters. We set up back boards on the girls Netball courts and quickly became a popular addition to the town's sporting culture. One other team was the High School, coached by a teacher, Peter Jeffery. As school holidays approached, Peter, who would not be in town over the period, asked me to take on the coaching of his team. Conflict of interest did not arise as the Alley Cats did not clash over the holidays. Peter and I became firm friends and have remained so for over 50 years.

Once again, my allotted time ended, and I was told I would be transferred to another country branch, Kojonup, some 100 odd miles south of Perth. I had already organized a weekend trip for a Perth team I knew to play in Harvey, so when I told everyone that I was leaving, promised that if basketball had not arrived in Kojonup I would get it started.

Kojonup is a prosperous centre of sheep, grain and cattle country, known as the Blue Wool country. I was boarded out with the town's hairdresser, Hank and his wife Bunny. Hank and I did not get on and I left after a few weeks to rent a room in town. Many years later in South Australia I met a man from Kojonup who told me Hank was still there, but no mention of Bunny.

Kojonup life quickly became 'full on'. I played football for the town team, sometimes in the Firsts, sometimes in the Reserves. Weekend football always meant drives of up to 100 kms, sometimes necessitating overnight stays in country pubs. One memorable visit to a local Greek Café in Katanning after football had the Coach march in and demand, "22 Steak and Eggs and make it snappy". Many years later I was watching a TV program on country towns and Katanning was featured as a town which welcomed many refugees and migrants, some 80 different nations represented in a population of about 3500; a welcome change in attitude from the 1950s and 60s.

The football season ended, cricket and tennis took over, and my basketball promise began to take shape. I approached the football club with the reasoning that basketball was a great way to keep footballers fit over summer, to which they agreed. Next to find a place for a court. A beer in the pub one night led to discussions with the Secretary of the Hospital board, which owned a block beside the town sale yards, and he said, "Take it". The block was on a slope, so next was recruit some local farmers with trucks to cart many loads of soil to the site and grade and level it. Having now a site, next to seal it with bitumen; once again to the pub, spoke to the foreman of the council road gang, no problem; one afternoon whole area sealed and fenced. Next morning Tim, my flat mate, woke me with the news that a farmer had brought a mob of sheep to the sale yard and rather than take a 50-yard detour, had taken down the fence and run his sheep through the wet bitumen. Council guys repaired it, all ready to go. A local businessman paid for a score board, basketball established as promised.

Having struck up a friendship with Phil Gurrin, a school teacher, I moved in to his shared house, along with two other teachers. Phil Gurrin became a lifelong friend up to his death aged 80. One night we won a 35- pound turkey in a raffle, just in time for Christmas. The turkey was far too big for a normal oven, so it was cooked in the baker's oven. I arranged for us both to go to Perth for Christmas, so Phil riding his motor bike, me a passenger and turkey on the fuel tank made the 100 plus mile trip no problem. We spent Christmas with my parents, sister Carol and brother Brian; a rare occasion we were all in the one place.

Shortly after this in the Kojonup pub I saw a newspaper article about my father; he had been expelled from the Law Society because of a problem with his Trust Account. Dad assured me that this was an accounting error, which he had been reported for by a woman client. She subsequently tried to withdraw the complaint but was unable to do so. The resultant expulsion stood, and Dad was never able to re-join his profession. Without ever really knowing the full story, I have always suspected that 'the powers to be' are quick to condemn those lower on the food chain while protecting their own. Another afternoon newspaper story, a girl friend of mine in Perth featured on the front page as winning Thirty Thousand Pounds in a Lottery, a huge sum in the 1960s. Because her name was published she was soon forced to leave the State because of the deluge of begging letters and approaches.

Social life was nonstop. I became 'an item' with Rose, the Belle of the district, rich farmer's daughter, and this caused some jealousy with some local lads. Sport of course again plays a major part in country life and I represented the town in both football and cricket. The newly formed Apex Club, a service and social club for males also occupied plenty of time, particularly as I was the Treasurer. My belief that the only way to appreciate country town life was to be fully involved became a source of friction between myself and Bill Trevaskis the Teller in the Bank, who with a wife and young baby hardly ever got out socially. One day in the Bank this boiled over with Bill swinging punches and the Manager having to pull us apart. Some fifty plus years later in a small town in Tasmania I came across a statue of a local man Bill Trevaskis, no relation. We got over it. Apart from the social whirl, money was an item that seemed to pass through my fingers without touching the sides so when annual leave became available I spent the three weeks working as a farm labourer helping get in the wheat harvest. Shortly after that I received the inevitable transfer, this time back to Perth.

One day in my new branch one of my mates, Digby Bellett, came relieving. I casually asked what he was doing at Christmas. "Going to England". Quickly getting the details, next morning I raced into the Perth office of the Greek shipping line, Chandris, and booked my passage for 115 Pounds. Five and a half weeks to Southampton. Next problem, I did not have any money, so I called Bill from Kojonup, now in the Bank's Staff Department and got a posting to Relieving Staff, which gave an allowance of 10 pounds per week. By this time Phil had moved back to Perth and had a flat in Cottesloe, Perth's premier beach, and I moved in. Some country postings enabled me to save some money but did not stop life going on.

One night while out drinking in North Perth, myself and drinking companion were approached by a young girl keen to secure an overnight transaction. The girl was about 18 and was just up from the country, only that day. Naïve as we were we decided that this girl did not deserve to be flung into that life in desperation. We spent some time talking to her and managed to get her to agree to go to a Convent to spend some time to reconsider; we then called the St John of God Convent and explained to the Sisters what we were doing. They agreed, if the girl would go to them voluntarily; at the Convent gate we let her walk to the waiting nun, hoping that we did the right thing.

Two Qantas stewards I knew thought a drive to Carnarvon, about 1000 miles north was a good idea, so I joined them. Carnarvon at the time had one of the two whaling stations in the State. One night the catchers brought in two whales, but only one could be processed at a time. We watched the whale being dragged up the slipway, which was flanked by foot deep gullies, crawling with thousands of maggots. The second whale was tied up at the foot of the slip, but next morning all that was left was bones. Sharks had feasted. The other whaling station was south, at the bottom of WA in the town of Albany, one of my relieving branches. Once again, I was there when a whale was caught, dragged to the flensing deck and 'processed', the deck slippery with blood and oil while we tourists gingerly walked across. The Cheynes Beach Whaling Company was owned by non-other than

Geoff Reilley, my childhood friend from Mount Lawley. When whaling ceased in Australia, the whole station was donated to the town as a tourist attraction. Fifty years later only two countries operate commercial whaling, Japan and Norway, much to the disapproval of most of the World's population; Japan, trying to convince the World that their catch is for 'scientific research', later withdrew from the International Whaling Commission to enable them to continue their slaughter.

The time for departure for England was rapidly approaching, and with only a few weeks to go I was taken off relieving staff and posted as second officer to an even more remote wheat belt town, Kondinin. When asked if I had a car, I was told that my 50 Pound Ford Anglia, was 'half a car', but it made the journey. When just short of the town I realized that my Anglia was going to need a drink, and I ran into a line crew for the Post Office. My radiator was sated by one of the linesmen who, when I reached my boarding house was also there, Phil Bussanich, who with Trevor 'Spider' Holme also became lifelong friends.

My first night in Kondinin however had to be spent in the local pub. Next morning, after coming back to my first-floor room from the communal shower, I realised I had left the key in the room and was locked out. The best efforts of the waitress with a large knife were unsuccessful, and as she had to go to the dining room I was left with a towel wrapped around my waist and a life-threatening choice. My room was on a corner on the first floor; in the corner room was a shearer wanting to go to breakfast. The windows are sash, and my top window was down. Securing my towel as best I could I studied the situation from the shearer's window. It was a leap of about six feet. The hotel staff and some guests gathered below, but the waitress could not look. The shearer wanted to know if I was jumping or not. I jumped and scrambled over the sash window. It would not have been a good look to be late on my first day at work. Later that morning the local Police Sergeant came into the Bank, asked my name and said, "12 Pounds or 12 days". He was chasing up a Parking Fine which I had incurred and paid. I arranged to show him the receipt in the pub that night.

Welcome to Kondinin. He later urged me, on return from overseas to join the Police Force.

Kondinin did not have the pleasure of my company for long. I resigned from the Bank about two weeks before sailing and returned to Cottesloe. While I had mostly enjoyed my six years with the National Bank, I had for some time formed the opinion that if I was still in the bank by age, say 28, my life would be 'ruined'; my vagrant tendencies would not have adjusted well to the structured existence of a bank officer. Although not particularly political, I was coming to the belief that Australia was on the verge of much needed change from the complacent '50s'; easy life, plenty of jobs, little social unrest. Even in the early 60s change seemed to be in the air, especially 'overseas' and I and many other young Australians were keen to experience it. I naively thought that things would be sorted out by the time I returned, whenever that might be.

FAREWELL AUSTRALIA

Time was now running short; I had the necessary inoculations and applied for the equivalent of a British Work Permit, but because it had to be issued from Melbourne I had to pick up my Passport on the way through. I joined Digby and the other member of our group, Jim Odgers, a journalist and State Champion middle distance runner. Last day in Australia, of course what better way to spend than in a giant Pub Crawl around Fremantle with a motley crew of friends.

Time at last to go to the ship. The party continued in our cabin, until the call came, "All visitors Ashore", at which a couple of journos thought they would stay aboard till Melbourne. Pandemonium ensued as the cabin was rushed by several Greek crew members under instructions to get rid of the non-passengers. This created a problem for me, as with no Passport and no ticket I fell into this category. The other miscreants and I were hustled up to a hatch in the side of the ship which was closed and therefore needed to be opened. Protesting my innocence was not cutting it with the crew, so I broke away and bolted for the upper decks. Planting myself at a rail I innocently enquired from the woman next to me what the fuss was all about. At this moment, the hatch was opened. The ship had now cast off and was a few feet from the wharf. The male stowaways made the jump but the biggest cheer from those on the wharf was for the girls, who had to hitch up their already miniskirts to make the leap. And so, the journey began.

Having made the acquaintance of the ship's Purser, I established that I was a passenger and quickly settled into life aboard. We spent Christmas between Fremantle and Melbourne. This was a migrant ship, and so many of the passengers were Greeks heading for a new life in the Land Down Under, along with plenty of young Australians off to the Old World.

There were also a small number of returning disaffected British migrants, one family of which we became friendly with. I remember his complaint about Australia, that we lack "heart". While of course disagreeing, I did over time come to see the issue from his perspective. Australians can be abrasive, thin skinned, racist, insular, intolerant as well as open, kind, friendly, generous, welcoming; as indeed are most people in the world. All this means that generalizations only work in the eyes of those with preordained opinions.

Melbourne an overnight stop, we had a party to go to in St Kilda, an all-nighter. Ship due to leave in the morning. This was a weekend, British Consul closed; frantic phone call got someone to open and give me my Passport. Rushed taxi trip to ship, arrived just as the gang way was being pulled up, and managed to scramble aboard, legal at last. Next stop Sydney, called out to Mosman to see my Aunt Sylvia, not home, left message, on to pub in city, back to ship; Sylvia left gift of books in my cabin; up on deck as ship pulling out, in time to fling a proprietorial arm around my current shipboard romance, much to the consternation of her farewelling parents ashore.

Australia departed, next stop Singapore. The ship always seems to arrive at night and depart next morning. We had arranged to meet friends of Jim for a meal in Bugie Street, eye opening encounters with the famous and beautiful boy-girls. Our new friend Tom the Tasmanian Trumpet playing Taxidermist meanwhile found a group of Chinese wharf labourers playing Mah-jong, so decided to join in. When we arrived back from our dinner Tom had the Chinese playing Two Up; another Australian cultural triumph.

Shipboard life was far from restful. A Singapore purchase of a portable record player and assorted records became the focal point of our Aft Deck Action Club, which kicked on after ship entertainments had closed for the night. Jim was perplexed that one of my records, 'The Brothers Four' seemed more popular than Odette. It was a rare night when regular sleeping hours were kept, to such a degree that on our last night before Southampton my cabin steward insisted that I get out of bed in the morning to allow him to, for one night at least, make up my bed.

Next stop Suez. As the ship had to pass through the Canal, an all-day bus trip to Cairo was the highlight. The Egyptian Museum, tour of the City then Mena House and the Pyramids, the Sphinx. By this time my Egyptian money was gone, but the camel driver did not believe my 'mafeesh floos' and insisted I ride his horse up to the Pyramid. At the top, he demanded money which I did not have, so he gave the horse a crack of his whip, and off I took over the sand hills at full gallop. Lawrence of Arabia had nothing on me. The horse stopped, and I walked off waving to the running horse owner. Back to ship in Port Said.

First day in the Mediterranean, half the passengers' sea sick. Piraeus port, tram to Athens. Tommy had desire for a beer and enquired from a Greek man where to go. Told he needed a Fix. Tom was adamant he did not need drugs but saw a poster advertising Fix Beer. Toured the Plaka, Acropolis, and then a night club where I was fascinated by a band in which the only non-electric instrument was the drums. I still have a photo of me dancing on a table top with an African beauty. Last port Lisbon, quick day trip around City, then back to ship for last leg to Southampton.

HELLO WORLD

Arrived in England in late January and the coldest winter since Napoleon invaded Moscow. The master stroke of booking in Australia was joining the Overseas Visitors Club in Earls Court, which gave us a week's accommodation. One of Jim's friends was a nurse who took us out to a Pub as an introduction to London life. After 8 pints, and lots of London Life I finished the night with a London Lass on my knee; and a feeling I could get to like London. On the other hand, Jim insisted that we help in his training, so Londoners were treated to the sight of shorts and singlet clad mad Colonials running around the streets of Earls Court trying not to freeze to death.

We met up with some of Jim's friends, one a fellow journalist. Jim was very interested in nuclear power: at the same time in London the Russian Spy drama was unfolding and one comic feature was the story of the birthday cake on a naval base in the form of a submarine. Jim started making enquiries by phone of various aspects of nuclear power and somewhat surprisingly received a call from MI5 re. his interest, however he was able to convince them that he was not a spy. Burgess and Maclean had already departed for Moscow.

Another of Jim's friends was an Australian nurse, who did 'specialling' for some patients; one of these was a Saudi Prince who, as time to return home arrived, asked what she would like as a farewell gift. "Oh, how about an E-type", she casually replied. Next morning, a knock on her door, and she was handed the keys to a shining new E-type Jaguar.

London in the dead of winter rapidly lost its appeal, so Spain won the vote. I left most of my luggage in storage with the OVC and bought an Army kit bag for travel essentials; in my innocence I had never heard of rucksacks. On the ferry from Dover I managed to lose or have my camera stolen, the first of many disasters my photographic records have experienced over the years. Bought another in Seville. Chatted to a South African girl who was a sales person for South African oranges, but lamenting that her product would be overtaken by Vitamin C pills.

We caught the train to Barcelona via Paris. On arrival greeted by the numerous hotel touts and quickly settled for one just off the Ramblas, described on the card as 'The Main Drag.' A few days to acclimatize and enquire of possibilities. Ibiza sounded good, so caught the inter-island ferry. This being February, hardly the peak season so we found a house, called Casa Cibeles, to rent just out of the main town. Rent was US$10 per month each. Jim was joined by a girl friend who was very vocal in the bedroom but otherwise a good house companion. We quickly settled in to life, made friends with local people, ran around the roads, started learning shorthand for some reason. Learned that the well in our yard had recently been the hiding place for an axe which had been used for a murder in Barcelona, but why it had been transported back to Ibiza was a mystery.

The local bar scene was quickly explored, and we discovered a bar owned by Pepe Cabrit, a fabulous Flamenco guitarist. We would warm up in a cheaper workers' bar then spend the rest of the night at Pepe's. Pepe became friends and when we had a party he would come and sit in front of the fire playing. Another of our guests was the daughter of Raymond Massey, Ironsides of TV, who had a propensity for lifting her blouse on her bra-less breasts while dancing, to universal approval. Pepe declared that he would always come to our home but did not like Americans for some reason. Pepe opened my eyes and ears to Flamenco, for which I remain grateful.

Another local expat was Clifford Irving who wrote the fake autobiography of Howard Hughes. Irving would shoot baskets with us in the town square. Life on Ibiza was a total revelation to a young lad from Perth Western Australia. On a trip to nearby Palma de Majorca I was sitting by the dock looking at a beautiful but deserted two-master and got into conversation with a local man who told me it was the 'Sirocco', which had been owned by Errol

Flynn; the man told me how Flynn had had trouble at one stage with crew, who left him to man the boat by himself, and Flynn had brought the Sirocco, under full sail, into a perfect docking at the wharf, a great feat of seamanship. Another of his talents was described by a US judge in one of his many paternity suits, "A Sexual athlete of Olympian proportions".

Ibiza had not yet become the island disco it now is, although The Rolling Stones were the trend setters by renting a house in the northern town of Santa Eulalia Abad. Sunday mornings we would gather in the town square for a meal and gossip. One morning the peace was shattered by a loudspeaker announcement by the local Bishop, telling the local people they should not employ an American girl we knew as an au pair as she was a non-Catholic sinner. The Catholic Church at the time was all powerful in Franco's Spain, but even then, the locals' reactions were a portent of the future anti-Church attitudes of especially the younger Spaniards. I think Ireland, Italy and Spain have reacted against the Church in much the same way. Recent statistics in the UK reveal that more people register as having no religion, a huge problem for the established Churches, especially with the growing appeal of Islam with large numbers of increasingly disaffected youth in France and the UK.

The rise of such lunatic fringes in the 21st Century such as ISIS and Al Qaeda has some roots in the religious and Colonial politics which the West had foisted upon the mainly under classes in their Colonial possessions. The rulers in such countries as Saudi Arabia, Egypt, Iran and now Turkey all claim Islam as their guiding light, but really politics and force are their tools. I believe that one of the main drivers of Middle Eastern politics is the respect the average Arabs have for strong leaders, actual or perceived; Russian people are also similarly inclined, as the power of a bully like Putin demonstrates. The Islamic religious preachers, who often distort the lessons of the Koran to inspire hatred of 'Infidels' are simply using such 'teachings' as political tools. Such distortions are certainly not confined to Moslems; atrocities from Myanmar to Africa, Asia and Europe are often stirred up by 'leaders' supposedly invoking their religious beliefs.

After one month in Ibiza, time to move on. My radical travel kit consisted of the kit bag, a sleeping bag I constructed from a blanket I had stolen from the ship and a piece of canvas sewn together to make a very heavy burden. The kit bag had to be carried over the shoulder by rope, which cut into the shoulder and was relieved by using underpants as padding; a trail of lost underpants across Europe resulted. Jim and girlfriend returned to England, Digby and I caught a train to Seville, to go to the Fallas Festival, one of the main festivals in Spain. On arrival, we checked out the accommodation possibilities, but decided they were too expensive, so spent the first night sitting on chairs in the city square. Next day got tickets to the Corridor de Torres, my first bull fight. After the first of 6 bulls, the huge crowd suddenly got very excited; Jayne Mansfield and husband Mickey Haggerty appeared in the ring, walking around to where their seats were, just in front of us. The crowd was delirious as Jayne, in a tight white sweater was lifted, back down, famous breasts up, over the rails to her seat. Calm was restored, and the main event proceeded. Not long after this Jayne Mansfield was killed when her car drove under a large truck and she was decapitated.

Digby now decided to return to England; I headed off 'on the road', going south. With my rudimentary Spanish, I embarked on a career of hitch hiking, staying in cheap hotels and hostels on the way to Alicante, Malaga, Granada, spent two days exploring the Alhambra and Granada city, climbing the wall on the non- free day for the Alhambra. Wednesday was then the designated day when locals could enjoy their own attractions without paying.

Malaga on the Costa Brava was the favourite holiday destination for English tourists and my first encounter of a fish and chips machine. The hotel I checked into featured only one hook on which to hang clothes, and during the night it became apparent why only short time stays were the norm. Further around the coast a cheap hostel in Jerez de la Fonterra, home of the famous Spanish Sherry found me in a large room by myself until the early hours when suddenly 100 plus field workers descended for a few hours' sleep. Further on to Portugal across to Madrid.

Backtracking around Spain, one bullfight in a small city, the young Matador seemed too courageous for his own good. The banderilleros on horseback, who normally place 6 banderillas into the bull's back were, for one bull, removed and the matador took the banderillos himself, but as he placed the second pair, one fell out. The crowd began chanting. "Mello, mello", meaning half, so he then broke the remaining banderillas in half and placed the remaining three which was very dangerous as he had to arch his back over the charging bull's horn. The crowd by this time were ecstatic as he took the muleta and made several passes, at one stage kneeling in front of the by now exhausted bull before finally the kill, called the Estacada. The crowd demanded the matador be awarded the maximum trophy, two ears and the tail, which the President accepted. Later, having coffee and cognac with some older Spanish men, they were sure that this matador would surely die in the ring. Young matadors are desperate to make a name for themselves, but competition is fierce.

I was on a train heading for Madrid and a young would be matador showed me a photo of one of the posters for the famous El Cordobes, telling me he had worked as a banderillo with him. The ticket collectors were making their rounds and my friend leapt out of the carriage, hanging on to the outside of the train till the coast was clear. All I could offer was a share of my sandwiches. Many people deplore bull fights as being cruel, but I take the view, probably influenced a little by Ernest Hemingway, that the bull is in hot blood and not feeling pain much more than they would in an abattoir. The average time for a fight is 10-15 minutes. The mistreatment of greyhounds and horses in Western sporting circles, although not as public, is surely crueller.

While hitching in Normandy I met up with a young Israeli who was escaping from the Army draft and lived even more frugally than me. At one stage, we started a road side fire to boil a billy and cook some sausages. We were invited by a young couple who owned a village shop to sleep in their store, and early in the morning my companion awoke and started stuffing his pockets with packets of biscuits and food against my protests. He was determined to steal the food and as my choices were to stay and confess to the owners or leave, to my frustration and shame I left, but left the Israeli immediately.

On to Paris where I stayed in a school in Guy Moquet converted to a hostel for the summer, and spent a couple of weeks enjoying the delights of the City of Light. Apart from The Louvre, Les Invalides, Muse des Artes Modern, Eiffel Tower, Notre Dame, Versailles etc, nothing much to see! My introduction to American Express consisted of utilisation of their mail service, latching on to the tail end of the various tours in Versailles and other attractions, which sometimes attracted hostile looks from the, usually American, paying customers. I also made a very useful purchase from an American, a blank Student Card, which I filled out as a student from UCLA on an American Express typewriter. One of the fellow hostellers, a Syrian artist introduced me to the delights of Middle Eastern food at the base of the Eiffel Tower. An American girl I had met in various places in Spain and France was due to go home. Her father had sent money, so she could spend the last week in Hotel George V but after one night she returned to the hostel, saying the hostel was much more fun than a luxury hotel, a truth I have believed and lived by ever since.

Hitchhiking around Europe became my lifestyle de jour, and took me around most of France, Spain, Portugal, Germany, Netherlands, Luxemburg, and Austria. While on a highway to Brussels one evening with fading prospects of a lift I bought some French Fries with their delicious mayonnaise, so I began offering motorists a chip; so, to my surprise a car stopped, and a young priest took me in. In Brussels, he offered me a room and I stayed there for a couple of weeks. He was quite well known in Brussels, having folk singing and non-sacred music in his church. He took me around with him to many places I would never have been introduced to normally, meeting both wealthy matrons of society and others much lower on the social scale. One memorable night we went to the Airport to farewell some young Nuns on their way to The Congo, which was at the time immersed in a savage civil war, and I was extremely moved by the emotional occasion; young Nuns, many of whom seemed no more than teenagers heading for a very uncertain future, where recently others of their friends had been murdered.

From Belgium to Holland, staying in a village called Broek in Waterland, trips in to the City to Rijksmuseum, Anne Frank's home, Heineken Brewery where they provided not only free beer but postcards and postage for all the cash strapped hitch hikers. I also did a canal trip, where a young boy ran alongside our barge till he got to a bridge under which we had to pass; he got there just in time to spit through an open section of the roof; not all Dutch people loved tourists.

Walking the roads of Europe with my unwieldy kit bag, speaking some Spanish and a few words of French became a liberating experience, although of necessity a frugal one. My finances consisted of about 150 Pounds in my London account with the National Bank. On a couple of occasions, I marched into French and Spanish banks, produced my cheque book and told bemused tellers I would like to cash a cheque. Before their protests became final I would ask them to call London and tell them a tall, skinny Australian would like to cash a cheque. Most of the time they even forgot to charge me for the phone call. How primitive were those days compared to today's credit cards, ATMs, electronic transfers etc.

A FEW BEERS IN MUNICH

Oktoberfest in Munich has always had its attractions for young Australian males and I have managed to attend three altogether. The first was with Digby and a friend who came down from London in an old Ford with a faulty fuel pump, which on one occasion in heavy rain needed a manual operation via a piece of string threaded through the windscreen attached to the pump and worked with a well-timed pull to inject fuel into the cylinders, if that if fact was where fuel needed to be injected.

Oktoberfest was preceded by a day in Dachau concentration camp, very sobering experience. A headline in a US Army journal from the War; *'Deutschland Alles Uber'*, an unkind take on the National Anthem.

One year featured a group of Australians who decided that they should take over a tram; locking the doors and ensuring they had a good supply of best Bavarian beer they drove this tram up and down on the same track, followed by several irate policemen. When eventually the beer ran out, they opened the doors and were arrested. The consequences did not stop with them; Australians were declared persona non-grata in Munich and for the duration of Oktoberfest Australians in youth hostels, camping grounds and hotels were ejected from the city. Fortunately, I was not there that year.

My last Oktoberfest was the most memorable. I arrived at the Campingplatz Talkirchen, in south Munich, this time with my backpack, tent and proper equipment. I walked along the outer fence till I came across an open space, asked the two Americans nearby to watch my pack, threw it over the fence, walked back to the park entrance and back to the Americans. When they asked what was happening I just said, "You don't think I would pay do you?" A couple of minutes' contemplation of my wisdom decided them. They packed up their gear, checked out and returned 'over the fence'.

First day in the Hoffbrau tent in the fest grounds I was drinking with a group which included a blond American girl with whom I was making great progress while sipping on my stein; a South African in the group was also sipping on my stein, and after the third time I said, "mate stop drinking my beer". He took exception to this and threw a punch and of course I retaliated. A couple of more swings and the table we were at collapsed; the blond vanished, and I saw the Security Kontroll approaching. I grabbed a beer stein and joined some German women at a nearby table, thus avoiding any altercations with the Kontroll. The South African was not so lucky. He and his friend were not only ejected they were arrested. I did visit them in jail where they were for a week.

The consequences of the first day were that a few of us who were staying in Talkirchen decided we would set up our own beer store. Two Australians, the blond American and an Australian girl set about finding a beer supply. This meant going to the Munich breweries, of which there are many; 1500 in Bavaria. We were looking to buy a daily 100 litres of beer. It took a few breweries as none had the wooden tap needed to tap the kegs, until we got to the Lowenbrau office where they found the last one; we were in business. On the way back to the camp we were driving in front of a jeep with two American soldiers; after opening the back door of the van, showing a 100-litre keg and a couple of attractive girls, they took off their ties and followed us back to camp where we quickly became the main attraction. We set out the rules; 10DM for as much as you can drink, knowing full well that very few will actually be able to drink that much. My main role in the 'Syndicate' was to buy bread rolls from the camp store and steal as many soft cheese packs as needed for breakfast. Every day we would return the empty keg to Lowenbrau and get a fresh one and the Syndicate members did very nicely.

Beer kegs occupied the day, but at night the Hoffbrauhaus bar in town, site of Hitler's Beer Hall Putsch, was the main attraction. This was shortly after the Rome Olympics, and three of the Australian swimming team were also part of our group. Ilsa Konrads was the most successful and we were in the Hoffbrauhaus when Japanese tourists spotted her; we all did well with free drinks. Linda

Magill, more famous as a Cross Channel Swimmer, shared a lot of the cooking in the camp with me. I decided that I wanted a bier stein and would slip one into my jacket, tied at the waist which I called my stealing jacket. One night as I was leaving with a stein, the Kontroll asked me if I would not steal one that night. When asked why, he said that there were a few Australians in and there would be a fight. I asked how he knew and he told me that this group had been coming for a few years because, in their words, 'this was the only place in Europe they could get good beer and a fair fight'. I gave back my stein and said goodnight and good luck.

Oktoberfest can also have its dark memories, one of which occurred when myself and another Australian guy went back with Beth the blond and the Australian girl to the room where they were staying. We were all in the same room with the lights out when the door burst open and we were surrounded by a group of very aggressive Greeks throwing punches. The punches were having little effect, but I could see that an older man standing to the side seemed to be 'the boss'. I spoke to him and said we would leave and he called his boys off. I was pretty sure that the reason they were there was not because of outraged morals, but we were in no position to argue. Outside my stupid mate said he had left his watch on the bedside table, so we went back and knocked on the door; stupid had picked up a stick which he held behind his back, which I had not noticed. The older man saw this, closed the door and quickly he and another came out the door holding bottles. We backed out onto the cobbled street where stupid was quickly put on the ground, and the old man broke the end of his bottle off on the cobbles and came at me. I tried to get over to the other two and avoid the broken bottle, but things were not looking rosy when a car came along and slowed, which sent the Greeks away. The German people in the car took us to a nearby Police Station, where we were informed that there had been a murder at that house recently, and they would want us to testify in court as to our experience. The Police drove us back to camp and next day came looking for us, but I did not fancy having to wait around in Munich waiting for a court appearance, so made myself scarce.

TRAVELLING ON

Munich being quite near to Austria, later spent a few days in Austrian Alps at Westendorf, then a week or so in Salzburg for the Mozart Spiele, Cafe Winkler and then to Vienna where Austrian friends had an apartment. Years later in Sydney I was telling an Austrian girl how my friends lowered a basket to the baker, milkman and others from their 4th floor apartment to buy necessary supplies, and she could not believe this was done in Vienna. How primitive it seemed to her.

Munich was and is an important Base for US and NATO forces, including Air Forces. Germany had equipped its Air Force with the US Starfighters and had attempted to make this plane an 'allrounder' that is a fighter and bomber, and also used it as a night fighter, much to the annoyance of Munich residents who objected to the planes taking off and landing during the night. One man decided to do something about it and set up a large catapult near the runway. As planes came in to land he would fire potato dumplings at them, usually without success, but eventually he managed to hit the fuselage of one and put a potato dent in it. The US Airforce decided to modify its night flying. Some fifty years later I met a US Veteran flyer in Tasmania who confirmed my recollection.

Hitchhiking can become a haphazard occupation, depending on whims, companions, opportunities and luck. Quite often a decision as to destination is made before breakfast and even then, is subject to change. There are also unspoken rules. One day waiting by the road for a lift, two young girls stopped 100 metres in front of me, which was pretty rude. A German lady passed them by and picked me up. When I asked her why she did not pick up the girls she told me that I was 'a professional'; they were only part timers. On a later date in Genoa I was walking down the city street wondering how far it was to a possible lift when a truck pulled up and invited me in. When the driver asked where I was heading I said, Pisa. He was going to Firenze, which I did not realize was Italian for Florence. I asked him why he had picked me up in the middle of the city and was told that the law required all trucks to have 2 drivers, and so I was driver number 2. About lunch time we arrived at his home in the countryside and stopped for lunch; altogether one of the best lifts I have had, although I have never got to Pisa. He dropped me at a local youth hostel which was all marble and opulence; it was once one of Mussolini's palaces. There I met up again with a girl who had started cutting my hair a week or so earlier when the lights went out, so she finished the job in Firenze.

Firenze became to me a source of wonder. I teamed up with a young American art student who taught me so much about medieval art, even how to tell the difference between how hands were painted in the 14th and 15th centuries. Naturally now I would not have a clue. Spending hours in the Uffizi, Duomo, Galleria, Ponte Vecchio, Palazzo Vecchio and many other churches, galleries and public art works was a bit overwhelming for a young lad from Perth WA. After having spent a couple of weeks in Firenze, one evening I was looking over the River Arno and was approached by an American woman who asked if I spoke English. I replied, "Yes, a little". "We have been here since lunch time and have seen all there is. Is there anything else to see?" I replied sadly, "No". I decided she was on a tour from probably Kansas and felt sorry for her and also grateful to have the alternative opportunities I had given myself. My student mate and I crowned our cultural sojourn by stealing a bottle of whiskey from one of the overpriced tourist shops, settling down on a gutter underneath the huge statue of Zeus to have a drink, much to the disgust of some passing US sailors.

Some rather haphazard wanderings found me back in France and Spain mainly in the area around the Massif Centrale in France and Northern Spain. I have often found that getting lost gets me in situations where I have more fun and meet interesting people. Arriving late one evening in La Spezia in Italy, had to climb about 300 steps to the Youth Hostel atop the town. Not surprisingly I was the only guest, made welcome by La Signora and about twenty cats. Her boudoir, all red velvet drapes, candles and lamps, seemed more fitting of Arabian Nights, but altogether an exotic base while exploring the city, an Italian Naval base and also where the poet Shelley drowned. Another time a young French family picked me up somewhere in France and I stayed with them for a few days doing nothing in particular but enjoying their company and the experience.

By now money was getting low, so decided to head north looking for a job. Spent a night on a train journey with several Spanish men heading for the Cote d'Azur and waiting jobs in hotels, where they said they had to pay to get a job but could expect to make good money in tips. The French Riviera sounded like a good place to head for.

Marseilles was a hot bed of French colonials having been evicted from newly independent Algeria, and frequent clashes between Police and demonstrating crowds shouting "Algerie Francaise" and my first view of how brutal French Police could be, wading into crowds with shields and batons, bashing heads and limbs. I stayed on the outskirts, preferring the more mundane pursuits of Chateau D'if, Moorish architecture, old port, Notre Dame del la Garde, etc. Booked into a youth hostel overlooking the city. Among the other hostellers were Canadians and Americans. One Canadian challenged the Americans to name the ten Canadian provinces, while boasting he could name all 50 US States. He won his bet. One of the Americans remains in my fond memory; Mary Beth Roberts from Dallas was so keen on our company that she invited any of us who came to the States to call her from anywhere in America and "Daddy will send a plane to bring you to Dallas". I wonder if anyone took her up on it; unfortunately, I never had the chance.

AND SO, TO WORK

Tim from England and Tommy from Norway were also heading for Cannes, so we decided to meet up there. I set off hitching, arrived in Toulon in the middle of the night after a very quick ride. I heard next day that a motorist the same night on the same road had been cut off by another car, chased it for 60kms and shot the offender. The French can be very emotional. Next day met up with Tim and Tommy. I was the only one with any money, my last 50 New Francs. Tim thought we should have a decent meal, so I gave him the 50 with instructions to bring back change. He of course returned with a feast to be consumed on the Cannes breakwater, but no change. Where to sleep? After dark on the harbour side beach we found a few wooden pallets and made a quite substantial 'cubby house'. Our sleep was interrupted by loud banging on the roof accompanied by threats of 'Gendarmes', so we had to dismantle our home and sleep on the beach. Revenge some weeks later of owner of said pallets, a muscle-bound playboy who would tie up his two bulldogs to a park bench while he promenaded along the Corniche; when we released the dogs, they took off in joyful freedom with their strutting owner in panting pursuit; a petty revenge but sweet nevertheless.

The issue of jobs was resolved next day. Tim as the most experienced sailor got a job on a sailing yacht, Tommy and I on the *Cypress*, a 50 foot all wooden motor cruiser, me a deck hand, Tommy as cook; our skipper, David, ex Merchant Marine. *Cypress* was a beautiful boat, built in Belgium, ideally suited for the Mediterranean cruise market. David never seemed to have much money and while we never got paid much, we always ate and drank well. When we had guests, we would sail to St Tropez, Villefranche, Nice on day trips and usually the left-over wines etc would be welcome additions to our daily fare.

Work on the *Cypress* was hardly onerous, keeping everything clean, serving meals for guests, trying to look as if I knew what I was doing. There were occasions however, when we had guests, that I worked 20 hours a day. David never had any money and was always promising to get some. David had a girl friend whose mother was an Hungarian Countess who once got stuck in the plug hole of the bath and had to be quite forcibly extricated. David's lack of money never seemed a problem, and one day he had scraped up enough money, 50 NF, for the entrance to the Cannes Casino; he and a couple of mates put on the tuxedos and went to town. Next day his friend arrived back at the boat with the news David had won half a million francs and had decided to stay on and "play with their money". Needless to say, he came back a day later broke but happy.

Life in Cannes was never dull. Moored next to us was a very famous 12 metre yacht, *Stormvogel*, owned by Hank, an American poet. A sail on her was an exhilarating experience even though Hank was a much better poet then sailor. At one stage, he put her up for sale, and a Texan millionaire expressed interest. *Stormvogel* was moored on the second row which meant access had to be gained by stepping on a line to bring her in a little closer. When the Texan saw this he promptly lost interest, declaring he would not make the 3-foot jump.

One night, having a late coffee in a Quay side bar we were startled by a man running madly towards the water, hotly pursued by two police. When he jumped into the harbour the cops emptied the guns after him. He did not surface, and I have no idea if he ever did.

Another regular was Jock, a Scot who had a hand-made MG built on a solid oak chassis which he had left on the quay for a few months while he was somewhere else. When he returned he simply reconnected the battery and the MG was alive again. Jock never had any money and the car only had a few litres of petrol in it, so all he could do was take it around the quay. At this time the US 6th Fleet flagship, the carrier *USS Enterprise*, normally based in Villefranche until 2017, was in port and we had a cruise to St Tropez booked for several of their pilots and their girls. The rest of the sailors would always be in admiring circles around the MG and Jock would sometimes drive one or two of them around. Once too often, as it happened; a gear change saw the casing of the gears break. Not to worry, the *Enterprise* had plenty of gear to fix that, so they duly took it back to the ship. We took the cruise and on arrival back around midnight Shore Patrol came to collect all hands. All leave cancelled, a crisis in Lebanon; the 6th Fleet and Jock's gear casing gone before dawn. Despair, until around midday a helicopter landed on the quay, gear casing repaired and returned courtesy of US Navy.

About this time the Cannes Film Festival was coming. I had a girlfriend, the beautiful blonde Isabelle from Hanover, who was an au pair for a French doctor and family. Of course, I had no clothes suitable for the Festival but was in the process of borrowing some, but could not get tickets anyway. One night Isabelle said her doctor's family was away for the weekend, so she had the run of the house. A night of delights promised. We had just settled in to bed when a car arrived in the garage. Isabelle leapt out; family returned. While she went downstairs I had to dress and make about a 15-foot leap onto the lawn, fortunately without injury. A half hour walk back to the boat not what the night had promised.

About this time David had told me that he had promised my job to a Tasmanian who would be arriving in the next couple of weeks. There did not seem to be any jobs going around Cannes, but I heard of the possibility of a job in Villefranche-sur-Mer. With the hope that I could get it I packed up my gear and took a bus to Nice and on to Villefranche. When I arrived, it was night and the job had already been taken. I joined the skipper and some others in a nearby bar and after a couple of beers needed a light for my cigarette which was offered by a Moroccan albino whose look over the flame made his desires very obvious. I decided to decline and took to the road back to Nice. By this time there were no buses, and I only had enough money to get the bus from Nice to Cannes anyway. A long walk in the middle of the night with my kit bag slung over my shoulder, suddenly stopped by a Police car, surrounded by four cops who obviously thought they had caught a burglar with his loot stuffed into the bag. My explanations in my best French that I worked on the 'Petite Bateau in Cannes' was not looking good. I offered my second last cigarette to a cop, who declined, so then I asked if they could give me a lift to Nice. Meantime they had opened my bag and I hoped that while plunging hands down the side of the sleeping bag, an up- pointing fork would not come into play.

No lift, so trudged on to Nice where the Music bowl on the Corniche offered shelter for what remained of the night. In the morning while sitting by the sea was joined by a German guy who soon produced a pistol and tried to persuade me to join him in going to Algeria where he said he had been in the Foreign Legion and we should go there and 'Kill Arabs'. Naturally declined this offer, caught the bus back to Cannes. Back in Cannes life settled back to normal. Tim had inherited some money and was having a boat built which he intended to sail around the world, starting for Mombasa in Kenya where he knew someone who could get us jobs in Customs for winter, then off to Canada and USA, and I was part of these plans, however timing was becoming an issue as I had no money and the job on Cypress would soon be gone.

About this time, I met John and Norman. They were travelling together; John McNamara from England heading for Australia and capable of being the oh-so-superior Englishman, Norman Simpson a Canadian Naval Officer just travelling, very organized and multi- talented. Over a few beers they learned I had been in Spain and spoke some Spanish. They were wanting to go to Spain and thought they may be able to find some work; would I like to join them? Quick decision, Yes! They were travelling in a Ford Transit van with enough room for three. I did not have time to see Isabelle before we set off next day or even to collect a sweater that a woman in our favourite cafe L'Esquif was mending for me. No need to give David notice, he was probably happy to see me on my way. I left a letter for Isabelle in L'Esquif without much hope of ever seeing her again and we hit the road for Spain. I still have Isabelle's letter, sent to Spain, dismay and disbelief at my sudden departure.

TRAVELLING ON

After two days' drive, we arrived in Spain on the Costa Brava, a little town on the coast called Malgrat de Mar where we stopped at a camping ground, Camping Kuffert. While talking with the son of the owners, Carlos Kuffert, we established that we were all talented young guys looking for work, and before bedtime all of us had a job. Norman had competence with electric motors; the Kufferts' generator was always giving trouble so he became its saviour. I, because of nothing in particular, became the chief digger of holes in which to plant Australian eucalyptus trees which would be accessed from Barcelona; John for other labouring tasks. I was paid 30 pesetas a one cubic metre hole in hard clay. I could do at best 7 a day. Our food and board were also included, which meant lunch and siesta. On day one I thought the Spanish were pretty lazy taking 3-4 hours off in the middle of the day, but by day two I was completely converted. Starting work again at around 4pm till about 7pm, then off to restaurants and bars for the evening seems very civilized.

My career as a digger of holes was fairly short lived. I was introduced to the owner of one of the hotels in town being renovated, where the owner assured the foreman that I spoke Castilian and not Catalan. He stood in front and speaking from his full height to approximately my navel issued instructions, concluding with the reasonable "Entiendo?" At my response of "No Entiendo", without more words he led me up to the first floor where the tiled floor was covered with blobs of dried cement, a trowel placed in my hand, my single "Entiendo" sufficed and a day of cement chipping ensued; but this career change was also short lived, next day I was promoted to Night Receptionist. In the 1960's Catalonia nationalism did not seem overt; unlike the situation in 2017, but in the 60's Franco's repression was very evident.

The Costa Brava was and is a popular destination for British and German tourists, and my less than onerous duties consisted of looking after any guests between afternoon and midnight, without any dramas. On one occasion, a young guy came in and asked something in Spanish which I did not catch, so he grinned and took the typewriter. I assumed and hoped that he had reason to do so and was relieved when he returned it next day. My Spanish clearly not up to the complexities of typewriter repairs.

Papa Kuffert was German and had lived in Spain since marrying Mama during the Spanish Civil War and told us of having to take a gamble on which passport to show when stopped at Republican or Falange checkpoints. The wrong one could be fatal. When a town or village was taken by Falange, ie: Fascist forces, the roads in and out were signed with the bunched arrows of Falange. Spain at this time was still governed by Franco and very much a Police State.

The road leading into town was a Roman road flanked by beautiful trees. One day we awoke to see all the trees on one side had been cut down. When enquired Why? the answer was the Guardia Civil and Air Force had done so because they said smugglers used the road and could not be seen from the air. Guardia Civil members regularly stopped at our camp at night for a drink and chat while on patrol. I was fascinated by their black hats which were flat at the back; the explanation given that when in a street fight with their backs to the wall their hat would not fall over their eyes.

Life in Malgrat was very pleasant; work, beach, night life, train trips to Barcelona or Sitges. I became friends with an English travel guide who regularly accompanied groups from Northern England, but one day was told she was in a plane crash from Manchester and had been killed. Encarna, the very attractive washerwoman, was becoming increasingly insistent on sharing my bed but unfortunately the opportunity never arose before we left.

After a few weeks John and Norman decided to leave for a trip around Spain then North to France and Germany, and I joined them. Carlos had decided to leave the family home and headed for Alicante in the south. Mama asked if we would track him down and persuade him to return. We said we would try. We did find Carlos, but he was in no mood to head back to Malgrat.

A trip around Spain for a month or so, back to Granada, Cordoba, Madrid, Seville, Alicante, Torremolinas, Malaga, always camping out with the van. One morning we awoke to see an apologetic policeman asking if we would mind moving as we were in the middle of police firing range and they wanted to start shooting.

Time and money demanded a less than leisurely trip north, so quickly through France and Germany. In Switzerland John had a friend who worked in Geneva. We were pretty much broke but still headed there and found he worked for the United Nations; a day observing the conference of the International Labour Organization, which mainly consisted of the Third World delegates walking out, followed by fabulous meals at a very classy restaurant, courtesy of John's friend; altogether a diversion worth taking. Back on the road we called in to a Swiss farm to ask if we could camp on their land but was told it was too cold; the farmer showed us his barn into which we drove the van and spent a much warmer night.

A YEAR IN GERMANY

We drove to Mainz where John had a friend from his Army days who introduced us to the US Army where we were told we could have jobs fixing tanks but would need German Work Permits. We arrived in Frankfurt on a Friday afternoon. We found the Internatzianal Arbeitsampt (Labour Exchange) and set about asking for jobs. The German staff explained that we could not get a job in Germany without the right visas. We had letters from the American Army saying they would give us jobs fixing their tanks, but this was not good enough. They were getting a bit desperate as this was late Friday and bier beckoned and told us that the only people exempt were North American students. Norman announced that he was a North American student, I quickly confirmed that I also was a North American student, as did John. 'Ach so, no problem,' we were presented with a choice of about 400 jobs and quickly decided on a forest in Bavaria owned by a Prince who also owned one of the best breweries in Germany. One of the many blessings of (German) POETS day (Piss Off Early, Tomorrow's Saturday). So, began my next career, as a forester.

The Furstal Thurn und Taxis owned among other things, The Thurn und Taxis Brewery in Regensburg and Forstampt Thiergarten in the nearby village of Sulzbach am Donau. The Thurn und Taxis ancestors also started Europe's first mail service, and sometime later in Brussels I came across a plaque commemorating this service from Munich to Brussels. We arrived at the forest and were greeted by the Manager and installed in the hunters' lodge, along with some authentic North American students on work exchange. Wallace from North Carolina, Tucker Smallwood from Washington DC and Charlie from Chicago. Quickly introduced to the forester, Herr Gurtler, who would give us our daily duties and generally oversee us. The lodge had been built by Franz Josef, Emperor of Austria and had catered for large numbers of his, and others, guests on hunting holidays. Among the trophies displayed on the walls were some from Himmler, Goering, Bormann and Goebbels. The main objects of their attentions were deer and wild boar. The kitchen featured an array of stoves extending the full length of the lodge, about 60 feet.

Cutting fire trails through the mainly pine, fir, beech and birch forest began around 7am. After a hearty breakfast, we drove to the designated start following Herr Gurtler on his motor bike, who would give us the directions and would commence the day with his standard order "Stzuck Stzuck" and we would proceed to cut a fire trail about 5 metres wide to the daily target point, also clearings to enable younger trees to establish themselves. We worked with a few local Germans who were content to go at a pace which would get us to the target by the end of the day, but we would usually work at a decent speed, get to within a few feet of the target and relax with a book or shoot the breeze.

I thought at the time that the general belief that Germans were more hard working than us Australians was a myth, but as the forest Germans were much older and had been working in that forest for years the comparison was unfair. Years earlier back in Australia I was working in country towns with the Bank, and local farmers who needed labourers to do work such as rock picking in paddocks would not employ Australians, preferring Italians who were much harder workers. Later still when the refugee and migrant issues were creating rifts in societies around the world, hard line opponents of humanitarian treatment of refugees seem to persist in refusing to accept that refugees are generally highly motivated to work and succeed, although because of language and cultural reasons this sometimes comes to fruition in the second generation. Australia is, after all, a migrant nation.

Forest work was very enjoyable, most of the trees could be brought down with one or two cuts with a machete or with a hand-held saw. One day I was working alone with a saw and being bothered by wasps. I took a swing at one with my saw and managed to put a cut in my wrist from which a large spurt of blood erupted. I called "Norman", "What?" "I have cut an artery". Norman came crashing through the trees and we managed to stem the flow and apply a bandage. I spent the rest of the day reclining in the van reading George Orwell's *'Down and Out in Paris and London'*.

Forstampt Thiergarten was essentially for us, a working holiday. We were treated very well and paid well, about US$30 per week, plus very good food and board. We were asked what weekend excursions we would like, and a couple of highlights were the VW Plant in Wolfsburg, a steel mill and a porcelain factory near Frankfurt. Transport and weekend accommodation provided, a great incentive for North American Students to like Germany. I was particularly impressed with the VW plant in Wolfsburg, where a vehicle was turned off the production line every 12 seconds. An old copy of Der Spiegel told how after the War, Wolfsburg was in the British Zone and the first Post War VWs were produced by the British Army, after they had released the slave labour. Under the surrender terms the British Government had the opportunity to own VW, but the British Parliament turned it down, as a 'Peoples Car Concept' would never work. I think they preferred a Daimler in every country estate.

Tucker's father was the chief of the local American Institute in Regensburg, whose mission as explained to me by him was the "Re-education of the Germans". To this end various functions were held in his home, which was in a medieval tower, of which Regensburg had lots, as it had pretty well survived the bombs of the War. We students were on the guest list for some and enjoyed cocktails and canapes with German and American 'important people'. Tucker was, and hopefully still is, a dead ringer for Sammy Davis Junior, and as a left-wing African American student sometimes had some lively but civilized discussions with Wallace, a Southern conservative. Wallace once told me how he had gone on Freedom Marches, sat in the back of buses, sat in on segregated burger bars and other protests of segregation, but after few beers one night he confessed, "Goddam it Dan, I AM prejudiced".

Another day in the forest we were discussing the various cultural qualities of cities, principally London and Paris. John with his very English accent announced that the last play he had seen in London was Agatha Christie's *"Ten Little Niggers'* (subsequently changed to *'Ten Little Indians'* for obvious reasons). A shocked and hushed Tucker said, "You could not say that in America", which John replied, "We live in the land of the Free". John at his imperious best. One night we went to a restaurant in Regensburg where the manager refused us entry because I was not wearing a tie. John towering over him proclaimed, "Du bist ein kleine Hitler", as we left. Charlie was a little more aloof from these moments but was a great favourite with the school girls from North Germany who came to the forest in school holidays. He entertained them with drawings and games while practicing his German.

Wallace was the man with the life outside the forest. His girlfriend was the daughter of George Wallace, the Alabama Governor who ran for President on a very racist platform and was later shot, not fatally, for his trouble. Wallace heard from her that she would be in Munich with a school group so one weekend he took off for Munich and met her for a couple of days of clandestine passion culminating in midnight returns through hotel windows. By far his most impressive weekend however, was to meet Steve McQueen who was in Munich filming 'The Great Escape' and he and Wallace spent a couple of days on Steve's bike roaming Munich and surrounds.

The forest, which covered some 700,000 acres, was more or less feudal in that the Prince owned everything, but the farming land was leased out to the workers who shared the farm machinery; farm work such as harvesting was carried out collectively. On a day of winnowing hay, we were rewarded with a case of beer at the end of every row. The consumption of the chemical free Bavarian beer by the forest workers could be quite prodigious, the foreman would regularly have 4 litres before breakfast.

Catholic Bavaria is quite conservative; swear words are 'Sacrament' and 'Crucifix'; at Mass women sit on one side of the Church, men on the other. One Sunday the priest gave a virtual order that the vote in a coming election should be for the Christian Democrat, CDU, candidates. A walk through the Lodge gardens revealed a small chapel built for the Franz Josef family. None of this however deterred the forest workers and their families from enjoying the life stimulus of the great German beer. Although we were generally working in separate groups to the other forest workers we all got on very well and regularly joined in after work drinks at one of the local drinking houses. Hans Fuchs and his wife Maria often had us in for dinner.

The time being the early 1960's the War was not a distant memory, although Bavaria escaped much of the devastation of North Germany. One day I was walking through the forest with Herr Gurtler and came across a rusted out Schmeiser machine gun; when I pointed this out to Herr Gurtler he dismissed it as 'Ein Straggler'. Kurt, one of the other foresters told me how in 1945 he was 12 years of age in school when the SS came, put a cap on his head and a machine pistol in his hand, led him to a bridge and told him to shoot the approaching Americans. The Americans duly arrived, and a big black soldier took his gun, patted him on the head and said, "Go back to school son". Kurt passionately told me that he 'Loves Americans'. On another visit to Regensburg I was drinking with a local man. There is a very famous bridge over the Donau in Regensburg, the Steine Brucke, Stone Bridge, built by the Romans in the 12th Century. During the War one of the central spans was destroyed and is now made of pre-stressed concrete. Locals have always blamed the Americans; but after a few beers my companion confessed that it was actually him, ordered by the Army to impede the approaching Americans, and he implored me not to tell anyone as this would make his life very uncomfortable.

One of the Post War conditions imposed on the Germans by the Allies was that Germans should be made aware of what actually happened to the country under the Nazis; going to the movies meant having to watch a documentary on such things, Kristallnacht, concentration camps etc., and one could feel the atmosphere in the audience tensing. The Bavarians were very conscious of the race between the Americans and Russians to control territory. General Patton was reputed to be racing ahead of his Army in a jeep, armed with his pearl handled revolvers, proclaiming the territory to be for America. Not all, however, was rosy; one of the forest workers who had served in the Afrika Korp referred to Americans as 'Autobahn Soldaten'; I refrained from reminding him who won, as I remembered a bit of British soldiers' sing along to the tune of *'Colonel Bogie'*:

> Goering has only got one ball,
> Hitler has two but very small
> Himmler has something similar,
> But poor old Goebbels has no balls at all.

Sulzbach was very close to the Czechoslovakian border and a road running through a steep ravine was, I was assured, mined from one end to the other in case of invasion if the Cold War became hot. The Border was manned by Czech soldiers who were quite friendly, and we would chat and give them newspapers and other little gifts from the West.

Apart from trees, the main activity in the forest was the hunting of boar and deer. The boar did not have much natural food in the forest, so they were fed with mashed potato in special troughs, called Futerungs which we also helped build. To facilitate the boar hunting for the intrepid hunters we had to build shooting platforms in the forest; peasants would then brush beat to force the animals towards the 'hunter' who would despatch the beast with his high-powered rifle and retire to celebrate his conquest. One night, about 2am, we were summoned to collect one of these trophies which had inconsiderately decided to die in the middle of a swamp. Getting a 400-kilo boar on to a wheel barrow in the middle of a swamp was not the easiest task we had been set as foresters, but eventually we got it to the butcher's room where it was hung and processed.

Winter was now approaching, which meant that the forest work would be in abeyance till Spring. The Germans would retire to their homes, collect unemployment cheques and work their way through their supplies of mulled wine. The alternative was the sugar mills processing the crops of sugar beet. Wallace had been told of the death of a distant cousin in Georgia so had to go back for the funeral. Southern 'Rules' gave no leeway for being 8000 miles away at the time. Tucker headed back to college; Norman decided to head back to England; John who had met and fallen for a very beautiful reporter on the *Suddeutscher Zeitung* thought teaching English would be good; she had visited the forest and published an article headed 'Australianische student sag "Ich Liebe den Deutschen", together with my photo; somewhere the article survives. I had decided to spend the winter in the sugar mill. John went in for an interview with Berlitz Sprachenschule in Regensburg and I went with him. At his interview, I was asked my accent, to which I confessed 'Australian'. Margaret, an English girl also applying, said 'None'. I told her she had a Home Counties accent. At the time, I had spent a total of two weeks In England so of course knew everything about accents.

At Berlitz Frau Ricke the Principal simply looked at me and said, "Why not you?" I accepted and so commenced my career as a teacher. Regensburg was the main school, where John taught. In the meantime, Digby came down from London with 3 mates and we spent an intervening week in Munich for Oktoberfest. I was to teach in nearby Ingolstadt, a city of some 65,000 people and the city of the auto manufacturer Auto Union, now Audi. Ingolstadt is also the 'birthplace' of Mary Shelley's *Frankenstein*, because of its famous hospital and museum; also, in 1508, the birthplace of Germany's Pure Beer standard.

Being the last to leave the forest I was given a memorable send off at a local Gasthof, 14 litres of beer and 14 schnapps and a walk back to the lodge through trees that assumed very strange shapes. I left next day for Ingolstadt where Frau Ricke had organised a room with a family. John's Canadian girlfriend Carol had now appeared and was also lodged there, in a separate room. After a couple of weeks, the hosts became apprehensive that illicit relations were being conducted and we had to leave. Carol went back to England; I got a room in the city where I stayed for the next 9 months. John had in the meantime decided to return to London, with the beautiful journalist to follow in a few weeks.

Berlitz have a very simple and effective method of teaching language; they start with 'a book'. "This Book", "That Book" and go from there. Most of my classes were in the evenings; in daylight hours, I had the children of American contractors who were building oil refineries nearby; I had grades 4th, 5th, 6th and 8th. All my children came from either Louisiana or Texas; getting them to pronounce Double You instead of Double YA was a challenge.

Settling in to my new 'profession' was made easy by the other teachers and staff. Tony Kachami from Lebanon taught French and Commerce; Marie Claude also taught French. Frau Ricke was very helpful as was her secretary Heidi. I had English classes every evening, mostly young adults. Germans have 8 years of English in school, but very little conversation; the Berlitz method of gradual build-up of sentences and usage is very effective. Grammar and spelling is introduced as lessons progress. Dictating essays allowed me on occasions to introduce some Australian themes.

Now that I was in employment I became a German Taxpayer. I had to have an annual chest X-ray and dental check-up, all on Social Insurance. Tax is split between Income Tax and Social Insurance; a couple of years later I was amazed to receive in my Australian Bank account a full refund of the Social Insurance component, the Claim Form for which I had forwarded from Addis Ababa; German efficiency strikes again.

Life in Ingolstadt revolved around the school and particularly the students. Generally, every evening after the last class myself and some of the students would repair to a Gasthof or restaurant. One evening we would all speak German, the next English. My classes grew in size, to the extent that after a few months Frau Ricke informed me that one of my classes was the largest in the whole European Berlitz system. Pay was monthly and as month's end approached the number of 'homework' assignments increased as each one was paid an extra 60 pfennigs.

One night we were in a café when an announcement came over the public address which I could not properly understand. One of the students told me that they had just announced that President Kennedy had been shot. The shocked patrons soon left, and the café was closed. On that same night, I subsequently learned that the Munich Opera House was re-opened with a Grand Opera performance for the first time since the War; in the interval, an announcement was made, and the performance was cancelled. Germany went into a period of mourning; President

Kennedy had only recently made his much misquoted "Ich Bin Ein Berliner" speech at the Wall.

My American students were following a curriculum from the States which was easy to teach, although I had concerns with some aspects. In all the classes only two had any history; one was a simple Greek mythology, the other in 8th Class American History. I had a bit of trouble with one chapter in this which listed several inventions, which the course claimed as American. Included in the eight were; radio, television, telephone, motor cars, radar. I conceded the Wright Brothers, although years later a documentary on the German inventor Gustav Whitehead seemed to prove that he preceded the Americans by two years. I pointed out the actual inventors of these five were actually Scottish, Italian, English and German. Next day one of the parents came in the school to complain that I was 'Un-American'. Shades of McCarthy.

One of my great triumphs, probably the only one, was a breakthrough in teaching poetry. Susan in 8th class led the pack in declaring that all poetry was boring. I asked her to read 'How They Brought the Good News from Ghent to Aix' by Robert Browning, which she did in a flat Southern drawl. I then went back, stanza by stanza, inflecting the rhythm of the ride; and 'Glory be' the class actually GOT IT.

Every morning we would do the ritual of telling of the previous day's events. Mary Beth, eldest child of a large Catholic family, one morning announced; "Mr Moloney, my mother and father have two lovely beds at home but only ever sleep in one of them". I simply asked her to get out the arithmetic books.

Winter had now arrived, with it snow and ice on the moat which had once surrounded Regensburg. Skating and Curling contributed to the city's enjoyments. I also at times had to drive to Munich and had the use of the company car. I had never driven on icy roads before and had a salutary lesson on an iced over cobble stone street in Munich one night. One touch of the brakes and a 360-degree spin convinced me to never touch brake again on ice. On another occasion, I had been out with one of my Private Students and was returning with some of my normal students when another car raced past us and had a collision with a pole.

This necessitated a report to the Police where I was asked my opinion as to whether then speed on the other car was too fast. I replied that that was for the Police to decide. Policeman to me, "Das ist ein typische Englander antwort". Me to Policeman, "Ich bin kein Englander, Ich bin von Australien". My students were delighted with this as they were not in the habit of answering back to Policemen.

Christmas was now approaching, and as the school would close for a couple of weeks, I decided a holiday in London would be good. Booked the train from Regensburg to London, having arranged to stay with Lorraine, my girlfriend on the ship, who had a flat in West London. The train trip meant an overnight stop in Brussels, where I teamed up with a young English guy with whom I shared an hotel room. Winter was in full swing; the streets were inches under snow, but we found a cosy Pub for a few beers. After an hour or so I said to my mate "Do you realize we are the only two males in the place?" The scene was getting a bit tense, so a strategic retreat was in order. Shortly after we left there was blood on the snow.

The rest of the journey proceeded without incident, but on the re-entry to England in Dover I was in the queue with an expired entry certificate; In front of me was an Indian family with all the documents necessary when the Immigration official, without even looking ordered them to stand aside. My outrage on their behalf was tempered by the fact that any inspection of my Passport would give me some trouble. This was only the first incident of what I came to recognize as the English racism against, particularly, Sub Continent and West Indian people. A later newspaper headline referred to them as the "Visible one percent".

A pleasant but uneventful couple of weeks in London came to an end, back on the train to Ingolstadt. Most of the journey was at night, and none of the stations had eating facilities open and my travelling companions were two German ladies who were quite understanding when they could not understand my German as I was from Bavaria, so I was well fed during the night.

Winter began receding over the next couple of months and my classes seemed to be growing steadily. My social life was also very active, particularly with two girls. Ingrid from Holland was in a choir and I attended several recitals with her. German people seemed to me to be much more classically orientated. Years later the movie *Schindler's List* had a small illustration; two rather brutish German soldiers were climbing stairs to arrest some Jews; a radio was playing music and the soldiers were debating whether it was Bach or Brahms. Ingrid, when listening on the radio to Beethoven's 5th Symphony, shuddered at the opening chords. I asked why, and she explained that the chords were the Morse code signal of V, which during the War the BBC broadcast as the Signal for Victory and as the warning to Resistance members that coded messages would follow. Ingrid's brother was in the Dutch Resistance and had been killed.

My other 'girlfriend' was Elfriede Sauber, who lived in Neuburg. Elfriede had a Messerschmitt 3-wheeler in which we cruised around the countryside; one memorable Sunday driving the Romantischer Strasse, going to Wurzburg, Heidelberg and Rothenburg, among other towns. Rothenburg was a highlight; famous as the home of The Brothers Grimm, a walled city beautifully preserved. During the Thirty Years War, it was besieged for many months. After this time, the leader of the Swedish enemy decided to bring matters to a 'head' so talked to the Rothenburg leader and challenged him to drink a large stein of beer, about half a gallon, without stopping. Duly accomplished, the siege was lifted. This feat is commemorated every hour by the clock in the Rathausplatz; one door opens with a large bottle of wine, the other with a man downing the beer. Another town, Dinkelsbuhl, was similarly besieged and not doing well. The town's children decided to take matters into their own hands; they dressed in uniforms and marched out to the besieging army singing. The enemy commander was so impressed the siege was lifted. If only modern wars could be so decided.

One Sunday at Elfriede's home I was invited for Sunday lunch with her parents, who lived in a house overlooking the Donau River. Elfriede's mother became a little excited as she told how just across the river, during the War, was a Luftwaffe base which was regularly bombed by the RAF. After each bombing the local people had to repair the runway, carrying loads of soil in baskets. Frau Sauber became agitated as she told how the day after repairs were completed "Kompt der furdampter Englanders und Bombe, Bombe, Bombe". Elfriede gave me warning look 'Don't Smile'.

One of the great delights of working in a city like Regensburg or Ingolstadt is its proximity to so many of Bavaria's cultural icons. Apart from the cities medieval churches, buildings, markets etc, I have never seen so much gold in a church as there is in the Cathedral in Regensburg. The Danube river cruises to such gems as the Kloster Weltenburg Monastery, where the monks still make some fabulous beers, Walhalla Hall where German Poets, Scholars, politicians, statesmen are commemorated. Kelheim Bewfreiungshalle celebrating the defeat of Napoleon. Another weekend train trip to Berchtesgaden, site of Hitler's *Eagle's Nest*. One place I never got to but one day must is Neuschwanstein Castle, King Ludwig 11's Grand Folly. One of the many stories I liked about Ludwig is how he inspired a near Civil War by putting up the tax on beer by 1 pfennig to help pay for this. Bavarians are passionate about their beer; at the time, there were 2500 breweries in the European Market, 1500 of them in Bavaria; all of those I had sampled produced great beers.

Easter arrived, a long weekend holiday. Heidi wanted to go to Milan, two of our Italian students were going and offered us a lift. They drove a hotted-up Ford Cortina and we took off over the Alps as only Italian drivers can; flat out. Careering along Alpine roads with thousands of feet drops inches away had Heidi hanging on for dear life, but we made it all OK with all limbs intact. More sedately in Italy through Verona, Triento, Brescia. My most memorable day was spent early in the Milan Duomo for Easter Sunday Mass where the singing of the choir was simply superb. Milan's other highlight 'The Last Supper' and the Quadrilatero d'Oro shopping malls, the gardens of Orto Botanico kept me busy for the weekend, then back for another trip over the Alps, this time via Lake Como; Heidi this time resigned to whatever her fate may be.

By now I had been in Ingolstadt about nine months. My German was 'passable'. I could hold conversations with not too many lost looks. One of my students, who had escaped from Czechoslovakia after the War, had told me how when they walked into Regensburg, starving and desperate, the population, who were not much better off, had shut the doors on them, but now he was a happy German. One night after a few beers we were walking home singing some German drinking songs when I decided to enlarge his range by bursting out with the ribald version of "Our headmistress her name is Jane, she just likes it now and again, and again, etc." I don't think the sleeping citizens would have been appreciative, even if they did not know the translation.

BACK ACROSS 'THE DITCH'

The decision about how long to stay was made for me; my 'shipboard' girlfriend Lorraine sent me a letter inviting me to join her and some friends on a tour around England, Scotland and Wales in a hired car, an invite I quickly accepted. The American children were due to return home, so I gave Frau Ricke and my favourite classes a few weeks' notice and after a round of farewells, headed once more for England by train. I stayed with Lorraine a couple of days, met our companions, a couple from Brisbane and Peter Jeans from Perth. Some forty years later in Sydney came a knock on my door and there was Peter, having tracked me down by the Electoral Roll. He was a school teacher, and author, having written a book about his trip riding from Singapore to London on his Norton bike. We renewed a friendship and whenever in Perth I would visit him and his wife Judith. One day he announced that he had 'mild dementia', but a short time later he passed away. A talented man taken far too early.

One month driving around Britain, staying in hostels, looking for a 'lone piper playing a lament on a Scottish hill,' (unsuccessfully). 'Beating of the Retreat' at Edinburgh Castle, sniffing snuff in Stirling Castle, York, Canterbury Cathedral, Oxford, Cambridge, Carnarvon, Loch Ness, Liverpool and lots in between made for a great way to get to know Britain.

Back to London for the more serious business of finding work. Couple of days with Lorraine, in her flat in Knightsbridge, where her door on the first floor was directly opposite John Lennon's. We would put pictures of the Beatles under his door and would get them back signed by all the Beatles. Unfortunately, mine disappeared with the rest on my possessions when I left England about 18 months later. One day while sitting on the window chatting with the group of young girls waiting below on the street I said to them, "He won't be long girls, he is just in the shower". The response in middle finger salutes was immediate.

Leisure time over; time to look for a job, which in London seems to be very easy for Australians. First one offered, attending window box gardens for some of the elite members of society in the West End, including Rudolf Nureyev. I informed the owner that gardens were not really my thing; he protested that all Australians have Green Thumbs, but I assured him that this did not apply to me.

Next job more up my line; barman in a pub. The pub is the 'Warwick Castle' in Maida Vale, by the Regents Canal. The pub was built in 1846 and is listed with Historic England and over the years many well known figures have been regulars, including Richard Branson. Ken the owner was off to Australia for a three- month holiday, I would live in and help Bob, the Scottish manager, and his wife Anne. Quickly settled into the daily routine, setting up the bar for the morning session, then closed after lunch, evening session from 3pm. Opening hours North of the Thames different from those South, but seemed quite civilized.

Our patrons were a mixed bunch; great actor Roger Livesey and his wife Ursula Jeans, Irish navvies, journalists, antique 'manufacturers', couple of Lords and Ladies. We rang "*Time*" with a ships bell. One quiet afternoon I was chatting with a gentleman who told me he brought his barge down the Regents Canal from Hampstead Heath and that he had plaited the rope attached to the bell. In between drinks Bob asked if I knew who I was talking to, then informed me that the man was the Speaker of the House of Lords; certainly not someone who gave themselves any airs of superiority over mere mortals.

We served bottled drinks off cold shelves, but the Irish would always want their Guinness room temperature, even of the hottest summer days. It took a few months of 'suggestions' but finally one day they tried cold Guinness; a few considered sips then, "Begorah Paddy it's not bad." Another evening I got into a discussion on Tchaikovsky, how old he was when he died. In the ancient days before Google settling such questions as this meant calling *The Daily Telegraph* who provided these services from their libraries.

Question resolved, 54. Couple of days later I was chatting to one of the journalists; asked him what he did; "I sometimes work the night shift in the Library; couple of days ago someone rang in and wanted to know how old Tchaikovsky was when he died." I promptly bought him a pint of Best Bitter.

Warwick Place is close to St Johns Wood, and Lords Cricket Ground, home of cricket. I could go to a couple of Test Matches there, one against Australia, one against New Zealand. On the Saturday evening of the New Zealand game I was in a nearby pub when the New Zealand team emerged with their Captain, Bev Congdon in a wheelbarrow. Test Cricket seemed to be more relaxed then than now, where there is so much money involved. One day during a Test someone pointed out to me an old man in wheelchair, Jack Hobbs one of the greatest English cricketers from the 1920's. On another occasion, I turned up for the cricket only to have rain stop play. What better to do than go into Parliament House for Question Time, which seemed a lot more civilized than the Australian version.

One of my lifetime missed opportunities also arose; for some reason which I am a loss to remember I was picked in a team to play a match at Lords, home of Test Cricket, against the cast of the TV program 'Z Cars'. Spent the day waiting for the rain to ease off, listening to actors complaining about Pay and Conditions. It would have been my great boast to be able to say, "I played at Lords". Managed to see two Tests at Lords and one at The Oval in South London.

Many years later, on a river cruise in The Ukraine, I mentioned to a retired English policeman that I knew Eric Reid, patron of the pub and at that time head of Scotland Yard's Murder Squad and was surprised to hear him dismiss Reid as a 'Television Cop'. Eric Reid to me was much more than that; he was the father of Joan. Joan and I quickly became 'an item'. She, being Scottish, was a champion Highland dancer, a chiropodist and a great girl. She spent many days showing me London; Greenwich, HMS Victory, Westminster, Richmond, etc. One day in Westminster Abbey an American, who was a patron of the Warwick Castle, appeared at the doorway with his two young sons who wanted to explore;

"You have ten minutes", said Dad. So much for British history I thought, standing near the tomb of Isaac Newton.

Joan had a friend, Dereck, who managed one of the few "Gay" clubs in Soho, the A and B Club. Went there with her one day where a large Texan called out "Hey big boy, how about a roll in the hay?" My holding hands with Joan quelled his ardour. The A and B was reputed to be the only club in London where one could get Bacardi rum; a similar anomaly to the belief that Levi jeans were not available. Another night in Dereck's flat some kids started shooting air rifle pellets at his window; I offered to go down and put a stop to it, but he declined. Homosexuality had only recently been made legal in Britain and some of those affected were still nervous of some members of the public.

Another of Joan's friends was Angus Lennie, the Scottish actor, at the time starring in the TV show 'Horizons', as well as many other TV and stage shows. One night in his flat he offered to show me to the toilet, and once there made a polite but physical advance. I just tapped him on his shoulder and gave a shake of my head. The last time I saw Angus was when I saw 'The Great Escape' in Beirut, where he played 'the Mole' and was shot on the wire trying to escape.

Bob and I had a sometimes 'interesting' relationship. He, being Scottish, had during the War been in the famous Argyles regiment stationed in Singapore. When War with Japan broke out and the Japs were making fast progress down the Malay Peninsula, British and Australians were in retreat, hoping for evacuation from Singapore. Bob related to me with a degree of malice how he watched the Australians on the Singapore docks steal and drink as much beer as they could lay their hands on. Considering what lay ahead for many of them in Changi I could not blame them. Another time after closing, and in front of the Reids, he demanded I do something, I cannot now remember what, which I refused to do and told him to do it himself. To be fair to Bob he was up every day early to prepare the cellar and kegs, while I lay in bed. We generally managed to be civil to each other. Another time a genteel lady asked for a Snowball; I was tempted to say this was the middle of summer, not having a clue as to the makeup; Bob quietly informed me it was an advocaat and lemonade.

One Sunday a Swedish man became confused about tips in English currency and asked me what ten percent of his order was; I said, "'Nothing, you don't have to tip here". This confused him greatly and he left more than 20 percent. Americans seem to be so accustomed to tipping they do it automatically. I have had a lifetime objection to automatically adding an amount for 'service'. Once in New York, having bought two slices of pizza for me and friend we were nearly out the door when "what about the tip?" followed. My response, "I will give you a tip; make a better pizza", had me out the door and down the street. Another time John, Norman and I were in Frankfurt Airport waiting for a friend's plane to arrive, late. Breakfast of coffee and rolls. The bill arrived with 15% Bedeinung (service) added. We refused to pay as we had received no service. Police were called but the issue was resolved in our favour. I suppose I have this Socialist? Australian attitude that people employed to do a job should be properly paid by the employer. Notwithstanding all that I mostly tip for friendly, above the call, service.

Three months was nearly up, Ken returned from Australia, I stayed on for a week or so. On one of my final nights the pub was packed; a large group of that most objectionable of English people I call the 'nouveau riche' were standing two deep back from the bar and ordering drinks one or two at a time. One of the last orders was for Scotch, which the English pubs served in wine glasses. I finally got the last order filled when our 'gentleman' leaned across two people with his scotch glass and demanded soda. I obliged by squirting soda into his outstretched glass, spilling a little. This provoked an angry outburst, calling me 'boy'. Ken had been observing this episode and immediately told the group, "you don't speak to my staff like that, you can all leave now". Some fifty years later when I was back in London I went back to the Warwick Castle; it seemed to have not changed at all. The new publican, when I told him of my past there showed me a photo he had taped to a wall, Ken pulling a beer. A true gentleman.

Hitch hiking around Europe resumed, usually meeting up with fellow travellers around the traps. One girl, the Hawaiian Princess, and I spent a couple of weeks in Switzerland, St Moritz, Zermatt and one night found ourselves at the foot of a very large, forbidding looking glacier with no evidence of humanity to be found. A long walk in the night before finally finding a remote hotel where they accepted a cold and hungry married couple. Zermatt at the foot of the Matterhorn was more welcoming, staying in the vacant youth hostel, a huge wooden barn, which, this being summer, was vacant. I never got to stay in the Alps during Winter but was happy to be in such beautiful country with relatively few tourists in summer weather. A few months wandering Europe in Summer a nice break from the restrictions of employment.

AND NOW FOR A 'PROPER' JOB, AND 'HOME'

Autumn was now approaching, time to think of getting a job and returning to England. An ad in the Overseas Visitors Club directed me to Fulham, 31 Gowan Avenue. An interview with the main inhabitants, Peter an accountant from New Zealand, David who worked for Mars and Graham a hairdresser from New Zealand went well, particularly as the final part was a few drinks in a local pub and singing around the piano with lusty renditions of such classics as *'Maybe it's because I'm a Londoner'*. Approval duly granted settled in to sharing a large room with Peter for about five pounds a week. The job part of the equation was a temporary clerk job with European Honda in Chiswick.

Honda had been in England only one year and in that time, had captured 45% of the British motor cycle market. Their marketing success was not mirrored by their accounting systems. Six of us 'Temps' were recruited to a basic job overseen by the Accountant, Derek Stevens, whose colourful and immaculate clothes changed every day. After one week in this job I approached Derek and proposed that I quit the agency and work directly for him, the savings being split between me and Honda. Derek agreed, next week I told him his accounts ledgers were a mess and I would fix the problems, but it would take me a year. So, commenced my next career.

Honda has 10 Sales ledgers and 10 Sales Tax ledgers, covering the UK and Europe, none of which had ever balanced. I had two girls working the Burroughs ledger machines, one English and an older girl from Ireland. My immediate problem was to get to a starting point then have the machines altered so that that a monthly 'balance' could be obtained. I arranged for the Burroughs mechanic to install the needed part, and while discussing this with the girls, they said Derek would not agree. I said Derek would do as I wanted, just as he walked in behind me, saying nothing. Changes made, and I set out on my project.

Derek and I developed a friendly and efficient relationship. When I expressed interest in music and opera he got front stalls tickets to Covent Garden for seven shillings and sixpence, which now costs hundreds of pounds or more. While reading *The Telegraph* one day, an article on Covent Carden stood out; an American was observed in a Box without a tie and was hissed by some in the audience; "Standards Old Chap".

Derek once called me in to the office, behind closed doors, to ask what it was like in Australia for "us". I said that as far as I knew Sydney was the place to be. He would have loved to be in Sydney later for the Gay Mardi Gras. Derek was always helpful as were all at Honda. I once asked for an appointment with the Company Secretary, John Miller, to ask for a raise. John was on holiday; when he returned, I informed him that in his absence I had already received a raise; no problem I could have another in the form of unlimited overtime to conduct an inventory of the Company office furniture. I filled in several Saturdays so doing.

John was not your normal accountant; a few years earlier while in South America he had driven from the bottom of Argentina to Venezuela, pioneering what became the Pan American Highway. He also owned what I consider to be the most iconic of cars, a 3.4 Litre Jaguar, and I accompanied him in it to Nottingham where we did a stocktake. After some time in the Company I seemed somehow to have achieved some level of respect; our major dealer in UK, from Liverpool, when he asked for John, who was out, asked for me as, in his words, I was the only one who could talk sense. Don't know where he got that from but was flattered.

The work force at Honda was typically British; people from around the World. The Japanese workers seemed to be together in a separate room and did not mix with the other workers. In the accounts, there was a mixed lot. One man, 40 odd years old, had never been further from London than Birmingham; another from the West Indies, who had more Accounting and Business degrees from, among others, Harvard, was working as a cost clerk, a menial job for someone with his qualifications. When I asked him why, he simply said it was either this or he would be 'on the Buses'. Another girl, a very black Nigerian, very beautiful and very accomplished, was promoted to a position where she would be dealing with the 'Public'. Jerry Comber, the Staff Manager, was on holiday when this occurred and when he returned he reversed this appointment. I was appalled and told him so. He took me out to lunch and tried to explain that the Public Image was the overriding factor.

As an Australian I often feel that racial attitudes are not a strong point, but the more I come across the "Whites are superior" attitudes, the more I am repelled. On another occasion, I was with my current girlfriend, strolling around Hampton Court when she remarked on the number of Jamaicans and Pakistanis, with obvious disapproval. My words were, "You Poms have been going around the World for 300 years telling all you conquered that we are all part of this great British Family, and now that some of the family are in the Motherland you don't like it". She was the daughter of a RAF father who served in a lot of overseas postings which had obviously affected her attitudes. I don't think our relationship survived that. On the other hand, one Saturday, after having spent the morning doing my 'overtime', friends had arranged tickets to a gymnastics competition at White City, North London. They were going early and told me they would leave my ticket at White City Station. I duly arrived and was pouring through the Station exit with hundreds of others when the diminutive Jamaican girl collecting tickets asked, "Are you Dan Moloney?", and gave me the ticket. It must have been my height that stood out.

Race in England in the 60s was becoming more of an issue; time has seen many changes in attitudes towards race, not only in Britain, but much lingers on. Fifty odd years later I was staying in the Youth Hostel in Oxford, sharing a four-bunk room; 1am, became aware that the noise I thought was coming from the street was actually a bunch of German students in the hall outside having a post party chat. When I asked them if they would kindly do it somewhere else they readily complied. Next morning, one of my roommates, a very black Englishman thanked me, saying he would not have been able to do that. Hopefully his apprehension was misplaced, but he would know better than me.

Life at Honda continued at an even keel, ledgers worked on and gradually becoming balanced. At Fulham, social life was always lively. Peter had many girlfriends, basically one for every week day, and often had them around for dinner. One evening when he was entertaining Thursday, Tuesday arrived at the front door; Peter, not one for dramas, took off over the back fence, later announcing that he would have to fill the void. His best girl was an English Rose, named Sarah. One night as I lay sleeping he brought Sarah into our shared room. Sarah was anxious that I might be awake; no, Dan is a heavy sleeper announced Peter as he lit the gas heater with a loud Pop and proceeded to ensure that the least of Sarah's concerns was Dan's sleeping habits.

Among the Audits Peter conducted was The Courage Brewery, whose emblem was a Golden Cockerel. Peter had a few of the Company Ties featuring Golden Cockerels on a blue background. We residents of 31 Gowan Avenue would sometimes go to parties all wearing the 'Company Tie', while Peter would favour some girl with his oh so subtle "Do you get them down, and if you do, do you?" Swinging London of the 60's and Peter were the perfect combination. Meanwhile my love life was also anything but moribund, to the extent that there was Joan one, two and three; never, I hasten to add, at the same time.

Gowan Avenue home life was very communal, dinner was shared around the dining table, usually watching TW3, *That Was The Week That Was*, with David Frost. One night an unknown group just off the boat from Australia appeared on TW3 and sang; I declared that they were very good and would become stars. David said I only said that because they were Australian, but I was soon vindicated when The Seekers began topping the charts, sometimes even at the expense of the Beatles.

The core company at 31 Gowan Avenue was Graham, Peter, David and me, and occasionally another came in. We had one guy from Queensland, who stayed a week, did a bus tour of Europe, came back and announced he was going home as we could not cook like his mother. David worked for Mars, his father was an Anglican Bishop in Yorkshire. A couple of years after I left David wrote that he had moved to Huddersfield and bought a three-bedroom house for Two Thousand Five Hundred Pounds. Those were the days!

Geoff from Adelaide worked in insurance. We would sometimes visit pubs together. One pub, the Kings Head in Kensington was a favourite. They had a Golden Cockerel plaque on the wall of the bar, which Geoff was dying to steal, but never managed to do so. There was also nearby a famous restaurant called The Stable Inn, below street level, with a sign made from a slice of tree trunk, indicating the downstairs location with a downward pointing arrow. This became Geoff's target. One late night he persuaded me to carry him on my shoulders while he detached the sign from its moorings. Back home the ideal place was in the hallway indicating the location of our own dining room. One Saturday afternoon before one of our parties, we had a brewery truck deliver our supply of beer; it was a big party. A passing Bobby stopped to enquire, I happened to answer the door. He kept looking over my shoulder at the sign, thinking 'Where have I seen that before?' but more concerned with the quantity of beer being delivered. "You would not be charging admittance to this party would you Sir?". I assured him that we were Australians and that this was our customary hospitality. On another occasion, another Bobby noted the two 'Metropolitan Police – No Parking' signs we had installed outside on Fulham Football Club's home games, probably assuming that some high-ranking officer was inside. Some months later I was chatting to an English airline 'hostie' in Kuwait, who mentioned that her favourite restaurant was in Kensington, The Stable Inn, but sometimes had difficulty locating it as the sign had disappeared. I did not enlighten her as to its fate, though the Stable Inn no longer exists.

Life in London, never a dull moment between Pubs, parties, Covent Garden, Saddlers Wells, West End theatres, concerts in the Royal Albert Hall frequent and very affordable, even one of Bob Dylan's. Whenever I think of London Philharmonic concerts I am reminded of Sir Thomas Beecham, who was reputed to have commented to a cello player in rehearsal, "Madam, you have between your legs something which can give great pleasure to millions, and all you can do is scratch it".

One Easter weekend a car trip to St Ives in Cornwall, via Stonehenge at dawn; being the only people there was a memorable experience. Pasties in the modern Jamaica Inn, Mont St Michele, Bath, Cornish coast, a great trip. Back in London, Winston Churchill died. Attending his funeral was a must. We spent hours in the night, waiting to file past the coffin in Westminster Hall, then rushing up to Ludgate Hill at dawn waiting for the funeral procession to come to St Pauls Cathedral, where among others our Prime Minister Robert Menzies and Charles De Gaul accompanied the gun carriage and coffin; De Gaul overcoming his War time animosity towards Churchill to attend. A quick breakfast on the Embankment, back home to watch the ceremonies on TV. Many years later completed the 'circle' by visiting his birth crib in Blenheim Palace.

My allotted time was coming to an end. I had balanced all ledgers, except one where I could not find the last elusive Penny. I told Derek that I would write it off, he was horrified but eventually agreed. James Callaghan, Chancellor of the Exchequer in his latest budget had increased the Tax on cigarettes by six pence a pack. The household decided that we would all give up smoking, and each put in One Pound with the last one to weaken winning the Pot. I won but decided that I would continue not smoking. I managed to stay off cigarettes for six months.

I set about preparing for my departure, buying a new rucksack, 2-man tent, sleeping bag, air mattress, boots and basic clothes, and importantly 5 books. I left my remaining possessions in storage at the Overseas Visitors Club. Peter Jeffery from Harvey in WA was now working as a teacher in England and over time managed to recover some of my possessions and send them back to Australia. A last visit to the dentist to deal with an impacted wisdom tooth. This involved a two-and-a-half-hour torture while the tooth had to be cut in half with the drill while I counted bricks on the outside wall, dosed up with Morphine; on leaving I enquired if they really wanted the One Pound NHS fee. It was waived.

Geoff had also decided to leave, and I arranged to meet up with him in Pamplona where he wanted to go for the running of the bulls. In the meantime, I decided that I should insure a camera with Geoff's company. The fact that I did not own this camera I justified in my mind by saying that I had already lost or had stolen two cameras which were not insured. I described this in a letter home, as a 'business transaction' which I hoped would reap me about $300.

BACK ON THE ROAD AGAIN

June 1965. I caught the ferry from Southampton to Cherbourg and set off down the road. No lift by nightfall so headed into a paddock and set up my tent and camp. Next morning awoke to hear a farmer on his tractor announcing that he was calling the Gendarmes. I packed up within 5 minutes and left him to his worries. Plenty of easy rides down the West Coast to Pamplona. Met Geoff who had in the meantime got into films. Two big movies were being shot around there so Geoff parked himself near the Casting Director's caravan until a very distinguished gentleman started chatting and soon told the Casting Director to "Give this young chap a job." Thank you very much Sir Alec Guinness. Geoff's role in *The Battle of the Bulge* was a German soldier getting killed on his tank, while his role in *Doctor Zhivago* was a pair of boots walking past a grave. Hardly Hollywood but a pay day.

Geoff had a mate, Jim, who had a VW, so we left Pamplona for Madrid, then Portugal where we spent a week, mainly in Lisbon. Met some British sailors off the aircraft carrier *Centaur* who gave us a tour of the ship. A Portuguese bull fight which drew the scorn of some Spaniards because of the bull not being killed, which it is but later outside the ring. Further down to Jerez where a lot of Spanish wine, sherry and brandy helped the journey on. Further on to Gibraltar where we arrived at night. The border was closed due to another dispute between Spain and Britain, so we just parked on the border, rolled out our sleeping bags, hung our shirts on the gates and waited for the morning. The Spanish Police thought that was hilarious. Spent a couple of days on The Rock, which I did not manage to climb all the way, had my Passport stamped with an illegal Gibraltar visa.

We left the car in the care of some street kids in Algeciras and got the ferry to Ceuta, Spanish Morocco; a bus to Tangier where we found a room with a local family and set about immersing ourselves in the local culture, which to young Europeans largely consisted of getting Dope and finding ways of smuggling it back to Spain. The Cafe de Paris was the main focal where young Germans, British, etc. would discuss possibilities, such as filling shaving cream containers. At one stage, a local guy wanted me to be his 'manager', the details of the function now somewhat vague, but somehow, I made a profit from this. What really impressed me in Tangier was the quality of the fruit and vegetables in the local markets rather than the fraught Dope markets. Although I have smoked small quantities in several countries, it has never really appealed that much. As Tom from Wisconsin later informed me, my drug of choice is beer.

Tangier time at an end, time to return to Algeciras and find the car in the street, but as our watchmen were not around, quickly in and off, no protection money paid. Then further North to Seville and Barcelona where I left the car and went back to Malgrat where I stayed a night with the Kufferts, was offered a job again, but declined. Next morning put out the thumb and was picked up by an American driving a brand- new Rover. Asked where I was headed, said Hamburg; he was going to Strasbourg, more than a 1000- mile trip.

We quickly settled in for the long drive, me doing some of the driving. (I did have my International Licence). Quickly through southern France. During our chats discovered that my host had lived in Australia and actually went out with a barmaid from my local Pub in Cottesloe in Perth. Just another example of the Small World we live in. Night was approaching but there was no way we were to slow down. I was driving through the hills near the Swiss border, narrow winding roads, no white lines or sign posts. Going up a series of hills, I was urged to go faster. The top of one hill on a sharp bend, confronted by headlights of a large truck, 10 metres in front, only one way to go, over the cliff. We crashed over the cliff leading to fields below, through a wire fence and stopped on level ground. Quickly checked that my companion was OK, and within minutes we were surrounded by people from the village. Apart from some damage to the doors caused by the fence, the main damage was to the casing of the transmission. The villagers assured us that it could be repaired in the village and they disappeared. We walked in to a now seemingly deserted village at about midnight, and I found one house with a light on. I explained to the lady inside that we had had "Un Accident" and she led us to a room with a large double bed. Overcoming my companion's fears, we fell into sleep. Next morning the car was towed into the village and repairs made.

As the journey was continued I started worrying that I would somehow be asked to contribute to the repairs, which would have destroyed my travelling plans. My worries were put at rest when he picked up a young couple of Swiss hitch hikers; I thought he was a tiger for punishment but gave a silent prayer of gratitude. The rest of the trip proceeded without further incident and we parted friends in Strasbourg, where I quickly got a lift with a Danish truck driver, who offered to take me all the way to Copenhagen, but as time was becoming an issue settled for Hamburg, early in the morning.

While wandering the streets got into a discussion with a Wurst seller about the WW1 sea battle off the West Australian coast, between *HMAS Sydney*, and the German raider the *Emden*. He was quite insistent that the *Emden* had won, but as both were sunk I called it a draw. Years later in Geraldton, West Australia where there is a very impressive memorial to the 634 sailors lost on the *Sydney*, I was talking to some young German girls there who were not aware that the War had got to this part of the World.

After a few days in Hamburg I met with Sven Paterson. We spent a few days sampling the delights of Hamburg, particularly the Reeperbahn district. A few visits to rather sad strip clubs, at one of which a bouncer referred to us as 'Gypsies'. I assured him that we could Buy and Sell him, although I am not sure if he understood my challenge, probably fortunately. Our most successful stop was at the Star Club where the Beatles regularly played. When challenged Sven informed the bouncers in his best Swedish that we were members of The Vikings, the famous Swedish Rock Band, which gave us privileged entry.

Sven had a bike and we set out together, with probably too much gear to be safely carried on a bike, but headed for Hanover, where I was unsuccessful in locating Isabelle, then on to a nearby village of Elze where Sven had friends.

Sven was an ex US Marine, recently released following a tour in Vietnam, prior to the major US deployment in that country, and was very scathing of the US Army there. The US was ostensibly in Vietnam as advisers to the Diem regime, but according to Sven did nothing to endear themselves to the Vietnamese. Sven described one US tank barrelling through a village and running over people with no regard for the "Gooks"; not a good Hearts and Minds approach.

That was a 'hot' war, time to tackle the Cold War. Leaving the bike with the friends in Elze we hit the road for Berlin. Getting a lift to the Border no problem, but everyone was reluctant to give a lift to foreigners till finally one of the Border Guards got us a lift with a young German guy, after we paid DM 10 for the use of the autobahn. A night in a camping ground staying in my tent, a couple of days in West Berlin exploring Magdeburg Gate, Kongress Halle, Russian War Memorial, which was fenced off with barbed wire in case the West Germans tried to wreck it.

We found, next to the Wall, an RAF base, vacant until the British came to Berlin for manoeuvres. This was our hotel; showers and ovens in which to stow our gear in during the day. Altogether we used the facility for 9 days. I also discovered that the phone line to England was also open and one night asked for a call to be put through to Australia, which was done. With free accommodation, we set out to enjoy the sights and sounds; bier halls, Checkpoint Charley, monuments, but East Berlin beckoned. The S Bahn is basically the only way in, and involves full Border Control, including having to exchange, at criminal rates, at least DM10, which must be accounted for on leaving; any illicit money changing attracts severe penalties. East Berlin was a drab town; we found what was supposed to be a good restaurant, serving cold schnitzel and potato. Gas goes off at 7pm.

We wandered over to Alexander Platz where we met a couple of students and two Vopos, conscript soldiers. After a few beers, it was 9pm which they said would be the end of the night as all bars would close. I had earlier seen a bar by the Station which looked like a working man's bar, so we went there and found the place was rocking. We settled in, paying for the beers with illegal West DM. The young soldiers were very keen to learn about life 'Dar Uber', over there, and we gave them some West German newspapers, postcards. We were attracting the attention of a large jovial man, who wanted to join us, but the soldiers told him to Piss Off, informing us that he was Stassi. The students became very nervous and departed, the soldiers stayed till closing, me wearing an East German Army hat, one of the soldiers wearing my Australian Army slouch hat. When we parted, we made sure that they got away before Stassi could find out who they were, but Stassi had not finished with us. When we got to the station for the return to West Berlin the Border guards were waiting. They made Sven turn out his pockets, and the note book where he had the soldiers' addresses was placed on a table under an overhead camera. Whenever they used the foot switch Sven closed the book, until they warned him that we could be there all night. The last attempt he managed to wave his hand across at the crucial moment, hopefully blurring he addresses. By the time it got to my turn they had had enough and after a short interrogation we could leave, but almost certainly with Stassi files.

We left Berlin separately, hitching out. I was standing on the Auto Bahn entrance when a very large policeman informed me that, "Auto stop auf die Autobahn ist Verboten", I protested that I was not on the Autobahn, but the Einfahrt. Hands on hips he assured me that, in German, "When I say you are on the Autobahn, you are on the Autobahn". He left, and I resumed my place and soon got a lift with two brothers who had earlier escaped from the east. When the truck passed over the mirrors used to detect people hanging on to the underneath of trucks, they spat on the mirror, in full view of the Russian soldiers manning the Border. When asked if this wise they said the Russians could not care less. Sven and I caught up again in Elze and set off for Vienna where he had friends. Austria still in the pseudo Eastern bloc, and not happy or prosperous. Sven's friends had an apartment but had to sell books every few days to buy food.

Sven decided to stay on in Vienna for a while, I headed for Munich for the third Oktoberfest. After 13 days there, money needed some replenishment; back to Forstampt Thiergarten, where I was welcomed and offered work for as long as I liked. I stayed 2 weeks, and on the first day worked with a gang building concrete feeding places for the boars. They had me going all day pushing barrow loads of cement up and down planks, pretty exhausting. Next day and for the next two weeks they said that I had worked hard enough and would not let me do any more 'heavy lifting'. The 2 week's pay made up for my Oktoberfest, so off to Italy.

After spending six days in Florence, once again soaking up history and art, then off to Rome where I spent another two weeks in galleries, museums, the Vatican, Roman Forum, the Coliseum and many other of Rome's historical attractions, made more accessible by having a Youth Hostel card which the Italian Government allows holders of to get into museums etc for free.

While hanging around the Coliseum I met a girl from Rhodesia who was being pestered by an Italian man, whom I told to get lost. She had a club foot and was not only strong but beautiful. She also had an invitation to a General Audience with the Pope. We duly turned up at St Peters a couple of days later to join the hundreds of enthusiastic pilgrims; she was in the front row as the Pope was working his way along the barrier. I was a couple of rows back when she turned to me; "Dan, this guy is goosing me". When he realised who she was talking to, he slithered away through the crowd, all this with the Pope a few feet away. The rest of the time in Rome mixing and meeting at places like the Spanish Steps, Trevi Fountain. I spent a whole day in the Roman Forum with a Japanese guy; I mentioned to him that he did not seem all that impressed, to which he commented, "This is your culture, not mine". Another lesson in world diversity.

Time to move on. A quick trip down the Autostrada to Naples. Days spent exploring Pompeii, climbing up and into Mount

Vesuvius, and deciding Naples, by reputation alone would be the ideal city to stage the culmination of my camera 'business transaction'. Finding a park with a nice stretch of lawn I lay down for a few minutes then leapt to my feet with a cry of outrage that someone had stolen my camera while I slept. This performance was met with complete indifference by fellow park attendees, so I decided that I would have to find my way to a Police Station to report this heinous crime. Back in the City I finally found a Policeman on traffic duty, who told me he would be off duty in a couple of hours and I could in the meantime make myself comfortable in his wooden cubby house on the corner. Finally, back in his Station I made some detectives aware of the Crime of the Century, and they sagely deduced that what I needed for insurance purposes was a Police Report. They were too busy to do it but provided me with the necessary form and a typewriter. Report completed and signed I set about returning all the details to Geoff, who was now back in London, while I awaited the 'Fruits of my Labours'.

A few days wandering around Sicilian villages, a trip across the Bay of Naples to the Isle of Capri to the Blue Grotto, a couple of days exploring Pompeii; climbed up and into Mount Vesuvius again, which was still able to produce some activity; by blowing into a rock fissure, steam was forced out of a crack about 100' away. Leaving Naples, on to Bari, from where ferries go to Greece.

The ferry stopped for almost a full day in Corfu, which allowed for a pleasant stroll and chats with locals, who seemed to outnumber tourists by huge margins. My passage was Deck, and as the ferry sailed through the night, I woke to watch the ship seeming to pass through the Straits of Corinth with inches to spare, the walls of the Strait towering above. The history of the Canal makes fascinating reading; First proposed in 7th century BC, but not finished until 1893. The philosopher Apollonius of Tyana prophesied that anyone who attempted it would be met with illness. Three Roman rulers considered it; Julius Caesar, Caligula and Nero all met with violent deaths.

Somewhere in Greece I met and teamed up with Tony from New Zealand and we travelled together on and off as far as

Nairobi, but I was mainly on my own in Greece. Got lifts to Olympia and while I was walking into the village decided to pick some of the abundant oranges; no sooner had I arrived in the village when I was offered as many oranges as I liked. Guilty again. For some reason, probably the time of the year, I was the only foreigner in town and spent a few days chatting with local people, exploring the museum and sites; ran the 100 metres? track but broke no records.

Departure meant hitching but with lifts virtually non-existent I was on the verge of taking anything in any direction before being invited to join a few pigs in the back of muddy truck. I still have the photo of the large boar trying to stay upright long enough to eat me. Another lift was with a load of chicken cages packed on to the back of a truck as it climbed up the mountain one evening to Delphi. I think I paid my way by keeping the cages from falling off. The Oracle was not around but sitting in the theatre at dusk with only a circling eagle for companion, looking over the plain to Patras was an experience the Chickens and Boar could not diminish. My true station in life brought back into focus a little later when I joined a couple of Americans in the restaurant; I bought a tub of yoghurt in the shop next door as it was one drachma cheaper than in the restaurant and asked the waiter for some sugar. The Americans shook their heads in wonder, but the Greek waiter just grinned.

Further wanderings in rural Greece on the way to Athens. One late afternoon, in drizzling rain I was standing by the not busy road when a VW Karman Ghia stopped just in front of me. Breathing thanks, I leapt into the back seat, preceeded by my 40-pound rucksack. The startled look on the driver's face indicated that I was not the object of his intentions. I hastily apologised, but he asked where I was going; I think it was Athens, so he told me to stay; back at his nearby home I was introduced to the extended family, sat down to a great meal and later a comfortable bed. In the morning, the highlight was a cup of tea from a pack of Bushells Tea from Australia. Wherever one goes in Greece there is someone who has a relative in Australia. It is said that Melbourne is the second largest Greek city in the World.

In another village, while walking through, was suddenly surrounded by a dozen children who informed me I was, on the orders of their teacher, to go with them to their school. The waiting teacher, the most beautiful girl I had seen in Greece, asked if I would talk to the students in English. If she had asked me to be her slave, I think I would have agreed. I arrived at another village late evening; some men noticed the slouch hat which I had secured to my pack and invited me for coffee. They told me that they had known Australian soldiers during the War and then showed me a wall of the village church bearing many bullet holes where they said Germans had executed some local men. Altogether me being Australian was a big plus with them. My slouch hat however, was destined to remain in Greece; exiting from a car one evening, placed the hat on the car roof while retrieving my pack, the car took off with the hat stuck to the damp roof.

Athens finally. Staying in a hostel near the Plaka. I had somehow, probably from some European toilet seat, got a dose of the Crabs. Various ointments and pills had so far been unsuccessful in dislodging these unwelcome fellow travellers, but a young English guy, similarly afflicted, suggested a trip to the Greek Public Health clinic would be worthwhile. When we informed the young Greek nurses of our situation they were somewhat surprised and amused that young good-looking foreigners such as us needed their assistance, but they readily came to the rescue; each of us were given a brown paper bag of very green DDT powder. A prompt application of said powder to the appropriate nether regions, saw the rapid exodus of the dead and dying 'crustaceans minute' from our relieved bodies.

Highlights of a week in Athens, apart from the Acropolis and many ancient theatres and monasteries, finally got to see "Gone with the Wind". Bought an old US Army radio bag in the flea market which I used as a shoulder bag. It later gave me cause for grief, being easily accessible, and being another contributor to my talent for losing cameras. Met some other young foreigners who had arranged to work as extras in a Greek movie, dancing and singing; the pay was, I think, 30 Drachmas a day, not enough; we went on strike and were promptly replaced by Greeks.

Spending a few days heading North and once again enjoying the friendliness of Greek people. Arriving in Thessalonica late one night I was wandering about lost when I was met by a man who turned out to be the local chief of the tourist board, who found a bed for me. Over the next few days I met practically every day with him and his friends for coffee. Our group consisted of him, the Police Chief, the Mayor, the wrestling champion and the Postmaster, making it hard for me to be on my way. Being late November, snow was becoming a daily event. One day I was having coffee with the group and another man who was an international truck driver. I mentioned that I had an Iraqi visa that had expired. No Problem; as requested I handed him my Passport and he set to work with pen and razor to adjust the offending dates; an excellent job which fortunately was not detected by Border Control.

DESTINATION JERUSALEM FOR CHRISTMAS

Finally left friendly Thessalonica, caught a bus to Istanbul. In Turkey, heavy snowfalls but could not but be amazed by the sight of a one-legged soldier of advanced years standing guard over what looked to be an empty paddock. They breed 'em tough in Turkey.

Weather in Istanbul was much better, and I found the International Hostel near the famous Souq Waqif. Over the next week spent every day exploring Topkapi, Blue Mosque and the Old City, across the Bosporus by ferry. There was always a lively crowd at the hostel, including Tony who arrived shortly after me. A Pakistani Army officer and his family were on their way to England, hoping to join the many others seeking a better life in the UK. A Jugoslav man who was a University Lecturer in Belgrade, was heading to Beirut but spoke no English or French, and as he spoke German offered me a lift; Istanbul to Beirut, another 1000 mile plus lift. I accepted only if Tony was also included. We set off next day in his Mercedes car.

Central Turkey was by now in the middle of Winter, snow everywhere. We drove all day to Konya where we booked into a hotel. The driver, whose name I cannot recall, was paranoid about Turks, and produced a pistol which he said was for protection, but it only fired gas bullets. He was too afraid to leave the hotel room when we suggested a meal and drink, so Tony and I went exploring. We soon met some young Turks who took us to a few bars and a restaurant, and then remembered they knew someone who was getting married, so of course we had to go to the wedding. Lots of people, food and drink, and even got to kiss the bride, who did look a little surprised. Even provincial Turkey in the

Sixties was a lot more secular than what the present Government is pushing, taking the country back to pre-Ataturk days, President Erdogan playing the Religion (Moslem) card for all its worth.

Back on the road, because Tony did not speak German, our driver tried to talk me into dumping him somewhere and continuing on with me, at which I of course told him no way. I told Tony, in English what was said. That night we crossed into Syria, climbing up into mountains. We stopped at the Border post, and I put up the tent for Tony and myself, while driver spent the night in his car. Next morning, he woke us early and sat in the car with the heater on while I packed up, with fingers sticking to the freezing aluminium tent poles. Revenge was needed.

Down from the mountains to the Lebanese border. The Border police quickly found the pistol; they also had a large canister which had floated up from the sea. They could not decipher the various military writings on it, thinking it may be some sort of bomb. I assured them it was only a rescue cylinder. The officer in charge asked our driver if he was taking the Mercedes to Beirut to sell, which he was, but denied it. I told the officer that he certainly was. The pistol then became the focus, so they told our driver that the cylinder may be a bomb and they were going to confiscate the pistol and his car, and check bullets. They set up the cylinder on the beach and fired all the bullets at it. Fun over, they put a soldier in the car with us and directed the car to be delivered to a holding yard in Beirut dock, along with all the other Mercedes which were brought into Lebanon to be sold. We parted in Beirut. Tony and I found a hotel in East Beirut. Next day, while having coffee in the City our driver joined us, desperate to be friends, but was told his past performance disqualified him.

Christmas was now not far off. Walked to the outskirts of the city and got lifts to Damascus and on to Jerusalem. The last lift was in a truck and another Australian joined us. He was, he said, a shearer from Queensland, a man of about fifty. We parted, but after a couple of days learned that he had been going around offering money to such people as hotel workers for information on Jordan's military and government; very unwise and he was soon arrested as an Israeli spy. Israel, which I called Disneyland, was not very welcoming to young travellers, unless they intended to stay and work on a kibbutz. Getting in was not that easy but the only way out was by sea or air, and not cheap.

Now about a week before Christmas, we found a room in the Old City with a Palestinian woman and set about doing the things people do in Jerusalem. The Al Aqsa Mosque, Wailing Wall; to Bethlehem and the Church of the Holy Sepulchre and just the streets and lanes of the Old City. Tried to organize Christmas lunch with the Little Sisters of Charity but they were booked up, so I got a few travellers together and booked lunch in an Arab restaurant; chicken and felafel and Fanta. On Christmas Eve one of the highlights was songs and food at the Shepherds' Cave, a couple of miles out from the city. Many people were walking out, and I joined them, but soon a Jordanian soldier on his bike asked if I would like a lift; gratefully accepted. Folk singer Julie Felix provided the songs, churches provided the food, shepherds' stew and bread, all very enjoyable.

During the Christmas holidays, Palestinian families separated by the War, are allowed by the Israelis to re-unite in Israel for up to two weeks. Their access is through a laneway in the Old City to what looks to be a vacant square in Israeli Jerusalem. A Jordanian Army officer brought me through, angrily deploring the whole situation. The Six Day War was still eighteen months away, so I hope he survived. Over the next fifty years the Palestinian Situation has got progressively worse, with Israel taking every advantage of every uprising/protest by stealing more West Bank land.

Tony had decided to go somewhere else, so I took off to head for Aqaba. Since reading 'Seven Pillars of Wisdom' and Lawrence's capture of the port I had made Aqaba an objective. On the way out, I stopped at the Dead Sea and camped on the beach. In the late evening, the sky was lit up with Sound and Fury, enhanced by the joint I was smoking. I wandered over to the Army Post to enquire of the cause and was told it was only the nightly artillery duel between the Israelis and Jordanians. Shades (?) of things to come.

Next morning across to the West Bank I came to the small village of Jericho and wandered in where I was greeted by a young guy who invited me in for coffee, and later lunch. His family owned the village cinema and he told me of the family history. As a young boy in the 1940s he was one day working in the family orchard beneath the hills. On his return in the afternoon he found his whole family had been massacred by the Stern Gang. His words "Do you think we like them?" All part no doubt of the Create Jewish Israel campaign.

On the road from Damascus I met up with a young American, 19-year-old Tom Kinney from Lancaster, Wisconsin. Tom and I teamed up for the trip to Aqaba. On the way stopped to chat with a soldier on guard duty who suddenly snapped to attention as a car drove past. On enquiry was informed that we had just saluted Prince Hassan, King Hussain's brother. An overnight in a tea house in Ma'an, picked up next day by a couple of truckies. After a couple of hours Tom asked if I would swap seats as one of the drivers was feeling his knee. Evidently, I was not as attractive. Dozed off and woke to see we were overlooking the plains, A dozen or so mesa top hills poked through the low-lying cloud, an almost surreal sight. On arrival in Aqaba headed for the beach which would be home for the next week or so, where we were joined by some other fellow travellers and set up our community, drift wood fire central. New Year's Eve party, Bill the Greek had a bottle of Haig whiskey which Tom, he and I killed between 2.30 and 6.30am. Tom broke the bottle in the fire, cut himself and passed out. He intended to go with Mike for India, but Mike left without him, and so Tom and I became travelling mates for the next few months.

They say it never rains in Aqaba, but over the next days that saying well and truly disproved. We alternated sleeping on the beach with the shed, which the Police tried to make water tight for us, only partially successfully. Pierrette and I sat up all night in the tea house, the owner of which was the cook for the 'Lawrence of Arabia' crew when they were shooting in nearby Wadi Rum. Someone took me to meet a man in nearby Wadi Rum, who I was told was the surviving brother of the young boy who was taken by the quicksand while travelling with Lawrence; by now a man of about sixty in his family Bedouin camp. At this stage, I had gone 64 hours without sleep.

Sunny days returned, and I spent a lot of time floating around on my air bed and diving on to the coral and kelp forests, also unsuccessfully trying to catch fish. Klaus, one of the Germans, helped a couple of Swiss guys, who did not speak English, to sell their car for $500. Pirrette, Tom and a few others left for Jerusalem. The Police had foiled my attempt to get a boat to Mombasa in Kenya, so I arranged to meet Bambi in Beirut and headed out, got the wrong road which meant a 5-mile walk in the hot sun, but Police got me a lift to Petra turnoff. Met an Aussie girl, Jackie, and a German gave us a lift all the way to Petra. The entrance to the gorge was lively with camel drivers, donkey drivers and various sellers of souvenirs. One man noticed my knife and demanded that we go blade to blade with his Damascus steel. I declined; although my Solingen blade was pretty good it would be no match for his. Damascus steel has for centuries been renowned for being the best.

The 4km walk in through the gorge opens out to the Treasury building of World fame; a little disappointed with interior, which is basically a very large empty space. The rest of the day we spent exploring the hills and caves. An Antiquities guide told us how he had organized the clearing of the gorge with the help of American money and how 17 French girls had been drowned by a flash flood three years earlier. A barrier has been built to prevent any repetitions. The walk out through the gorge under full moonlight was memorable for the fantastic shapes and faces on the moonlit walls.

Our German gave us a lift back to Amman. Jackie and I enjoying a romantic interlude in the back seat, but they left us at their Amman hotel about 1am; I found an expensive one, $1 per night. Next day found my way to the British Embassy on Jabaal Amman, collected some mail, then found a bookshop and a book. Back at the hotel got into a discussion with a Jordanian man and his two sons. He had worked for the RAF and was upset that Britain had legalised homosexuality. Another guest in the hotel was an Iraqi student and long discussions on politics and

Arab customs went into the early hours. He told us how, just a few months earlier, a crowd had gathered in Amman to protest about conditions, and were blaming King Hussein. The King heard about it and drove in his sports car down from his palace on Jabaal Amman to the crowd; he addressed them from his car, and won them over to the extent that they picked him up and carried him and his car back to the palace.

Next day on the way up to the British Embassy to meet Bambi, got called in to a shop for coffee by the owner, Artif, and while there met Abdullah, the son of an ambassador who had served in England and America. Bambi, Tom and Tony arrived. We decided to go to Kuwait, buy Ronson lighters to bring back to Jerusalem, having been assured they would be good earners. Meanwhile Artif cooked a great meal, my first with chickens' heads and necks, quite good. Abdullah took us to his house to listen to music and invited us to a party next night. Tony found another better hotel, also cheaper. Awoke at 1am to order breakfast, this being Ramadan. That night at the party, dressed to kill, even wearing a tie. Some girls were there and did some Arab dances, but Tony became the object of a potentially ugly incident by dancing too much, and too enthusiastically, with the girls, I warned him, and he settled down. A great night finished about 2am, driven back to the hotel.

The hospitality and friendship we were enjoying from Artif and Abdullah and friends seemed never ending. Tom has Asthma, and Artif knew an old man who could cure things. He gave Tom a medicine, which Tom found to be very good, but after a few days the effects were not so positive; but it was time to be moving on. Got Iraqi visas but were told to get Kuwait visas in Baghdad. Headed out next day with various short lifts, at one stage spent an hour or so with some Bedouins camped by the road, very friendly and happy people, but hitchhiking with 40 Bedouins would not get us far. Spent the night in a Shell Service Station in Ramallah on the Iraqi border.

Next morning a truck stopped with room for two; tossed a coin, I lost, arranged to meet in Baghdad. Tuned in my radio to the BBC, Test Cricket in Sydney and the Seekers 'The Carnival is Over' but hopefully not for me. The Customs man soon had a lift for me, an Arab who spoke no English, me no Arabic. The driver was actually a Russian I discovered; many Russians had escaped and landed in Iraq but could only get Passports for limited travel in Iraq, Syria and Jordan. He shared his food with me on the 21-hour trip to Baghdad, listening mainly to Radio Israel. At one of the Checkpoints while he was getting his papers checked I was put in front of a drunken Iraqi soldier who kept waving his revolver in my face until I told him to put it away, which he did.

We arrived in Baghdad about 7am, I thanked my driver and set out looking for Tom and Tony, supposedly at the Post Office, but of course No Show. After about 4 hours I went walking and found them wandering the streets. They had a hotel which was cheap at 150fils. Bought some cheap books 'The Citadel' and 'Rape of the Fair Country'. Went to a movie 'The Ipcress File'. Met a young student who bought me a meal; through the fascinating back streets of Baghdad where we were invited to sleep at his house, met his mother, another meal, before the streets resounded with the clashing of drums and dishes to summon all to Ramadan breakfast. Downtown we met an Iraqi Army Officer who took us to the fantastic Mosque with Golden Dome Al-Askari in Samara, a beautiful and fantastic place. Sunni insurgents bombed it and the Golden minarets in 2006 and 2007. We were not allowed in, being Christians, but could look from outside. Back in Baghdad our friend took us to his home for a wonderful meal prepared by the women, who stayed away in other rooms. Another Army Officer later gave us a Grand Tour of Baghdad, including some of the huge date plantations; Iraq at the time produced 1/6th of the World's dates.

Tom went off to a party, Tony decided to head for Kuwait alone. I met Abdul Wahad and friends who decided I needed a haircut, so they took me to a barber friend for a haircut and beard trim. When I asked Abdul Wahad about the " Lucky" ring he was wearing he immediately insisted on giving it to me, as I had momentarily forgotten the Arab custom that this was obligatory. Later I mentioned to him that he had a nice sweater, and had to decline three times, as custom demanded. Abdul Wahad, when walking with me in the streets, would often hold my hand which

I found initially to be a little odd, but it is quite normal for Iraqi males. Later met other students, more food and sweets. Another man invited us to his shop where we drank Arak and had many discussions on politics, Israel, Jewish clannishness. After plenty of drinks he became tipsy and made some clumsy passes at Tom. We left about 3am and determined to leave next day before we found more hospitable friends; no doubt many of whom would die in Saddam Hussein's Iran War or the great stupidity of the Bush Iraq War.

Next morning leaving the hotel, tried to pay. Evidently in this hotel one pays as much or little as one can afford; if that is nothing that is Ok. We paid 150 fils per night. I wonder how the Hilton would like that system. Tom and I finally found the bus to the outskirts of the City, met another guy who invited us to visit him on our return from Kuwait for meals and books. Another man, a school teacher, invited us in but time was short so he put us on the bus and invited us to return; really the Iraqis everywhere were fantastic. Out of town we were picked up by a truck which took us about 40ks but wanted money. Of course, we had none, so soon we were picked up by another truck, the driver buying us food and tea, and later a full meal. Just outside Basra we had to transfer the load to another truck as the pontoon across the river would not handle the weight. We arrived in Basra about 2am. Tom not feeling well had to make a rush to the river bank, then we found a hotel. In the morning Tom got some pills for the 'trots', the chemist told us of a good movie, so we went to see the Australian movie 'The Sundowners'.

Next morning to the Kuwait Embassy for visas. Hitchhikers had evidently been causing trouble in Kuwait, smuggling Hashish. They did their best to dissuade us from going, telling us the troubles, how we could not sleep out and would need 50 Pounds to get in. We finally got the visas for One Pound. Next day a couple of short lifts. I was carrying the two bottles of whiskey I had bought in Basra inside my jeans, a little uncomfortable. Iraqi Police got us lift to Kuwait Customs where we had to get out of the car; the bottles started slipping down my legs, I performed an elaborate pantomime of scratching the area in between while desperately restraining the bottles from any further southward progress, while the Customs man just grinned; Tom in the meantime had a more fatalistic approach by just leaving his bottles in his pack. Lifts got us to Kuwait City, walking around in the markets discovered that the price of Ronson lighters was about the same as in Jerusalem; another get rich scheme up in smoke.

IN KUWAIT

First night in Kuwait, slept on the beach. After leaving our bags in a shop, wandered around, found Tony and English John. Heard all sorts of bad tales about smuggling of booze, 4 men in jail for one month. Tried to sell my camera for $10, got offered $8. Had to find a hiding place to eat sandwiches, this still being Ramadan. A Kuwaiti found a sleeping place for us in a vacant office; leaving the door ajar in the morning so we could stay there next night, as the American who was also there had taken the key. Decided to hide our whiskey until a buyer could be found, so went to the beach and buried it in the sandhills, about 500m away. Went to the Blood Bank where I sold my blood, one pint for 10 Pounds. Our friendly grocer gave us room to eat our food without troubling the Police.

Met English couple Ronnie and Zena and their friend Zaid. Things had turned bad for them; a Kuwaiti magazine had put their photos on their front cover and written a very nasty piece about them, saying they were typical of the hitchers who came to Kuwait looking for Hashish. They were going to help us sell our whiskey but had to cool it for a day. Meantime we went back to the sandhills to check our 'stash'. Still there. While we were sitting watching the sunset, night quickly descended and what appeared to be a parachute came floating down into the water. Not being sure what it was, but, good citizens as we are, decided someone should be told. I raced up to the nearby American Hospital, the hospital that in the first Iraq War was looted for baby humidicribs by Iraqi soldiers; finally found someone to call the Police.

Back at our sandhill, sitting on our smuggled whiskey, we soon found ourselves the prime people of interest to the Kuwaiti police. A couple of boats appeared on the water, searchlights were sweeping the bay. This was very inconvenient as we had arranged to meet Ronnie to dispose of the booze at 7.45. Tom went up and postponed it for an hour. A large patrol boat arrived; I think it was the entire Kuwaiti Navy now on the water. Lots of Police, including the Chief Superintendent who insisted that we should take advantage of his hospitality by sleeping in the Police Station, to which we were duly carted off, and shown our accommodation for the night, a corridor. We said we were going out for a meal and quickly raced up to the flat. Tony was there and having seen all the Police at the beach had decided that we were 'gone for sure'. He said Ronnie and Zena would be back in an hour to collect the 'stuff'. Tom and I collected it from the now deserted sand hills and back at the flat we sold one and a half bottles for Ten Pounds and drank half the remaining one. Did not bother returning to the Police Station, Zena brought food and drinks and we had a party before sleep. Next morning went back and picked up our gear from the Police Station, nobody taking any notice. After all the drama, on reflection the parachute was probably a weather balloon.

I still had to collect my Blood Money, and we needed visas. That day was the last day of Ramadan, so back at the beach a lot of Bedouins were dancing to drums and flutes, waving their large curved swords to the beat. A long stay in Kuwait was not appearing to be the most attractive of vacations notwithstanding Naval and Police events. Post Ramadan was a three-day holiday, spent mainly in the Bazaar and wandering the streets. One day as I was walking past a large black Rolls, the rear window came down and the most beautiful young girl leaned out and said "Hello". I stammered a reply just as the very large Bedouin with a machine gun appeared. I left in haste. Another day I was having a nap on the lawn at a traffic roundabout when I awoke to see an apparition in a gold and green sari walking across. I wondered how many Arab women would be jealous.

While waiting around started playing cards with Steve, the American. We Played Pontoon and as soon as Steve got ahead he would quit and take his winnings from me to the market and eat. This continued every day and I lost enough each time for Steve to eat, until my last day in Kuwait I decided no more, but Steve wanted one last game; I won handsomely, about 2 ½ Dinar. Obviously, Steve had no money, so he had to bring out his kit to see what I could take in payment; I finally took his flashlight.

By now we had become a sort of floating tribe; Americans, English, Jordanians, Iraqis and some 'visiting' Kuwaitis. One night in a coffee house it was the monthly TV concert from Radio Cairo of the famous Egyptian singer Um Kulthum, whose concerts could go for hours, and sometimes one song for an hour, using all her four-octave range. One of the Kuwaitis, one of the throng who sat through the concert drinking coffee and smoking 'Hubble Bubble' said to me; "If the Israelis want to invade, tonight is the best time". Another Palestinian who owned a coffee house complained of the Kuwaiti law that compels every business to be 51 per cent owned by a Kuwaiti, who did not even have to put money up for this, which meant all a local had to do was collect half the profits with no input. Sounds much like how Globalization works. Most of the work was done by Palestinians, and they all hated being here as far as I could tell.

Two English girls, Carol and Min, moved into our 'apartment'. No-one had much money, but we all pitched in, Ronnie and Zena often bringing food for the parties. Zena brought the half bottle of whiskey she had been unable to sell, which Min promptly knocked over. Zaid returned from his holiday in Beirut and we sat around smoking the Dope he had smuggled in, being lucky not to have been caught. The girls tidied up the apartment. Chatting with some of our Kuwaiti friends to learn about their country and I learned a bit more Arabic. They said every male student spent weeks living in the desert to retain their culture. I asked how they could stand the Summer temperatures, often over 50 Degrees. One said one day they would just build a big glass dome over the whole city and aircondition it. After all, it is just money. I think even the Kuwaiti budget would have a problem with that. There was some confusion about whether Ramadan had finished; one said Yes, another No, but the embassies were closed anyway.

Finally, the Embassies were open; went to the Iraqi Embassy, but carelessly had left my knife still attached to my belt; the Police took it, but I was able to convince them that I only used it for cutting food. Had to leave my Passport there as everyone who wrote out visas was on holiday. Finally, after three days we all had our visas and decided to head off for South Africa. On the road, a Jordanian picked us up and asked us to take cigarettes through Customs, then took us to Basra. So, ended 12 days in Kuwait. The road to Basra was littered with burnt out bodies of the Kuwaitis' standard car, a Chev Impala, victims of a drunken weekend in Basra.

BAGHDAD AND BEYOND

In Basra, the Jordanian said he would give us a lift to Baghdad next day. We went back to 'our' hotel, met some students, drank Arak with them and they took us to a terrible Italian movie. The Jordanian came about 2am to see how we were. Next day sat around waiting, they did not turn up. Met some Army officers and spent the afternoon with them, eating, drinking, discussing books, music and movies. Next day the Jordanian turned out to be 'queer', so we did not go with him. The owner of the hotel bought us breakfast and we sat around talking for a couple of hours, and he told us we need not pay for the hotel, just another example of the kindness and generosity we kept getting. Setting off around midday in the rain, got a lift in a muddy little horse drawn cart, followed by a swarm of kids, who followed us for miles. Walked over the pontoon bridge, Tom got a lift with a Kuwaiti, Tony and I got a lift to Al Merah. Walked through the town, met two teachers who bought us a meal. Got a lift through the narrow streets with a Police jeep. Three Bedouin women carrying loads on their heads were following at about the same pace. One was very attractive, and we made eyes at each other the whole journey. She suggested I should go with her for sex, but the soldier on the last check point said she had a gun, and men who had followed her had not been seen again. So much for Romance. The Nairn Desert Bus arrived, and we were put on for the trip to Baghdad, 400kms, for no money. In Baghdad, the students took us to a hotel for 200fils, but very noisy. Next day back to 'our' tea shop where we met Mohamad and some others; we were now a 'family'.

Next day met Abdul Wahad, and changed to another hotel on Al Rashid Street, the main street north, noisy but better. Joe, our mate from the clothing store, took us to the YMCA for a great meal and a 3- hour chat. Next day went to the Syrian Embassy and got my 3-month visa free with my student card. Spent some time wandering around the City with Abdul Wahad. Baghdad had impressed as being modern and open, this being pre-Saddam Hussein. Shia and Sunni tensions did not seem overt, people were friendly and generous. Perhaps too many times we were the beneficiaries of their generosity, but I have never asked for anything of anyone, anywhere. The consequences of the stupid Iraq War; the creation of ISIS, the schisms of Shia vs Sunni, the political corruption of the Al Malaki years and the probable dismemberment of the Iraqi nation between Sunni, Shia and Kurds lay with Bush, Blair and Howard. In 2003 I took part in the only mass demonstration I have ever been in, against the War.

Tony and I set off for Mosel, Tom stayed a couple of days more. First lifts to Samarra, where a very large dam was holding back the flood waters from Mosel. I wondered how long it would be before water became the catalyst for more wars and troubles between Turkey, Israel, Iraq and other dependent Middle East countries. Rain made hitching out impossible. Went to a nearby transport tea house, where the proprietor gave us a free meal. A school teacher came in and invited us to stay at his house, but his wife and parents were away so he could not get in. He then took us to a hotel, late at night, where two Arabs were evicted from their room, against our protests, but Arab hospitality demands, and they left without a murmur. We felt bad but could not do anything about it. Our friend paid for the room next day. He took us to the spiral minaret, the only remains of what was once the biggest mosque in Islam, built in 858, now all that remains are the walls. It was damaged in 2005 by a bomb set by insurgents because Americans were using it as a sniper post.

We soon had a lift to Mosel, found a good hotel where we shared a room with two Arabs. Next day people took us to the leaning minaret, a holy site destroyed in 2017 by the retreating Sunni morons of ISIS. The small back streets of Mosel, an older version of those in Jerusalem and I think more interesting. Another rainy day, met by a man who worked in the hospital, who took us to see the movie 'Guns at Batasi', but he left right after the show; we later found out that he was embarrassed because in Mosel people do not like to talk to Europeans, and are very suspicious of them (us).

Walking down the street a man called out to us and bought us some yoghurt. His name was Albert, a Christian Army Officer who had a very dangerous job; he had to give all the Kurds in the City their marching orders. One of them had a café and spoke to him in the street asking to be allowed to stay, but he could do nothing. We sat in a teahouse discussing the position of Christians and Kurds in the country, neither of whom were comfortable. Albert came to our hotel that evening and read from the Bible, then took us out for a meal. He told us if we saw him in the street to ignore him; he said he was a dead man and we should not risk talking to him. He said we would not have to pay at the Kurdish café we had been eating at. Next day tested that out, and the owner would not let us pay, although we tried. The Kurds situation, caught between Turkey, Syria, Iraq and Iran, among others, is tough, while the regimes in those countries, with no help from past Colonial masters Britain and France, and more lately the US, allow the situation to drift unresolved.

Mosel, and North Iraq was very different to the south; people were generally reserved but polite, although one man who refused to accept money directly from my Infidel hand was the only person to openly show it. I in turn refused to take my change directly from him, making him place it on the counter; Islam One, Infidel One.

Next day, still raining, headed out. Got a lift to an Army checkpoint where everyone was being searched for weapons, but the soldiers got us a lift to Tall Kolchak on the Syrian Border, where the Police gave us a bit of a hard time because we had over-stayed our visas. Had to pay but had no Iraqi money so our friend paid for us. Into Syria where the country is very green and fertile, this being part of what was once The Fertile Crescent, stretching through Syria, Persia and Afghanistan, sadly no more; I am not alone in blaming goats, which eat everything. Found a hotel and I went out playing dominoes with some local Syrians. Next morning got a bus to Kamachli, together with two sheep and a goat. The country still very green; asked where we could buy some bread, but someone bought us a huge loaf and a tin of meat. Walking down the road, hailed by a couple of men in the John Deere shop. Spent a couple of hours with them discussing farming in Syria, and the Agrarian Reform Bill, under which most of the farm machinery had been appropriated by the Government for 'redistribution'; they could not import any tractors into Syria and so had no work. They said the farms around here were getting one bag of wheat per acre; I think they should get at least five. Later back at one of their houses for tea and sweets talked about Syrian history. One of our friends came to get us a lift to Al-Hasakah, where a Policeman took us to a very good hotel for one and a half Syrian Pounds, about five shillings. One of the Cops started waving a gun around, causing everyone to duck, no idea why. Tony had hurt his leg, our friends knew an old man who was a 'doctor', who manipulated it a bit for some improvement. A chemist gave him an elastic bandage.

Next day, heading for Deir el Zor, but no traffic. Discovered that the previous year trucks taking petrol from Iraq to Deir el Zor had started using a different route across the desert. We were persuaded to take a taxi, 200kms, cost about 4 shillings each. Deir el Zor was the town Lawrence of Arabia chose to enter disguised as a desert Arab to spy on the Turkish garrison, and where he was reputedly raped by the Turkish officer, leading to the rumours of his later homosexuality; it was also the site of the Armenian Holocaust where 1.5 million Armenians were slaughtered by the Ottoman government, which the Turks continue to deny ever took place. In later times it was overrun by ISIS and became one of their last strongholds until it was retaken by the Syrian Army in November 2017, by this time largely reduced to rubble. When we were there the highlight was Tony giving me a beard trim.

Next day a lift with a man who was a district manager for an oil company, who told us how the government had nationalised his car, about Syrian politics, about the cotton crop which the previous year was sold for 75 piasters a kilo, now the government was paying 40. Consequently, people were not planting cotton; no 'tote that barge, lift that bale' song here. He dropped us off at El Raqqa, where we stayed for a couple of days, another city reduced to rubble in the Isis war, then getting a lift to Aleppo. That night met some young guys who took us to a hotel, special rates again, then movie *'Zorba the Greek'* and cabaret, talking and drinking tea, eying the French and Spanish girls working there. Next day walking in a big park, met a local man who told us about Australian troops in Aleppo during the War; how they were not popular with the locals, chasing the women, stealing from shops and starting fights with locals. Reminded me of my Uncle Alan, who had been stationed in Palestine, describing the kibitzes as 'Love Camps'.

Met two Kurdish boys who took us to the Citadel, the huge Moorish Fort overlooking the City. There are 20kms of tunnels underneath for storage of food during a siege. Still reading *'Seven Pillars of Wisdom'*. Next day got a lift to Homs where we saw the Roman water wheels, still pulling water up to an aqueduct 2,000 years later. A student took us out to the road to Palmyra, but no traffic. Back next day wasted a couple of hours with some road workers, again no traffic, except for some Russian made tanks on patrol. We were joined by a young man who threw stones at them. We never got to Palmyra.

Back on the Damascus road got a lift in a truck going to Damascus. The owner was an ex-soldier who bought Army trucks and converted them for civilian use. Driving down the highway I saw a speeding Ford Consul approaching and said, "he is going to hit us", which happened. The car slammed into the truck just behind the cab. We all stopped; the occupants of the car were all Syrian Army. Heated discussions took place, some high-ranking officer declared that we were at fault. I put in my 'Two Bobs' worth, but our driver sadly said it was no use. I offered to give a statement or even go to Court, offer declined. The car was badly smashed up, our truck a broken axle and tail shaft. Our driver got me a lift with some passing friends, telling them of my offers of help. When we stopped at tea shops all other drivers were treated to my heroics and tea and meals were bought.

In Damascus, found Tom at the arranged hotel; he had been waiting five days. Met two Aussie girls, took them to the Jordanian Embassy where they tried unsuccessfully to get free visas. Went to the National Museum, saw many interesting things including beautiful Korans, and the stone on which the first alphabet was written. The girls had a guide who was very informative, especially about Saladin. Saladin became in my mind a towering figure in history; all I had ever read about him in the West was far less impressive, with the Crusaders being glamorised as heroes, rather than the thieves and murderers that they often were. On to the huge Souq where I saw many fabulous silks which I wanted to buy but as I was down to my last $30, could hardly afford to lash out. That evening Tom and I went drinking beer with an American Fulbright scholar from Istanbul, beer very welcome after nearly two months without. Next day back at the Souq meeting and chatting with several merchants, drinking tea and slowly getting their best prices on things I liked.

On the street, I was amazed by a demonstration of razor blades. One of the dirtiest street Arabs, with the roughest skin, was surrounded by a crowd as he was being dry shaved. He was either the toughest man ever or these were incredible blades. Suitably impressed I bought 10 for 5 pence. Naturally they were pretty ordinary. On the streets, Syrian women needed only their eyes, with the ones without the veil all stunningly beautiful. I said that I would love to be around for the emancipation of Syrian women, sadly not likely soon. Next day at the Embassy collected mail, including a letter saying 130 Pounds had been credited to my account for the camera. I immediately went back to the Souq, picked out the items I wanted, including a beautiful table cloth for Mum and other things for the rest of the family. Went back to the Tourist Office where we had left our bags, then to the hostel, to find we were lucky to have taken our packs out earlier as someone had broken in and stolen many things, including one girl's Passport and cheque for $200.

2013, protests erupt throughout Syria against Assad. When his father died, many people hoped that the son, English educated, and an optometrist, would be more liberal; sadly, misplaced hopes. As protests escalated into armed revolt the Assad regime, confined to Damascus and surrounds, became more brutal. Backed by Russia and Iran, Assad conducted aerial bombardments of cities such as Aleppo, Deir el Zor. As I watch the daily TV reports of the Syrian tragedy I feel hopeless rage at the evil that allows such things to blight the lives of innocent people, particularly children. ISIS was eventually blasted out of their Syrian strongholds, hopefully never to return, but unfortunately their moronic fanatics remain in cells. The image of women and children freed from their last holdout does not give encouragement. Burqa clad females stridently attacking any female who does not swamp her appearance and personality under this most stupid and ugly female garment. Meanwhile Syria continues to suffer under the barbaric rule of the latest al Assad dictator, together with Russian and Iranian backing.

Next day tried to set off for Beirut, but Tom had left his inhaler behind so had to delay another day. An American girl, Judy, joined us and next day a car stopped, Judy and I got in, Tony put his pack in, but driver said only two, so we took off with Tony's pack. Delay at the Border, Tony arrived, got his pack and passed us. Heavy snow in the mountains made for a slow trip, but eventually arrived in Beirut, where our driver took us to the Market where we had arranged to meet Tony. He arrived an hour later and so to the Hostel. Next day I went to three banks trying to get my money transferred from London, finally the British Bank of the Middle East got it and I bought US$290 in Traveller's Cheques and some change; Wealthy again! We enquired about boats to Egypt, one leaving next week, $18. Tom arrived during the afternoon. Next day Tony was ill, stayed in the hostel being looked after by a French speaking girl. Tom and I went walking, met some Aussie girls, had a few beers, finished reading 'Seven Pillars of Wisdom', started 'Life of King Farouk'; now there was a contrast.

Talked to a pretty English girl who made money drawing on the pavement outside the main Post Office. She said," Dan, I must be crazy! Today a Saudi man approached me, said he was the Secretary of a Saudi Prince who had seen me and wanted to offer 10,000 Pounds if I would spend one night with him, and I turned him down!" I said, would he be interested in me? Missed the 10,000 Pounds but sold my blood for $10. Picked up Passport photos, this was now Monday, boat leaving 10am Tuesday. Raced to Egyptian Embassy, told we could not get visas till next day.

Spoke to a German guy who said it was difficult to get through the Sudan.

Next morning up very early, bus to Egyptian Embassy, where we had to wait an hour for the Consul to come and sign our visas. The boat was now due to sail at 12 noon, visas signed at 9.55. Raced to shipping office, got our tickets. I had packed up my Damascus purchases and had to get them posted. Raced to the main Post office, which was not yet open, but a young guy said he could get me in the back way; in to the main mail room where I had to get special permission to post it, slightly overweight. Paid the postage and raced down to the ship. Needless to say, the parcel never arrived in Australia. We all finally got on board, met Gerry, an American who was having trouble getting his scooter on. Stewards took us in hand and found a cabin for us. Tony met a girl from Beirut and disappeared, Tom and I sat around the deck with Gerry who played his guitar and sang while we drank beer and relaxed till 2am. In our cabin discovered that one of the beds had been taken; Tony insisted that it was mine; I went off and found another bunk where someone lay awake all-night spitting on the floor, then at 5.45am everyone woke up and started singing Arab songs, which I did not enjoy, don't know why.

During the morning planned to deliver the crew member's cargo in Alexandria; altogether we had 21 shirts, 1 bottle of Scotch, 1 carton of cigarettes, 1 tablecloth, 1 box of apples, 1 fishing rod and a bag of unspecified 'goodies'. We finally got off, although Tony took two hours longer for some reason; Beirut girl maybe? Delivered our goods and were taken for a meal and a leisurely drive on a horse drawn taxi through handsome, wide streets to a hostel. Met three young guys who bought us beers and prawns, together with some heavy President Nassar propaganda; Tony got a bit 'antsy', but another bar, more beers and a taxi ride home made it all OK. Next day settled in to Alexandria; a stroll along the Promenade, chat with girls in Tourist Office, movie the Beatles 'HELP', met young Farouk, a mate from the ship, with his two cousins, more meals and beers, thoroughly enjoying the much more relaxed acceptance of alcohol in Moslem, and Coptic, Egypt.

Now thoroughly enjoying Alexandria, even though next day I was sold 2 bottles of whiskey; when I asked why they were so cheap, was assured they were 'Klefti; Klefti'; stolen. Perfectly wrapped and labelled, tea. Sight-seeing to the Roman Catacombs, Pompey's Pillar, the castle on the site of the Lighthouse of Seven Wonders of the World fame. On Sunday, I went looking for a Post office to mail some letters home, met a young guy who assured me he could take me there; a rapid walk through back streets and I was ushered into a bare room and given a beer and a joint. I assured him I had not realised that 'Post Office' was code for Hashish, so we had a laugh and another beer. Found the post office later. Alexandria provided time and space for movies and reading as well as just enjoying the City. Ismail, a young student in the hostel repaired my pack and sewed up a tear in my jeans.

FABULOUS EGYPT

The end of February, time to move on. We walked through the city to the edge, accompanied by a crowd of kids throwing stones, not large ones, at us; evidently the previous night the President had been on the TV making a very anti-American speech. The kids had a soccer ball which they made the mistake of letting come near me; I grabbed it and kept it until we came to the edge of the City. This stopped the stone throwing; at the city's abrupt edge I gave it my best punt and sent it sailing into the desert, pursued by the cheering kids. A truck ride with 6 Arabs to the middle of the desert, where we walked for 5k's before being picked up by a young guy who had studied in Vienna, who took us to a hostel in Cairo. Met an Aussie girl, Annette, who next day took us to the British Embassy where she had a contact, a Mrs Katba.

I had applied for a new Passport in Beirut, as mine was full, but had to wait until getting to Cairo to be able to collect it. This was also going to take some time. While waiting in the Australian Embassy listened to staff telling an Egyptian he could not emigrate to Australia because his English was not good enough. I had the Sudan visa in my original Passport, which meant having to go to the Sudanese Embassy in Cairo and explain to them that they should transfer it to the new Passport. This became a major issue, particularly as the office was packed with people screaming to get all sorts of problems solved; had to leave it with them, and it took another week to get done.

Back at the British Embassy for tea and cakes with Liz Katba who introduced us to her husband, Kamal, who was the most amazing man. Kamal was the head of the Egyptian Tobacco industry, and he quickly took us under his wing, so to speak. Kamal became our Host Extraordinaire; he took us for lunch in the revolving restaurant, Saladin Citadel, the Mosque of Mohamad Ali. When I asked Kamal why women were not allowed to pray with the men on the ground floor, he explained that men praying behind bowing women would become very distracted; probably not what the Mullahs would say but seemed reasonable to me. Afternoon tea at Kamal's home in Heliopolis to meet Lizzie again and his two daughters, and that evening to the Pyramids for a performance of 'Son et Lumiere', a spectacular show about the history of Pharaonic Egypt, narration by John Gielgud, lights and music fantastic. The number of beautiful women in the audience were very distracting. Kamal explained how things worked; if a woman fancied some male she would simply slip him her 'card'. Up to him to make the call. I got lots of smiles, but no cards.

We were staying at a hostel near Garden City, and next day Kamal picked us up for lunch at the Semaramis Hotel, the best in the City. Earlier I had gone to the Hilton to steal toilet paper which is not that easy to get. After lunch Kamal took us to the home of the ex-Crown Prince of Egypt, Hassan Sabari; a beautiful collection of rooms all done in different Arabic styles, magnificent woodwork, mosaics, furniture and art, sitting in the brilliant tropical garden, in which the Government has built a hotel. Kamal had asked us what we would like for dinner that night, to which Tony had replied 'Pork Chops'. I thought this was not on in Moslem countries, but no trouble for Kamal. At this time meat in Egypt was rationed, butchers only able to open on alternate days, but pork chops we had. Next day to the Pyramids in daytime, getting access to parts of the Sphinx where most people cannot, the house which Farouk used for some of his 'dates', now Mena House, then out to Sahara City, overlooking the desert and Nile Delta. Kamal's brother Peter and his friend Habib also took us around the Old City.

We now moved from our hostel to a house boat on the Nile with a few other travellers, one of whom was Charley Betancourt, a nephew of the Venezuelan President. I slept on deck as fleas were in control below deck. Kamal took us to his Club in Garden City, met Ursula, an Austrian girl who has been working in Cairo for two years, sat around drinking beer and listening to music, Ursula playing piano. Drove out to the Delta and Barrages, Kamal telling us the history, how Alexander the Great had come here with the intention of securing a burial place for himself. Finally got my new Passport and Sudan and Ethiopian visas. Changing money in Cairo a very haphazard affair, sometimes offered anywhere between 60 and 75 piastres to $. We became regulars at the Hilton, used as a Post Office. Got Yellow Fever shots. Drank coffee at our discovery, Riches Café.

One day sitting there congratulating myself on being in Cosmopolitan Cairo, a bus pulled up and disgorged its passengers from the Australian Women's Weekly World Tour. Finally found a map of Africa after trying for months. Watched work being done on the tunnel under the Nile, in particular 3 girls carrying baskets of cement on their heads with wonderful poise and grace; Parisian models would blush with envy. To the Museum to get our free Upper Egypt monument passes, also boat tickets from Aswan to Wadi Halfa on the Sudanese border, deck class for EP1.25. Wendy, an Australian girl who joined us, was going to go to Luxor for one day then get a ship to South Africa. Kamal took us to the station and was very upset at our leaving. He was the most wonderful man; I sent a letter to my mother asking if she could send him something Australian on my behalf, which she did. Later, after the Six Day War he emigrated to Canada, but eventually we lost touch.

Our train tickets were 3rd class; we tried to change to 4th class but they would not change, so we had to ride 1st class overnight to Luxor. An Egyptian journalist joined us and wanted us to leave the train earlier and go to Luxor later. He had evidently spent a lot of time in jail because of articles written against Farouk, but we had to decline. Arrived in Luxor early, checked in to a Hostel, met 2 American girls and hired bikes. Crossed the river and I discovered my bike had a flat tyre so left it with a young guy in the village. An Englishman, a visiting Professor in Cairo University gave me a lift in his taxi to the Valley of the Kings, uphill about 7kms, so I was glad I did not have to ride. Spent hours touring the Tombs, including Tutankhamen, Ramses 11. The others arrived, Wendy got a lift to the Valley of the Queens, I took her bike for the downhill ride to Temple of Hatshepsut, Tomb of Isis, the Ramaseum, the series of Temples and fortresses built by Ramses 1, while Wendy rode with the Professor, and I was mobbed by young school girls who wanted the Lucky ring from my finger, telling me that they loved me, to no avail; I kept the ring.

Managed to retrieve the bike, Wendy by now wanted to come with us but had already paid for her ship to South Africa. Took her to the station to see her off, promised to see her in South Africa. Joined our journalist friend for drinks in the New Winter Palace Hotel where we were joined by the chief of Luxor. Next day to Sphinx Alley and Luxor Temple and the huge Karnack Temple, the Sacred Lake where Pharaohs were sailed around seven times before being buried. More camera troubles, film stuck. I seem to have a lot of camera trouble; if it is not malfunctioning it is a lost or stolen camera, hence my photographic records are somewhat patchy, to say the least. My 'photographic memory' has also proved to have significant lapses over time, but the surviving diaries have largely filled the gaps; where I can actually read my writing. Letters to and from Australia and other friends throughout the world have also been a great boon.

Fabulous and educational days in Luxor were now at an end. Time to get the train from to Aswan along the Nile Valley. The dam was in the process of being built, with lots of help from Russia, and it was certainly an impressive sight. We caught a bus to the High Dam where we learned of the projected increase in cultivated land of 50%, 2 million acres, and Electricity 50% increase, at a cost of one billion dollars. Our budgets being slightly smaller, we brought provisions for the boat trip to Wadi Halfa, packets of dates from Iraq. The boat leaves from Shallal, and we were now a group of eleven, so we had a part of the deck to ourselves, leaving below decks to the rest of the passengers, who were camel drivers returning home after delivering their camels to Aswan, which is the biggest camel market in Africa and probably the world. Camels that survive the trek from Sudan finish up in Cairo as meat. Four days with 20 Sudanese and Ethiopian camel drivers below decks does not bear contemplating.

Among our group was Jeff, a New York Jewish Communist heading for Tanzania, where he hoped to find a job as an economist in the so-called Socialist Paradise led by Julius Nyerere. Jeff attached himself to us all the way to Nairobi. Jeff however had the only cigarettes among us and gave me a packet 'on loan'. I began reading 'The Blue Nile' by Alan Morehead as the desert drifted by, and admiring the desert sunsets, the sun being filtered through the dust haze creating spectacular colours of red and orange. We stopped at Abu Simbel, which was being re located from the banks of the Nile before it would be drowned, a major operation involving the carving up and re-assembling of the huge statues some 150 feet above their original location. Sun bathing on deck was great but had to be careful as my skin had not felt hot sun for about three years.

SUDAN AND AFRICA PROPER

When we arrived in Wadi Halfa we had no Sudanese money so had to walk about 3ks across the desert to the town to get money changed, and a hot meal of beans and meat. Welcome to Sudan. Because of the long queues we had no time to buy train tickets, and so got on intending to buy tickets on the train; this of course branded us as criminals; Passports confiscated. Long overnight trip through the desert, sleeping on luggage racks. Crowd of camel drivers appeared, displaying typical desert hygiene, spitting through closed windows and crapping on the carriage floors. On arrival in Khartoum we paid our fares but objected to having to pay 40 Piastres more and staged a sit down for two hours, but eventually gave up. The Police were very helpful and drove us to the University to get beds, but administration closed; come back tomorrow. Back to an hotel, got rooms, six of us to one room, Ray and Jessica shared a bed; it was Jessica's birthday. Next day met a Sudanese student who gave us a tour of the City, including the Palace where Gordon was killed by the Dervishes led by al Mahdi; the merging of the Blue and White Niles at Omdurman and other elegant buildings and Mosques. The tallest building in Khartoum is the American Embassy, at 8 stories; the rest all seem to be just one storey. One of these mosques reputedly has a relic of the Mahdi, his preserved penis, one of majestic proportions. Arab women are supposed to be allowed to see and venerate it; private viewings only, can't have any group titillations.

Finally made it to the University, which was closed for vacation, but got rooms for 60c US per night with 3 meals. Met some Students, including Gerry an American and Saif from Mozambique. Saif became a Moslem to make collection of funds for 'the revolution' easier. Later that night went to the whore houses. The girls were mostly from Ethiopia and wanted 1½ Pounds each. Very exotic evening. Next day tried to get my camera fixed but it could not be done. Decided to buy Tony's camera for $40, but it was also broken, aperture jammed. Kept it unrepaired, but it works alright, with limited flexibility. Another camera disaster; I had two rolls of slides all ready to be posted to England for processing, postage paid when they disappeared. Of course, whoever found them did not simply put them in the mail; visual records of Egypt and Sudan no more, it's all in the mind.

Settling in to life in Khartoum was not hard. The University, being Moslem, did not allow any public contact between male and female students, much to the frustration of the European and African students. There were several Africans who liked to describe themselves as 'revolutionaries', particularly when seeking funds from locals to support their 'revolutions'. Most Africans regarded them with contempt, as the only revolutions they had seen would be in movies. The day before I left Khartoum I told Saif of a movie just arrived which he should see. It was 'Zulu'. "What is 'Zulu'?" Saif asked. I told him it was set in Natal, a near neighbour to his home in Mozambique, a geographical fact of which he was not aware. "So, what is it about?" he asked. Basically, I said It is about how 150 white soldiers beat the crap out of 10,000 Africans. "I will picket it!" revolutionary Saif declared.

One of the Kenyan students, no admirer of those whom the Zambian President Kenneth Kaunda called 'Chicken in the Basket Revolutionaries', told me of his childhood where his mother used to smuggle him through British soldiers' lines to help Mau Mau fighters; a much more real involvement in anti-colonialist revolution. I shared my room with a young South Sudanese student, a Christian who often vented his frustration at the lack of social, i.e. female, life under Moslem society; an Anti-Christian feeling was generated by the Moslem Brotherhood. One day he suddenly declared he was leaving to go south to fight for South Sudanese freedom. Although no-one is quite sure who is on whose side; a member of one side caught by the other side is pretty sure to be shot. This was in the 1960's; people in the West seem to think that the South Sudan War is fairly recent.

After one week in Khartoum, time to move. We were now four, Tom, Tony, me, plus Jeff, our Communist New Yorker who attached himself to us, as he would have no hope of travelling alone. He was often sick, and we had to carry his bag for him. We found a truck at the Shell Service Station to cross the Nubian desert to Kassala, about 500 kms away on the Eritrean border, sitting on the back for about 50P. The driver managed to get bogged before leaving the station, but we eventually got under way about 3pm. A dusty two days ahead, my Bedouin shemagh very good at keeping out the dust. The road is merely a track, one of seemingly dozens. Our driver managed to get bogged a few times, and we had to get out and push. Jeff of course was too sick and stayed on board, while even an old man of 70 was helping. Stopping for tea at a couple of desert villages where one of our fellow passengers insisted on buying us tea as well as food. The country was mainly scrub, with occasional patches of irrigation, one of which we learned was the re-located Wadi Halfa after it was flooded by the Nile; a long way from the original. The people too were now very different; the men with fuzzy hair, long, plaited and greasy, with a carved piece of ivory in it. They carried large swords, camel sticks and some had boomerangs, which they used for hunting birds. Altogether they looked fierce, proud and impressive and, although I had a camera of sorts, I felt chary about asking to take their photo.

Our driver got bogged three times, ran out of diesel and got some from passing trucks; he did not seem fazed by his stupidity, so we were not either. On the second morning, we passed a huge mob of camels heading for their doom in Cairo, then a seeming apparition became the mountains of Ethiopia. We finally arrived in Kassala and caught a cab to Barclays Bank, where we had to plead to let us in as they were closed. They robbed me of 25P, commission, but we found a hotel where we could sleep on the floor for 5P, but they relented and gave us beds on the balcony. Kassala is a pleasant town between the mountains and the dessert; when Gordon was killed in Khartoum the British mounted their attack to re-take the Sudan from Kassala, thus consolidating their hold on Egypt and Northern Africa. A rather bizarre opportunity arose, the movie on in town was 'The Invisible Man', which was enjoyed by all, with Arabic subtitles.

Travelling with 'mates' has its ups and downs. Tony, for example was often annoyed with my late arising in the mornings; I have never been a Morning Person. On the day of our scheduled departure from Kassala I awoke to find Tony trying to persuade the others to leave without me. I let fly at Tony and a fight was imminent till Tom intervened to calm us down and restore peace. On the road Tony would usually be lagging behind the rest like a lost puppy. Tom, 19 years old, was usually placid and if any troubles flared would wander off, probably reading a book. Travelling together allowed us to exchange opinions, share experiences, jokes and in some cases to inspire a type of communal courage to do things that perhaps would not be attempted by a lone traveller. Later, when we had gone our separate ways, Tony wrote to me asking that I look out for Tom, as he was very young and inclined to wander into potentially troubling situations. Jeff, on the other hand, was nothing but trouble. In Kassala he was running a temperature, so we took him to the hospital, perhaps hoping he would stay there. His constant lectures about the beauty of Communism, his moaning, sponging and general helplessness were a drag on our collective spirits.

A COUPLE OF MONTHS IN ETHIOPIA

We caught the bus to Asmara, having caught up with Charlie and Nick at the bus station. A pleasant drive first through the desert then the foothills. Declaring our money at the Border Customs; Charlie had $5, Tony $10, Nick $30, Tom $50; only Jeff and I had more than $100. We found a hotel where we were given a place to sleep for nothing, although Jeff had a room because he was ill. The prostitutes here are very cheap, US$0.35; they mainly cater for the truck drivers of which there are plenty. The others indulged but I was too tired and disinterested.

Next morning, on to Asmara, but missed the bus because the clocks were changed one hour, so I went for a wander, finding an Arab cemetery, 12' high anthills, dry river beds with a series of locks and dams which had been constructed by Italians, a mongoose but no snakes. Took photos which I had developed in Asmara. Next morning up at 5.45 to catch the bus. Jeff of course had left his shoes, our map and a book behind; Charlie retrieved them. A very crowded bus, the trip taking 10 hours, climbing 7000 feet up through spectacular country, lots of rock apes, gazelles, an occasional empty shroud in trees, this being the burial custom for some of the tribal people. Lunch a very hot curry for 50c. I started to get a chill and by the time we arrived in Asmara was feeling pretty ill. We found a cheap hotel where there were plenty of willing girls, but Jeff discovered lice in the beds. We found another hotel, the Addis Abela where we had great rooms for $1.50 each. The pleasure of climbing in between clean sheets for the first time since Aleppo six weeks earlier was almost too much. Next day stayed in bed all day, Tom looking after sandwiches. Next day went with Jeff to a camera shop, where they fixed my camera for free. Jeff tried to spend his money buying a camera and radio. I got films developed with copies for Tom. Food was now completely different; huge steaks, vegetables, salads, bread, ice cream, fruit. A huge meal costing about $1.

Today was the beginning of the feast of Haj. I went to the mosque where the Moslems were praying and sacrificing sheep and goats. Got pictures from a nearby balcony, met a German, Henning, whom we had met in Khartoum; he had been sold bogus gold and tried to get his money back without success, but when he discovered it was actually silver was not too upset. I bought some Agfa film off him. Next morning up early to catch the bus to Axum. Jeff of course late so we left him; he managed to struggle on behind. The bus very crowded; Tom counted 29 people between the front of the bus and row 2. Sat with an Englishman who taught English in Saudi Arabia, typically in love with Arabs and Arabia, also typically arrogantly English into the bargain. Meanwhile our driver navigated the mountain road with all the style of Stirling Moss.

We arrived in Axum about midday, met a young fellow who had met Tony and Charlie, and took us to a good hotel. Tom and I went for a walk to the tomb of the Queen of Sheba which had been recently excavated by some Frenchmen. Years later I learned that she was actually buried in Nigeria, but as the stories about her and King Solomon fluctuate between Ethiopia and Yemen, who knows? One of the young 'unofficial' guides took us out into the wilderness to show us a pile of rocks which was reputed to be the tomb of an ancient Ethiopian King; maybe.

Back in Axum, which is the centre of the Coptic religion in Ethiopia and the ancient capital of Ethiopian kings, the Church of Our Lady of Zion, containing many beautiful paintings, also reputedly the Arc of the Covenant. The 'new' church is large and round under a dome, predominantly blue, set against a background of bare hills and gum trees, with the old church beside it. On the other side of the road were obelisks, some standing, most fallen, which were erected by kings, including Solomon, so we were told. The 4th Century Obelisk of Axum stands 24 metres tall, with false doors and decorations, so far undeciphered.

Met an Englishman on his way to Uganda by Land Rover. Had a meal and were introduced to local beer. Many places sell beer;

they advertise by placing a tin can upside down on a stick; if the can is white it is the cheap beer, red for the more expensive. We had red beer for 5c a glass and learned how to make it from barley and hops. They take their bread, very spongy, dark grey in colour, looking like dunlopillo rubber, put it in water with hops, left to stand for two days and the liquid is drained off; this is beer; not very alcoholic, not pleasant to taste but not unpleasant. While we were there the lady owner showed us her piece of silver, shaped like a large mechanical nut with designs on it. When a woman is married her husband gives it to her to wear around her neck. After much bickering managed to buy it for EP15. I still have it somewhere. Back at the hotel Jeff managed to get a discussion on politics going, in particular a savage attack on Germany and capitalism, directed mainly at Henning, which got me going. Would be OK in 1940, but not now.

Awoken next day by a young boy who wanted to show me some tombs. I walked with him for miles out of town. These tombs were a series of underground rooms, 8 in all, beneath the ruins of an old palace.

The vista, overlooking the mountains and plains was quite fabulous. The rooms were nothing special, having an occasional cross and Amharic writing to distinguish them, however they were interesting in as much as they were in the middle of Africa and constructed on European lines.

Today was Palm Sunday, and the town was full of people who had come from all over Ethiopia to attend the ceremony. People milled around the Church in their thousands; priests reading from their Bibles to crowds gathered around; beggars with horrible afflictions everywhere. People here seem to have a calcium deficiency, as we saw many people whose legs were useless. One had about five distinct angles in his legs, like a grossly accentuated hair pin. We removed our shoes and went into the Church where the people were gathered. Drums set up a throbbing, rather primitive beat, women set up a high-pitched keening resembling somewhat a Red Indian war-cry, only shorter and higher pitched. We were invited to sit at the feet of the High Priest on the central altar, where priests were receiving various people for 'a chat'. We sat for about 15 minutes absorbing the music and atmosphere, then went outside to watch the procession. The Gold Bible, 500 years old, crosses and the Crown Jewels were carried to the Sacred Oak Tree. The procession made a very colourful spectacle, with the priests dressed in brilliant robes and shaded by coloured umbrellas threaded with silver. I got some great pictures, some of which actually survive.

Walked back to the old church, then back to the hotel, where I removed the film from the camera and discovered that the diaphragm was stuck on F16 again. I had a brainwave and went to the Tourist Hotel where a German camera crew was making a film on Ethiopia. I explained my problem. They were from Munich and very helpful; they fixed one thing but did not want to take the lens off because of complications. They were very helpful, but I still had to use the camera on F11 all the time. Back at our hotel we persuaded them to let us sleep on the floor for free, had more 'good' beers. I had 4 but it seemed to make Charlie break out in hives. In conversation with some locals, heard about the troubles between Moslems and Christians. Axum is the centre of the Coptic religion. The Moslems tried to build a mosque, it got to about 20 feet high before the Christians tore it down. There were big fights and all the Moslems were thrown out of town, about 5 months earlier. They started a new town nearby and are building their mosque there.

We met some Peace Corp guys. Jeff was disgusted with the filthy affluence in which they lived. They get US$200 per month, man and wife, half of which is paid by the Ethiopian Government. They get 300 books and a place to live. They cannot take the money out of Ethiopia. I was told there were about 600 in Ethiopia and comprise 1/3 to half of the total teacher strength of the country. I met a lot of Peace Corp people throughout Africa and can only say that they all seemed to genuinely want to help the local communities as much as they could, despite what Jeff might think. Leaving Axum next day, we went out of town hoping for a lift, but were surrounded by crowds of curious people still. Every beggar in Ethiopia seemed to be there. We stopped by the reputed Tomb of the Queen of Sheba.

A truck stopped and wanted E$20 to take us to Gondar. We beat him down to $10. Sitting on top of the truck, stripped down to get some sun, but my milky white skin soon got scorched. I used my shemagh for protection from the sun. The mountains we were now approaching formed a jagged wall in front of us and by the time we began climbing them we were thrilled by their immense grandeur; in their ruggedness and immensity they were unchallenged by anything I had previously seen, complete with many strange and beautiful birds, monkeys, eagles and hundreds of donkeys. The road is one of the wonders of construction; it is wide, firm and climbs huge mountains with easy grades. Later when discussing this with a road engineer we met in Gondar he told us of its history. While expressing complete admiration for the Italians as road builders, he said they were hopeless fighters. During the Italian occupation, they decided to build the roads across the mountains. Italian soldiers on ridges above them to 'supervise'; above the soldiers' local partisans threw rocks and bullets at the soldiers; above the partisans Italian planes shot at the partisans. Through all this the roads were built, some 350 kms to Gondar. One of the valleys we had to descend, about 3000 feet deep and one-mile wide on an unsealed all-weather road; Italy's enduring legacy in Ethiopia.

We stopped overnight in a small-town high in the mountains. Trucks are not allowed to travel overnight because of Shifta tribesmen who sometimes hold up and rob travellers. A school sports meeting was in progress. One of the events would probably not make it onto an Australian program; six young boys were blindfolded and given clubs; they had to find their way to a tree from which were suspended six earthen gourds, which they had to smash. One contains a live chicken which is the prize for the boy who smashes that gourd. Makes the Australian Pub or Club chook raffle pretty tame. Dinner is spaghetti washed down with water I had 'purified' with Halazone tablets. Even the locals do not drink water, which contains all sorts of dread diseases.

Next morning early start for the drive into Gondar, through mountains even more magnificent than those of the previous day. The road hugged cliffs with drops of thousands of feet right beside us. Gum trees were everywhere, having been brought into Ethiopia from Australia some 70 years earlier by King Menelik 11, who defeated the Italians in the battle of Adwa in 1896. Gum trees provide much needed shade and eventually firewood for villages. We climbed up to a huge plateau about 8000 feet up and settled in for the run into Gondar. The country became green and populated with lots of horses and friendly people, with waves from everyone.

In Gondar, we put our packs in the Police Station where we arranged to sleep that night, and then walked up to the castle, Fasil Ghebbi, which was built about 400 years ago by Portuguese traders for Emperor Fasilides. A large, quite European style structure, it was here that King Theodore imprisoned Consul Cameron in 1862, thereby incurring the wrath of the British, who gathered an Army in India, complete with elephants and mounted a huge rescue mission. Having successfully rescued Cameron they promptly withdrew from Ethiopia, marking the only time that Britain invaded a country without colonizing it. Now it was used by HIM, His Imperial Majesty Haile Selassie where he kept his family of lions; lions being the embodiment of his title The Lion of Judea. They were quite friendly and allowed their keeper to give them cuddles. Over a meal met a local man who told us a lot about the country, its history and customs. Called in at a bar and chatted up some of the bar girls before retiring to our bunks at the police station, where the Chief promised us all the help we may need. Discovered my air bed was leaking, due no doubt to the floating around in the sea at Aqaba.

We left Gondar, got a lift to a small village, Addis Zemen, where the driver let us off before the village as he feared the Police, but they bought us tea and bread; the driver appeared and bought us tea before taking us on to Bahir Dar at the mouth of the Blue Nile, on Lake Tana, accompanied by lots of monkeys, exotic birds and baboons. A young teacher took us to the Police Station where we left our bags. One of the features of travelling in this part of the World is the lack of banks, or any places to change Travellers Cheques, which meant we were often without any money. At one stage, I used my last dollar to pay for all our meals, with no prospect of finding a bank. People, as poor as they were, were always buying us food, drink and accommodation, though we would try to pay our way.

The teacher's brother told us he worked in the local cotton mill, which employed 3000 of the town's population of 7000. Bahar Dar was not huge but was the centre of International attention as it was supposed to become Ethiopia's second city, based on the Hydro to be provided by the Tisissat Falls. The Russians built a big new Technical School, with training in engineering, electrical, physics and chemistry. The Germans built a hospital, where nurses were trained, with the Americans represented by the Peace Corp. Our teacher friend told me of the difficulties Russians were having trying to teach in English and Amharic, while locals mainly wanted to go overseas, but the Government would not let them. In the 2000s, Bahir Dar is the Capital of the Amhara region, and the centre for the Coptic Monasteries on Lake Tana, now the centre of a tourist boom, but still jealously guarded by Coptic Monks.

Tisissat Falls are about 30 kms out of town; Tom and Charlie wanted to walk, but my usual late start meant I decided to try for a lift. We were befriended by a Moslem tea house owner, Mohamad, who fed and watered us and gave us a place to wash up. Sleeping by Lake Tana was not comfortable, being eaten by bugs and fleas. Went to the Ras Hotel hoping to find transport to the Falls. The manager bought us beers and we chatted about tourists and Bahir Dar. The locals do not like Americans as tourists or as workers. They liked Italians as workers but laughed at as fighters. The Hotel Land Rover went to the Falls, but at $5 a head was too much for us. The manager told us the LR left at 6, and if we were on the road he would probably pick us up. A few beers in a bar, dancing with a local girl. One of the local boys kept calling me "My Dear", which had me keeping him at arm's length.

On the road next morning, the Land Rover arrived, the two American passengers had a debate about letting us aboard, but finally let us on. The other passenger was a middle-aged lady from Yugoslavia, travelling the World on her own, no mean feat in Africa. We passed Tom and Charlie sleeping by the road but did not have time to get them aboard. The Falls are about half a mile wide, but at this time of the year only about 25% flowing. After walking around, taking photos, headed back, passing Tom and Charlie as they arrived. The other passengers discussed in German how much we should pay, but I explained to them that we did not have any money, which they accepted. Back at the lake sat and watched the women washing, cleaning fish, collecting drinking water, ducking swooping eagles, boys swimming, all in the disease infected water. That night Mohamad sent us drinking with our teacher friend; local corn beer, made from roasted corn brewed with Hops; also, Tej, the famous Ethiopian drink made from honey and hops, with the kick of a mule. We managed to take our friend for a meal, the least we could do as he was buying all the drinks, then back to Police HQ to sleep.

Next Day was Good Friday. Headed for Addis Ababa on a truck. Standing next to a tribal man on the truck tray, who had a large, festering gash on his shin. Tried to do something about it by applying antiseptic and a bandage while he stood impassively holding his spear, looking ahead, but never at me. Hope it did some good. Next lift in a bus, which at one stage stopped and everyone trooped off to a beautiful lake in a small volcanic crater, which we were told was where Jesus had once come, not sure at what stage of His life this event was supposed to have occurred. Another site we stopped at had many obelisks covered in hieroglyphics which no-one has ever been able to decipher; this was supposed to be where King Solomon paid a flying visit from Yemen for a dalliance with the much travelled Queen of Sheba.

We stopped near dusk at a village called Bura, where we were told the Police Station was not far away, so off we trudged up a steep, rough track, fireflies all around, and a horrible noise from some animal nearby. The village in complete darkness. In the centre a group of children, after asking for money directed us to a bar, where a drunk joined us drinking Arak, and he won the fumbling session. I paid 50c out of our 4th last dollar. Finally met the schoolmaster who allowed us to sleep at the school, fleas included. Next morning one of a group of children, who spoke excellent English, guided us through the village, where we were picked up by a VW van; the driver took us about 30ks at breakneck speed; even the chicken I was sharing a seat with was worried. Next, a UN Land Rover, who took us to a Health Centre, including a new leprosarium, not yet open. There were 32 beds for an estimated 3000 lepers in the district. Next a bus took us to Debra Markos, where we found a truck driver who took us 75kms to Dejen, where the trucks stop before going on to Addis. Here, at the Police Station I put up my tent for the first time in 3 months, having been warned by the Police to be wary of the Hyena packs which often roamed the town at night.

Dejen is on a high plateau overlooking the Blue Nile Gorge, commanding a magnificent view. To pass the time I had taught the others Bridge, to the best of my knowledge, and Bridge became the main occupation when sitting around, so after playing cards that evening we went down to the church to take part in the Easter celebrations. Having assured two boys who took us down that we were Christians, and not Moslems, the priests gave us permission to enter. The church is a large circular building of wood; the centre seems to be blocked off, and a passage goes around the circle. We removed our shoes and were given candles, then joined the congregation in walking around the circle. Drums were beating, people singing and chanting, the women set up their peculiar, shrill whoop. The effect of the singing, drumming by candle-light as we shuffled around the Church, was both hypnotic and exotic, particularly that by a short, red turbaned priest who sang and played a long drum. He conveyed to me a scene from the Arabian Nights with his animated singing and Eastern appearance. After two circuits, the priests began a chant and passed around a golden cross, which everyone kissed. Ceremonies over, we all left, and I had a good sleep in my tent.

Easter Sunday slept in, too late for the trucks, local population looking a bit tired after yesterday's celebrations, gave my last 10c to a local beggar. A crowd of boys gathered, and to our great embarrassment took up a collection for us, 5 and 10 cent pieces, which we tried to refuse, to no avail. Finally, a bus arrived, and I was able to persuade the driver to accept a cheque for $10; off to Addis. While waiting half the town arrived carrying a huge thatch roof down the street, local DIY. I had expected a suspension bridge high across a deep and mysterious canyon, but down we went to a rather puny bridge across the Nile, where we delivered 4 tyres to an American woman photographer with an Italian guide; all their tyres were blown. The Blue Nile Gorge at this stage had only been accessed by US soldiers with helicopters. Our driver took off like a Formula One contestant, trying to keep ahead of a rival bus to get all the passengers. In Addis, a somewhat unappreciated grand tour of the city, before the driver tried to extract more money; we had already paid and got change so told him to go to the Police, who decided in our favour, and then showed us to a hotel, the Kagnew Sheleka, where we split $2 rooms, and settled in for what became 2 weeks in Addis Ababa.

We discovered a great eating place, Addis Abele, huge meals for 75c. Repairs to sleeping bag, air bed, boots and clothes the next project. Clothes were filthy and riddled with fleas. The hotel had an ornamental pool into which I drowned the sleeping bag for a day, which was successful in getting rid of the fleas. Settling in, the local food was great, the manager very friendly and the bar girls some of the prettiest whores in Addis, although sometimes they tried to cheat us. Meanwhile getting finances sorted was the priority. Tom and Charlie both had mail, with cheques, Tom's mother warning him to beware of prostitutes and syphilis in Eritrea. Went looking for the fine buildings in the City, including Africa Hall, Municipality Building, Commercial Bank, Addis being the headquarters of the African Union, but apart from the main buildings, shanties and single storey buildings predominate. There are more bars and whore houses than, it seemed, any other type of business, mostly run in conjunction with hotels, with many beautiful girls employed.

Tony met a Peace Corp guy, Ron, who said that a revolution was supposed to start in two days' time, while the Emperor Haile Selassie was away in Kenya, and advised us to stay with him. We settled in to his house and played a lot of Bridge, going from 9pm to 10am, memorable for me, bidding and getting two Grand

Slams. During the night, someone tried to beat down the door, and next morning it bore axe marks, but everything seemed calm. On checking with students at the University we were told that overnight the ring leaders were arrested by US troops, who were stationed just outside Addis setting up a communications base, but I have never been able to confirm this. I do know that the base was there; they were test transmitting songs, and I can still remember Dean Martin singing 'Houston' being stuck in my brain.

An Ethiopian boy took us on a tour of the City, a park where the lions were kept, and the Commercial Bank where Tom and Charlie changed their cheques and could repay me, as I had been acting as banker. Ron had seen Jeff wandering around. Eating at the Addis Abela, huge meals for US75c made it, to me, the best restaurant I had been to. We were waiting for Tony's money to arrive before leaving. Charlie decided to leave. Tom and Tony reported they had found Jeff, who came around. He had got $25 somehow but had spent it. He seemed to be completely incapable of looking after himself; paying $5 for meals where we were paying 75c. He declared that he had only $1, and wanted me to pay his hotel bill, which I refused to do. Tony abused him for buying a large roll with my money, and Jeff made a scene. I told him to leave quick. A couple of days later Jeff appeared and announced he had contacted the Tanzanian Embassy and they would fly him to Dar as Salam, and he would sell his radio and pay all his debts. Sceptical would best describe my reaction. Tony in the meantime had received a cable saying his money would arrive by mail, in about 7 days; Tom and I would leave soon, and Tony would catch up in Nairobi, or the Border.

Wherever we go, there seems an inexhaustible supply of people with tales to tell. In a tea house, over chai and bread we met a young guy with a tale of woe. His brother, who had been putting him through school, had been shot by a coffee merchant because the brother, an inspector, would not pass his coffee. He had then been thrown out into the world, unable to complete his education, and unable to get a job, without knowing someone in the 'right place'. He was now working on the Hilton Hotel construction site for $1.10 (US44c) per day. Although he had virtually no money he had paid for our tea before we could stop him. He had very few clothes, so Tony gave him a blanket he had acquired from a hostel in Greece. The boy then wanted to spend the last of his money on coffee for us, which we refused. His attitude seemed typical; if he has it, he spends it, and when he has no money, not to worry.

Addis can also be a place where due consideration has to be given to personal safety. One day, when walking back to the hotel, through the many markets, I became aware of two Ethiopians following, about 20 metres behind, stopping where I stopped, waiting for the right situation. After a while I just turned around, called to the two Americans who were about 80 metres behind me, and made sure the Hitler knife on by belt was visible. The stalkers promptly disappeared.

Back at the hotel Jeff appeared with a cheque for his radio. We talked till 5am, about Communism, Africa, Middle East, economics. Because of our long night, next day did not arise till midday. Now Jeff and Tony stayed in Addis, and Tom and I set off. Next morning, cashed a cheque and were picked up by 2 men in a DKW, who took us to Sheshamame, about 200 kms on the road South. We drove through dry country, plenty of small towns, neat and clean and looking prosperous. Now in coffee country; Ethiopia is the place where coffee originally came from, in the Province of Kaffa; Yemenis of course claim that coffee came from Yemen. After lunch in Sheshamame, another lift to Dilla, 120 kms on, the last town on the all-weather road. We drove through beautiful, fertile country, with many large and small lakes scattered around. In one valley, mile after mile of sisal fields, grown on co-operative farms. There were plenty of thunderstorms, this being the 'Little Rain' season. Coming in to Dilla, a spectacular view of a large lake with the sun shining on it, surrounded by fertile country of all shades of green.

In Dilla we were taken by some boys to a hotel, then to meet the Peace Corp girls, Bessie and Claudine, who then took us to meet the male Peace Corp, Dick and Doug, who took us for a meal and a tour of the town's bars. Today was the first day of the town's new electricity system, so people were very happy. Next day in the afternoon went up to the school and kicked a football around, where I discovered that the Americans could throw it further than I could kick it; very mortifying. While eating dinner in a restaurant, overheard a conversation with a German and an Ethiopian about the condition of the road. I got myself into the conversation, and the Ethiopian said he would take us some of the way next day. Next morning, he said he would be going about midday. His name was Teodros and was the only qualified sanitary engineer in the country, having studied in Chicago. He got us a lift to the next town, 65kms away, and drew up a map showing the route, distances, bus fares and said we would be better off to wait for him. The road south was said to be all mud, and very difficult to drive on until Yebello, then it became desert. Spent the evening with the girls, eating, talking and drinking cognac and Coke till 1am. Next day Teodros gave me all sorts of vitamins, cold pills, aspirins. Waited all afternoon for the Land Rover, Teodros finally arrived and said the District Governor had held things up by holding his monthly Court. They had to go and inspect the site for a new township. Met the Peace Corp Inspectors also. Told we were going next morning, carried our gear up to the boys' house, helped Doug connect the new electricity system, and swapped a book for 'The Once and Future King'.

Next morning, up at 6, took off with Teodros, The Governor, his escorts and others. After a short while it became obvious why it is a dry weather road; for 60 kms the Land Rover went through the most horrendous mud holes I have ever seen. Sometimes it bounced over huge ruts, then practically swam through small lakes on the road, churned through foot deep mud, and once got stuck in deep mud; we all got out and pushed it out. Many trucks were stuck, which bode ill for the future. Nothing but a Land Rover would have got through that mud. We got to our destination, a small town named Chelekletu about midday; the governor went off to inspect the new town site. Teodros insisted on buying us a meal, which we were half way through when a Land Rover arrived. Teodros tried to stop it, we got our gear aboard his vehicle and took off in pursuit, finally catching up after about 6ks of mud slides. They were German missionaries, and despite Teodros putting in a strong plea for us they refused to take us, so we had to retreat to Chelekletu. The German missionaries lived in a hill-top villa outside of the town, and listening to locals, they were not very popular. Teodros immediately started taking up a collection for us, to get us to Moyale, and collected E$25 from the mainly coffee growers who were in town for a market. We met the local teacher, who invited us to stay the night, discussing with him the problems of teaching in small towns; he had extra sessions every day in all subjects, with a wide range of age groups in his students.

Next day Teodros and the Governor had gone by the time we awoke but had collected another $32 for us. All this was somewhat embarrassing, but the total lack of any money changing facilities between Addis and Moyale gave us no choice. A Land Rover arrived, and room was made for us; altogether 14 people in a small wheel base Land Rover for the trip to Agera Mariam, 100ks away, through very deep mud; I preferred to look at what we had been through rather than what was ahead. About half way we climbed to higher ground and reached a plateau with a magnificent view of the valley and surrounding hills below us. In the town, we got rooms in the hotel, $1 each, but no food. After a sleep, in the evening looking again, met a man who took us to a store where we bought sardines and bread. He said he would collect us in the morning for a truck. Had a bad time in the night with a barking dog; dogs and snoring are my great sleep killers.

Next day a truck arrived, and after the usual haggles, agreed on a price, our friend wanting to take up a collection, but we would not let him. Finally, at midday passengers were collected, 24 in all. Only two trucks left that day, and we took off in pursuit of the other, which had left earlier. We soon caught up, as it was bogged. After being dug out we went another mile before being bogged again. The wonder to me was not that these Fiat trucks got bogged, but that they were not bogged 20 times more often. They were grossly overloaded, but ploughed through feet deep mud, lurching violently from side to side, mud up to the tops of their wheels. The first truck got bogged again and we took the lead and promptly got bogged in an open field, and this time made a good job of it; we were there for 7 hours. Everyone dug, chopped wood, carted sand to make a road out, and finally, at 7pm got out. We caught up with the other truck and made camp. I put up my tent, which suitably impressed everyone, but discovered I had lost my 'Lucky' ring. Dinner of bread and sardines. Woke at 6 and discovered we were parked in a beautiful rain forest; very tall trees, with a rather willowy look, as the leaves hung from the branches, rather than grew on them. A few shots were taken at a vulture with no success. We walked through the forest and came to a large open patch of ground, which looked solid, but was actually covered in water. Ate some sugar cane for breakfast, and came across the afore-mentioned camel, which refused to budge. I looked back an hour later and it was now free. The trucks now came; they burst through a track in the forest, wallowing in mud, horns blaring and everyone cheering. It resembled an Easter Parade.

We drove through the very beautiful forest for miles, till about 10am, the front truck suddenly stopped amid great commotion; everyone ran off into the trees, many with guns. We soon heard shots and ran down through the trees to where we found they had killed a young leopard, its eyes bugged out in terror, about 8 feet from nose to tail. Although I felt very sad, and over time have despaired at the destruction of wild life by many Africans, but could not do anything about this. No-one had a sharp knife with which to skin the animal, so they had to use my Hitler knife. We stopped at a small village for breakfast, bread, milk and Tej, bought for us by a Kenyan truck driver on his way home. My 'Lucky' ring magically appeared in a doorway.

Now our chief danger was trees overhanging the road; many had large thorns which caused some scratches. Tea in the next town, where a stretcher case was brought down for transportation to the hospital in Yarello but was refused as he would have been thrown off by the lurching of the truck. At Yarello the Police Chief met us and fixed everything. He took our Passport details, the first time anyone in Ethiopia had even looked at them. Next stop Mega. The truck driver wanted $4 each for the 120ks; I gave him $4 total. The country dried out, but the road remained terrible, not helped by the driver, who stupidly followed the previous track, no matter what the surface was like. Just above Mega, set in a beautiful valley between two hills and overlooking the lowlands, was an old English looking fort, which looked very out of place; as if anything could be 'out of place' in Ethiopia.

In Mega we met a Japanese boy, Gemba, and an Ethiopian, Johannes, who had been following us from Dilla. Johannes was intent on jumping the Border to Kenya, without a passport. They were staying at the Mission, where they had been lent a tent, so I set up mine for Tom and me. Dinner and Tej, long discussion on politics, particularly Ethiopian, which Johannes was disgusted with. He had come up against the 'influence' problem in getting education and a decent job; he tried to educate his three sisters, without success. Our next stop, a town called Hidda. There the Police said they would arrange an armed escort to the Kenyan Border; there were many Somali Shiftas about; the previous week they had stolen 8000 cattle and killed 150 people not far north. The Government of Somalia had recently been taken over by the election of the Somali Youth League, which Ethiopians said was trying to annexe Southern Ethiopia by having Shiftas force locals out; it was also said that the Youth League was the inspiration for the Taliban in Afghanistan. The Shifta conflicts in Ethiopia and Kenya raged from 1963-1967.

Up at the new, and very tidy, school we were given beds, bananas, tej and a radio. Next day went up to the Police Station, where the Police Chief was furiously addressing a bunch of men and boys, who were nervously holding .303 rifles. I asked Johannes what was going on, and he told me the Police Chief was berating the locals; last night a Shifta raiding party had come into the town and stolen more cattle. The Government gave the locals rifles and expected them to defend themselves and the town.

The Police Chief told us we could not get to the border by road because of the Shifta. Instead of a 20km trip by road, we had to take an 80km walk to Moyale, on the border. He told us we would have an armed escort. Shortly after, at 4.30pm we set out on the track, with our armed escort of two locals with spears. We had not gone one hour when we met a man on a donkey, accompanied by his servant. He told our escort that the previous night a local chief's son had been taken by the Shifta and skinned alive. The prospects of a leisurely stroll through the countryside were not looking that great, but there was no point in going back. In the evening we arrived at a village surrounded by an acacia thorn fence, to protect people and cattle, and settled in for the night. We were given hide mats in the Chief's hut; the chief and his wives had a square internal structure made of hides. I decided to sleep on the floor on my air bed; during the night it started to rain, and the mats were taken to be put on the roof, with only marginal success in keeping the rain off. Later I awoke to see Tommy sitting on a log; he invited me to check out my surroundings; the hut floor was now wet and a mass of maggots. They did not seem to be interested in climbing up my air bed so went back to sleep. In the morning they had gone. No-one could speak Amharic, only Gullinian, but somehow the chief got about 10 of my cigarettes and we drank some of their milk, which was supposed to contain TB, but it was better than the bug filled water.

Next morning, we set off in drizzling rain till the next village, by now without our 'armed guards'. Gemba got us a bowl of herbs which we saw cooking. Next village offered some thick, lumpy curds, which I declined. My taste for yoghurt had yet to be awakened. We were walking over very hilly country, from one village to the next, and not covering many miles. Sometimes villagers, mostly women, carried our packs for us, always wanting cigarettes; Tom had none left, and mine were very few. People were generally unfriendly, in most places we could not even get water. Last village for the day we tried to buy half a goat, but they wanted a ridiculous price, even after I said they could keep the skin. Tom went wandering and I found him sitting in a hut watching a woman cooking something; eventually she offered a plate of what was boiled tree roots, with milk. We slept on beds. Next morning discovered my Arab shemagh had been stolen from my pack; Johannes had lost a suit from Tom's pack. I became very abusive; they said that someone had come during the night and taken the things, which was an obvious lie. We made plain that we knew they were thieves and mentioned Police as we left, an empty threat, but we were still given 2 guides, a man and a woman.

Walking in light rain, but hungry, thirsty and tired. We had no water, but after about 3 hours came to a muddy water hole, and filled the only water canteen, which I had bought in Jordan. The water was foul, filled with bugs, but wet. We drank our fill. Later, we came to a dry river bed and I showed the others how to dig to find the water table. Further on I became very annoyed with Johannes, who had volunteered to carry my shoulder bag with the water and had drunk half of it. About midday we came to a village with a flag flying over it, a touch of civilization! A man who spoke a little English showed us to a tea house, tea and corn bread, even a little meat, most welcome. Went to the Police Station where we listened while a report was taken from a man who had been a prisoner of the Shifta but managed to escape. Three people had been killed the previous day. There were many Shifta around and the Police said we would be lucky to get to Moyale. They said they would give us an armed four-man escort next day. The district chief's brother had also been killed the previous day. Things looked black. Back to the tea house, Gemba had found some tej and arak. I went looking for a chicken, which kids chased around for; the first one they presented I rejected as too small. A feast of chicken, eggs, bread and tea. Back at the Police Station, someone objected to us sleeping inside, so under the verandah for a night nearly out of the rain. Guards were posted all around because of Shiftas.

Midday next day, still raining, about midday before we could hire 2 donkeys to carry our packs, $2 each. The Police said it was a 3 hour walk to Moyale. We had no Police escort, only the men who owned the donkeys and 2 women. A pleasant walk on an easy track. I was mostly about 400 yards ahead of the rest hoping the Shifta would still be sitting around the camp fires. I was joined by one of the guides who spoke a little Italian. We passed through a deserted village, where he said the Shifta had killed 4 people and everyone else had fled. Gazelles and a rare black panther, exotic birds, butterflies and caterpillars were the only companions I saw. Got more water from a river bed. About 5pm we came across many herds of cattle, then a large settlement with an Army camp, and over the next hill Moyale! It had taken us 2 weeks to get the 600 miles from Addis, walking the last 50 miles. We walked into town feeling like great explorers and found the Albergo. Mama from the Albergo promised us a good meal, after which we got stuck into the Tej. Gemba and Tom left first, while I got horribly drunk. Johannes virtually carried me back to bed. Next morning, back at the bar there were bullet holes in the wall; a Shifta raid, which I fortunately slept through.

Not feeling well next day, took pills which I think got rid of the worms which were in my stomach through drinking bad water. Washed my stinking body and had a meal and headed up to the Police Station; handed in our Passports to the Captain, an unpleasant bastard, no doubt thinking he had enough to worry about without us complicating his life. Shiftas were around and evidently the Army and some local people were going out to fight them. Back at the Albergo, Tony turned up; he had taken just 8 days to come from Addis, on trucks all the way. He told us that Jeff was still in Addis, his plane ticket had not arrived, he had no money, but was still acting like the last of the Big Time Spenders. Johannes made himself scarce, probably contemplating how he was going to get to and travel in the desert country of Northern Kenya, a not very welcoming prospect.

Next day met the Kenyan who runs the planes to Nairobi, who gave us useful information about the fare. 300/-, either To Nairobi or Mount Kenya. He wanted us to stay till Friday, this being Saturday, but we decided to go into Kenya and get the Wednesday plane. Moyale was virtually under siege, half of the town being in Ethiopia, the other in Kenya. The only meat was camel, which was killed as required and made into a very tasty stew. In Kenya, things seemed to be much better organised, British training no doubt. The Kenyan Police were very friendly, and we had no trouble with visas. We arranged to pay the plane fares, and settled in to the accommodation provided, which was a room in the Indian Agent's store. That night I slept on the floor and during the night was awoken by a consistent rustling sound, which, when I turned on my torch, was cockroaches. The walls, ceiling and floor was completely brown with them. Once again, my air bed seemed to keep them away, but next night shared the bed with Tom. The Indian Agent and his African girlfriend did not seem particularly concerned. Mosquitoes and fleas were the main sleep inhibiters.

After a few days in Moyale, time to fly. We had a truck to take us to the airfield. Because of the rain, the strip in Ethiopian Moyale, on higher ground, was wet so the pilot had to land there, load our gear and go to the lower, dry strip. Once again, the armed escort, this time two Kenyan soldiers who drove about a mile ahead of us; the plane, a Beechcraft Bonanza, landed, we scrambled aboard and departed Ethiopia after nearly two memorable months.

KENYA AND EAST AFRICA

We had intended to fly to Nanyuki, near Mount Kenya, but because of low cloud, diverted to Nairobi, after flying over Mount Kenya, Africa's highest mountain. Flying direct to Nairobi was not the preferred option, due to apprehension about Customs, but as Customs were not on duty when we arrived, no such worries were relevant. Got the address of a Hostel and took a bus. Gemba went direct to the Station and we never saw him again. Settled in to the hostel, which was out of town; the Secretary gave us bedding. An Irish girl was there, just up from the 'Cape'. Her companion had been travelling in Africa for 2½ years. Next day in to the Embassy for mail, Tony went off to get a new Passport. I priced the repairs to the camera, 6 pounds, have to put it off. Met an Australian serving in the RAF, transporting oil to Zambia. He told me the Zambians were trading it for Rhodesian coal, which I thought was rather pointless. The next highlight of civilization was watching 'Thunderball', and a dance at the YMCA, all very tame, till we met an American, Jim, who had some Pot. Back at the Hostel we played Bridge all night, 'under the influence'. Tony got the giggles, Tom was super slow, Jim and I normal till I 'turned on' in the early hours. Quite a funny night in all.

Earlier, in Khartoum, we had met a couple of men from British Guiana, who had travelled from Egypt with virtually no money, jumping on and off the train when Inspectors were checking. Met them again in Nairobi and they told me how they had progressed. They had gone South, through the Sud, the great swamp on the Nile, till they were arrested and thrown in the infamous Jubba Jail. They told me of the horrors inflicted on the Africans by the Northern Arabs; how they watched from their cell as African and Arab guards spent nights watching each other and sharpening their daggers. They were lucky to get out alive and make it to Nairobi. They were carpenters and were hoping to get work 'somewhere'.

I thought British Guiana must be a pretty desperate place for employment opportunities if the alternative was Africa.

Hitching into the City was now a daily event. Had to walk past the home, on the way, of the famous Colonel Grogan. The Colonel was a South African. Some years earlier he had been rejected by the then, 'Love of his Life', and to console himself, set out to walk from the Cape to Cairo, which he succeeded in doing. Sure beats going to a Pub and drowning one's sorrows.

My finances were now getting on the low side, so I wrote to Dad, asking for a loan, particularly to satisfy Border Control requirements that I would be able to sustain myself before getting a job, I hoped in South Africa. In Nairobi, a favourite watering hole was the New Stanley Hotel. During Mau Mau, according to locals I met there, this is where young farmers and others would gather for a few beers before going out on the hunt for Mau Mau. Many atrocities were committed on both sides, with the Black Watch Regiment featuring prominently in recollections. Beers were reasonably cheap, as was our staple diet of fish and chips. Kenya was now independent, and although these events were fairly recent, I never could detect much resentment from either side. Apart from such in-depth investigations on local history, I spent a lot of time writing letters, one to Maureen McKenna from Canada, with whom I had spent many happy beer drinking times in Munich. Decided to head for Kampala next day, May 16th. Tom and Tony were heading for Dar, and although we had vague arrangements to meet up, I thought I would never see them again; I was now once again a lone traveller.

Had several small lifts, some arranged by Police, passed through the Great Rift Valley, then beautiful farm land, pine and eucalyptus forests, and the lake covered by millions of pink flamingos. Two Indian traders picked me up, and I enjoyed music, strawberries, apples, and for the first time Pan; dried mango, betel juice and other spices wrapped in a leaf; the Indian tranquiliser. Border formalities non-existent; picked up by an Irishman who drove me the 50 miles to Kampala, straight to the Sikh Temple, where I was given a mattress and shown to a corner. After dinner of fish and chips, Britain's enduring legacy to Africa, back at the

Temple I was told I could stay months if I wished. Sikh hospitality demands nothing more than no smoking.

Long term stays in the Sikh Temple were not an option, however. Many lifts next day heading for the Murchison Falls Park, real source of the White Nile. One of my African drivers told me that many Africans would prefer that the British had stayed, rather than the unpopular President Milton Obote. Uganda's main tribe, the Buganda, were discriminated against by Obote, and they had many grievances. The Buganda who are settled mainly around the Lake Victoria region were considered to be the most advanced in terms of architecture and legal customs and had suitably impressed Burton and Speke in their 19th Century explorations. This situation was soon to come to the boil. I eventually arrived in Masindi, a very pleasant town where, with the help of the Police I pitched my tent and explored the town's parks and gardens.

That night was picture night for the town. Everyone assembled in the main park, and a screen was set up; a truck arrived with a projector, and as dusk fell the movie commenced. A slightly bizarre evening unfolded; the movie was a period French drama, set in probably the time of Louis XIV; powdered wigs, Court costumes. Every few minutes the projection paused while the standing crowd was given a Swahili translation of the action, such as it was. Adjourned for my first meal of matoke, the Ugandan staple diet, cooked mashed bananas, which was very tasty. Somewhere later I read that to get adequate nutrition, a man would need to consume 14lb of matoke a day. The café owner was Moslem, and over an hour's chat told me how good Moslems were and how bad Hindus were. Travelling in East Africa it becomes very noticeable how most of the shops and businesses are owned by either Singhs or Patels.

My usual late rising meant that I did not get a lift till 3pm, a truck going to the Park. Plenty of elephants and hippos before getting to the river, crossing and setting up my tent in the camping ground. During the night I awoke to the sound of some animal feeding right beside the tent. Thought it better to breath quietly. Next night discovered that the eating was being done by a herd of hippos. Hippos are one of the most dangerous animals in Africa;

163

get between them and water and you are dead. Next day caught the launch to the Falls; I was the only one on it and had a fabulous trip on the river up to the Falls, where the river is forced through a narrow gorge with tremendous force. The river is teeming with life; elephants, hippos, crocodiles, water buffalo, baboons, fish eagles, pelicans, flamingos. At one place I was thinking a huge croc resting on the bank was pretty docile, when it took off, diving just underneath our launch; fortunately, did not let go of the rocking boat. This part of the river was also a prominent part of the movie 'The African Queen'.

That day one of the wardens came in, told me I could not camp where I was, had to pay 5/- to camp somewhere else. During the evening one of the young Americans in the 10/- hut opened the door and I slept there. Next morning, up early so I would not get sprung for the extra fee; the Americans drove me down to the river, where I got a lift in a truck, but when we came to the bridge, a guard would not let us cross it as he was afraid it would collapse under the truck. Not being prepared to go back and pay another 10/- fee, I set off over the bridge, becoming aware of the herds of nearby elephants and water buffalo, but they were not interested in me. Gradually my brain came to realize that I was strolling through a Lion Park, in the middle of the day. After a couple of hours, I selected a tree under which to sit, one that I hoped would enable me to climb its branches should one of the local wild life wander past. I spent a couple of hours watching ants before at last, a car appeared. Making my intentions clear that I wanted a lift, I was soon in the company of two lecturers from Kampala University, John, from California, and Ian from Perth, WA. In Kampala John took me to his flat in the Uni grounds, met his wife Anne and had a few Vodka and lemons, before being invited to spend the night. Vodka, bed and bath, the first since Cairo, pure luxury. A restaurant meal, Scotch night cap.

Ian invited me to go on a picnic by Lake Victoria at Entebbe. Joined by John and Anne and another American woman, Fair. A great picnic and BBQ by the Lake. Later wandered through Entebbe town, a very pleasant place, but a lot of soldiers around President Obote's residence. Ian told me that the President had gone overseas, and the Buganda had decided to send a letter to the UN setting out their grievances, but he heard that someone had forgotten to post it. Trouble it seemed, was not far away. That night we went to see the movie the *'Flight of the Phoenix'*. Later in the evening sitting around drinking Scotch, listening to music and discussing the World. Civilized life starting to look attractive again.

Next morning Ian drove me down to the road out. The second lift was with an African priest. We had not gone very far, on a crest overlooking a town, when we were stopped by a boy who told us we should go back; people were gathering in the town and were about to over-run the Police Station. The Buganda were rioting about the Constitution brought in by Obote, which they say would strip the Buganda, and their King, the Kabaka, of many of their powers. The priest decided to go back; I looked back towards Kampala, saw a large black cloud of smoke and decided to keep going. I walked through the town, where men were gathered, their blankets not quite concealing their spears. I kept walking, smiling and greeting all with "Jambo", Swahili for 'I Love You'se all' and hoping they would rightly think I was crazy, and let me through; which they did. When I got back to Nairobi and read the news I realized how lucky I had been to get out of it. On the outskirts, a young Indian drug salesman picked me up and took me to Jinja, on the way stopping at a sugar mill owned by Madvahnis, who, he told me, made a profit of 10,000 Pounds a day, with the mill alone valued at 35 Million. In later years Idi Amin virtually eliminated Indian commerce.

In Jinja I was picked up by a Kenyan European, who had been stopped 4 times by knife and axe wielding mobs, finally getting through with a Police escort. He said if we got stopped again, there was a pistol in the glove-box. The prospect of confronting an angry mob of armed Africans with a pistol, seemed to me a good way of committing suicide. After lunch he dropped me in Eldoret, in Kenya, where I was picked up by a young guy, Peter, who invited me to stay on his farm overnight, which I gratefully accepted. The family showed me around the farm, and I settled in, a bath, huge farm hot meal. Peter and I talked about South Africa, which is where he was from, but did not like. He wanted to go to London. The family had not heard of the troubles in Uganda, until next morning when they heard it on the radio news. Next morning, several rides, mainly with a Mount Kenya farmer. Driving through some of the most beautiful country I had seen; coffee, tea, trees everywhere, old colonial homes set in spacious gardens, the epitome of wealth and gracious living, African style.

Back in Nairobi, got a lift to the Hostel, bought pills for Malaria, Tapeworm and any other bugs I might have picked up over the past months. Next day, 25th May, my 25th birthday. Met a dozen or so locals, and Jim and Anne at the Thorn Tree, very pleasant day, lunch, drinks. Returned to the hostel for an early night, much of which I spent on the long drop, hopefully getting rid of tapeworms in the fundamental way. Next day, not feeling well, hoping that this was not Malaria, consequently spent a lazy day reading and writing. Next day got away before 9, for me AMAZING! Got lifts to Uhuru Highway, there picked up by Peter from Eldoret to Arusha turnoff. A young Indian couple going to Moshi, returning from Nairobi from a holiday and banking course, with their charming baby daughter. They invited me to stay at their home at the foot of Mount Kilimanjaro, where I spent a pleasant night. Evidently the previous day some German tourists had been killed by elephants on the mountain. The Tanzanian Border, no problems; to my relief all they wanted was to see my Passport.

Driving through flat country, with lots of sisal plantations. Sisal is the main crop in Tanzania, owned mainly by Swiss, Indians and Greeks, having been taken from the Germans after the War. I was told that it is unlikely to be taken over by the Government, as it would be mismanaged, and lose out to synthetic fibres. I was also told that, after the election of Julius Nyerere's Socialist Government, many of the workers on the plantations quit, thinking that now all would be provided, without the necessity of having to work. How much credence all this deserves is open to much conjecture.

Next destination Tanga; several lifts, one of which needed me to change a flat tyre. Very beautiful country, before arriving in town and been taken to the Sikh Temple, where I was made very welcome. After a meal in town, back to the Temple, where there was a ceremony for one of the locals on his way to London. I had many interesting conversations with Temple members while I stayed there for a weekend, enjoying more festive meals before a lift was arranged for me to Dar. A teacher invited me to stay at his house, but I had to turn it down. The arranged lift on Monday never turned up, which was highly unusual, but after a three hour wait, during which I looked out over the Indian Ocean for the first time since leaving Perth, and observing that it was the same green colour here as in WA, as opposed to the Blue Pacific; never have got an explanation. Got a lift on a BSA 250 with John from Edinburgh, here investigating the possibilities of establishing a crayfish industry, which he rates as NIL. Back at his house for beers, then to the Yacht Club, more beers with a couple of German girls, who lived in an old and very stately German Colonial mansion. Back at the Temple had to awaken someone to let me in. Next morning, at 4am, my driver awoke me with breakfast, and on the way stopped often to make temporary repairs to a leaky radiator.

Finally, in Dar, found the Australian High Commission and the American Embassy; for once all my mail was there. Dad sent me a cheque for 150 pounds, lots of other letters. No room at the Temple, found a cheap hotel, which was quite good. Wrote a long and windy reply to Peter Jeffery in Perth. Back in my hotel, sharing with Indian truck drivers on the Zambian oil run; all of whom snored like saw mills. After changing Dad's cheque for travellers' cheques next day, read some papers at the High Commission, wandered around the town and harbour, had a couple of beers with George, an African cook in a bar. Met up with one of the men from British Guiana who was in all sorts of trouble with the Police, who were going to deport him to London. Also met Doug, a Canadian, heading for Zambia. I decided to go to the Tanzanian Immigration to get a stamp; they had me running all over the building for an hour and trying to get me to pay a cash deposit, which I refused to do, saying if I could not get a job in Zambia I would catch a boat from Mombasa to Bombay. Went with Doug to the Peace Corp Headquarters where we could sleep in a washroom. Doug had lent money to an Aussie in Djibouti, who had been sent back to Australia. I remembered seeing a letter from him to Doug in the Embassy. Doug then set about finding all the difficulties he would have getting a refund on his plane fare from BOAC. I decided to head for Lusaka in Zambia.

Next morning, on the road; got a lift on a truck going to Morogoro, where I discovered they were going on to Iringa, 310 miles from Dar, on the way to Mikumi, the recently established Mikumi National Park, fourth largest in the country, now the staging point for the Petrol Run to Zambia, which had now become a Boom Town. Bars had sprung up everywhere. Because of UDI, the Southern Rhodesian Unilateral Declaration of Independence by Ian Smith, petrol could no longer be brought in from Mozambique through Southern Rhodesia to Zambia, necessitating a system of trucks bringing petrol from Dar as Salam to the Zambian border, off-loading and having Zambian trucks taking the petrol from there. Hundreds of trucks waited around for loads, sometimes for up to a week, but making 200 Pounds a trip. The trip to Iringa at night, climbing up in moonlight through mountain passes, one five miles to an old volcano, which became less idyllic as my bowels began demanding immediate attention; my English, combined with emphatic sign language saw my moonlight plunge into the bush being just in time. In Iringa, after buying my driver some beers I slept in his truck.

Next day, while walking to the turn off, met two Australian brothers, Tony and Richard Peacock. They had left London 3½ months earlier, crossed North Africa, on to Addis then into Kenya by the West side of Lake Rudolph, then spending two weeks trying to cross the Omo River, finally getting their Land Rover across by making a raft of petrol drums; probably getting bilharzia, sleeping sickness, while swimming in the river with crocodiles. They told me they were heading for South Africa, hoping to join the mercenaries of Mike Hoar in the Congo. We all got lifts to Wangangina, a small village where some kids took us to the Peace Corp guys, Tony and Dave. Sitting around a camp fire telling ghost stories rounded out an eventful day. Next day the Aussies gave expert advice on the making and operation of the Long Drop toilet, as Tony and Dave spoke of the difficulties of teaching modern subjects to people who still believe in witchcraft.

Another day with no lifts, spent talking to school children about how difficult it was to get into secondary school. Then swapped two books with Peace Corp guys, got 'Officers and Gentlemen'. Next day lifts with petrol trucks; after a while noticed petrol leaking directly onto the hot exhaust. The drivers did not seem worried, but as we were sitting with the possible consequences, spent some time shifting the leaking drums. After a short ride we were stopped by Police who made us get out of the truck. I abused them roundly, but they would not budge. Walked a mile down the road with a group of Africans singing, on their way to Church, before a utility picked us up. We had not gone 10 miles before it refused to climb a steep hill; petrol pump problem. The Indian driver had no tools; we stopped a passing LR, but they could not help. The driver got a lift to Mbeya to get another car. With a lot of careful driving we managed to get the ute to Mbeya, much to the Indian's delight, who then bought us meals and arranged to set up beds in a half-completed building, with hot showers in the morning; Luxury!

Next day, the fun begins! Picked up by a farmer's wife who took us about 50 miles, telling how difficult it was to farm, because of high taxes, (where have I heard that before?), and the Government's anti-settler policies. More devastating to Tony was the news that the British Lions had beaten Australia at Rugby, 30-Nil. Two Indians then took us to Tunduma, the Border, which was situated in the one building. Left Tanzania walked 10 feet across the painted line into Zambia. My filled-out declaration stated that I was heading for Malawi, where I had a job as a teacher; they demanded a deposit of 40 Pounds from each of us. A storm of protest erupted; I said there was no immigration post on the Fort Hill road and would not be able to get the money back. The others had said they were going to Durban to catch a ship. I showed my traveller's cheques, plus a cheque book in which I had altered the progressive balances to show a healthy total. Tony and Richard had only 30 Pounds between them, and things were looking bad. This was now late afternoon, and while I was arguing with the African official, a European officer came, and against his colleague's protests, gave me a 14-day visa. I had to leave Tony and Richard, who were made Prohibited Immigrants, or risk having my good fortune reversed. A Swedish couple had tried to get around the border, but were caught, and did not know their fate, having their Passports impounded. I said goodbye to all and walked to a nearby little village. Here I met a bus conductor who boasted to me how he robbed the bus company of 50 Pounds a month. He was going to let me sleep on his bus, but suddenly took off with two women; obviously with better prospects; he did, however, buy me breakfast.

Walked to Isoka where the Tanzanian trucks transfer the petrol to Zambian ones. The driver of a truck, with a full cab, told me I would have to try the driver in the next truck. I stopped the next truck, with the same markings, and told the driver his boss had said he should pick me up. We set out for Lusaka, 600 miles. Midday we caught up with the first truck and stopped for lunch. The boss was an ex South African Afrikaner. He had the Africans set up a shelter for him of branches, cook a stew, and generally act like a real bastard. I was fed Hippo biltong, stew and brandy. At one stage, as he was chewing the black hippo meat he said to the African drivers; "Hey boys, look, I am eating you". Horrified as I was, I was in no position to protest, being 300 miles from anywhere. Back in my truck, after an embarrassed hour or so, the driver suddenly said, "One day that white boss", as he made the universal finger across the throat. I shook hands on the deal. We discussed education in the Rhodesias, now Zambia and Zimbabwe; although most children could not get through to High School, they were much better off being able to read, write and use basic maths. Not being cheated in the markets was a great plus of being able to count.

We arrived in Lusaka 2.30am and I stayed with the Afrikaner, where I had breakfast of steak and eggs, before he took me around town, asking various places if they had any jobs going, without success. Left him to go and look for a cheap hotel and try to phone the American Embassy to see if Tom had come, but not able to get through. People told me that Zambia has the World's worst telephone system. Looked for hotel, but evidently there are no cheap hotels in Lusaka. Went to a camping ground 3 miles out of town, where I made friends with a huge bulldog; put up my tent, before meeting the owner who told me it was 10 shillings a night, because of locals sleeping in cars and making a mess, but gave me a discount. Met Robin, a Scott, who was working here and said the money was great. Stayed in his caravan, after taking down the tent; Lusaka is freezing at night. Next day set out on the job-hunting trail.

After a few non-productive visits, was given the intro to the College of Further Education, where I made an appointment. Met the Principal, who left me with the Registrar, who practically promised me a job as Assistant Accountant, 1200 Pounds p.a., furnished flat P7/10/- per month, and I assured him I had no problem working with an African boss. During the weekend, met Werner, an Austrian architect, met his wife for lunch. While waiting, did some catching up; had a haircut, more repairs to the air bed, started reading Homer's 'Iliad'; finished the 36-page letter to Peter J. Went to the College where Mr Watson, the Registrar told me they could not take me on, because of Zambianization. He gave me the address of an Accountant, who would take me on, but first I had to go to Immigration. There I went to an office; me and a young African couple, where an official proceeded to 'Big Note' himself to by telling me I had four days to leave the country, "Our Police will find you wherever you may hide". I told him to call the Police while I was hiding in his office. Net result, a Prohibited Immigrant stamp in my Passport. Met Tom at the BIT; he had been refused by Rhodesia three times and had decided to try via Malawi. I had discovered I had developed Piles and decided to go home via India. Tom and I had quite a few beers on a final night. On the way home, I stepped into a ditch, one step in, one step out. Next morning, I went to check; it was at least 6' deep. The beers must have given me super stepping powers. Altogether, 10 days or so in Lusaka was a waste of time; jobs were available but offers had been withdrawn because of 'political' considerations.

Tom and I got lifts to our respective turn-offs, he to Malawi, me to East Africa. Tom and I had been together, on and off, for about 6 months, sharing many good and interesting times, and I was sad to see him go. When I returned to Australia I had contacted his parents, particularly his mother, and we exchanged letters. Even later, I suddenly decided to try and find him, knowing he came from Lancaster, Wisconsin. His father had helped build the family home with Frank Lloyd Wright, which is now a well-known landmark in Wisconsin, but efforts are on-going. Tom went South, me North East. I got picked up by the Police Chief from Ndola for 100 miles, then several short lifts, before next day Tommy, a South African, one of the Good Ones. He had bought four trucks for the Petrol Run and was now making P2000 per month profit. Wants to retire in six months and live in the Bahamas. Left him in Isoka, where he gave me two Pounds to help me on my way. Truck drivers would no longer give lifts, because the Police were getting tough on them. Soon got a lift with Norman, a young English surveyor who had just finished a job in Malawi and was going to Nairobi, a 1000-mile lift for me. We had no trouble at the Border; heard that the Swedish couple had gone to try Malawi, the Australians had gone back, and Jack, an Englishman was commencing his sixth week of waiting.

Our first stop Mbeya, where Norman treated me to a meal and beers. Next day had a broken engine mounting repaired, leaking radiator required plenty of refills. Shared the driving over terrible roads to Iringa. More repairs, on to Dodoma, through beautiful hill country, plenty of monkeys, zebras etc. Only room in Dodoma Hotel a double, so I had a free bed; more Luxury. Next morning Norman met Charlotte, an ex-Peace Corp volunteer from California, who came with us to Arusha. On the way stopped to see some rock paintings, of great antiquity. Norman and Charlotte booked into the New Safari Hotel, I slept in the car, after looking at all the photos of rich Americans and film stars who had stayed at the hotel. Next day, on the way to Nairobi, Norman told me that in the village I had walked through in Uganda, the mob had soon after attacked the Police Station and killed everyone in it. My timing was only just OK. To Nairobi this morning, some shopping, Norman bought Masai knives; me, cigarettes.

Arrived in Nairobi mid-afternoon, back to Hostel. Jim and Anne still there, had been trying to get a free plane to Addis for 2 months. Next day several lifts on way to Mombasa, where I arrived late afternoon, and went looking for the Sikh Temple, and fortunately went the wrong way. Called in at a shop for a drink, and two young Indians sat me down for food and drink. While there, several people came in to talk, and one asked me to go to the movie with him; I said I would have to find a place to sleep and was promptly invited to his house. His friend Mohamed Ali took me to Mohamed's house to meet his family. After a meal in town, the movie 'Our Man Flint', back to Mohamed's house, where I refused to take his bed and slept on the floor; I stayed with his family for a week.

Next morning, awoken early by the call to prayers from a nearby Mosque, then after breakfast met Ahmed Ali Shaeb in the market and spent the morning at his fruit and vegetable stall where I watched him selling, and met everyone in the market. When Ahmed needed a break, I manned the stall, making sales. After work, Mohamed came and took me for a ride on his scooter; after coming back from the Airport, I took over the control. I passed a van full of Police; at the main road I had to stop, then put the scooter into first gear and took off like a bucking bronco, leaving Mohamed standing on the road. The Police caught up and asked to see my Licence; my WA licence was not for scooters, and Mohamed had only a Learners Permit. They were going to charge Mohamed with allowing an unlicensed person to ride his scooter, but somehow, we got out of it; paperwork probably too much trouble.

Mohamed's brother Ramzan, and another teacher, told me of a Teachers' Union meeting, where they were thinking of a second strike. They complained about how difficult it was to teach African children, and how they were put down as 'Asians' whenever they offered suggestions. The next few days, Ramzan and his friends showed me around Mombasa, the Jesus Fort, Uhuru Gardens, in between Ahmed's stall, meals, meeting his friends, of whom he had many, getting used to Pan, and liking its soothing effects. Mohamed and Mohamed Ali had religious events to go to, one

Sunni, the other Shia, but I was not sure which was which. I never saw any friction between the Sunnis and Shia. Mohamed Ali's father wants to go to Europe, because he thinks Africa is finished for Asians, and he also hates the hot, humid climate in Mombasa. Ahmed was suffering from a fight he had been in; someone had hit him in the kidneys with an iron bar, and he had slashed the guy across the forehead with a knife. The other guy was jailed for two months. Ramzan's girlfriend was giving me inviting looks; none of the others liked her, saying she is a virtual pro.

Mohamed has been put in a position where he has promised to marry his cousin, although he does not want to, preferring to remain single. Mohamed Ali has talked him into it, saying his sick mother needs someone to help around the house. Marrying to get a housekeeper seemed drastic, but family demands are paramount. I had by now spent a week as part of this community; I asked Mohamed if I could stay one more day, before leaving for a Hostel and arranging Passage to India; he would like me to stay for a lifetime, as he regards me as his brother. I bought some African wood carvings to take home, which helped make my pack even heavier. Spent my final morning in Ahmed's stall before walking to the bus stop with Mohamed and getting the bus to Kipenbula, where the hostel is, 15 miles north. Once again, I reflected on how fortunate I had been in meeting so many wonderful people, and how many of them were Indians. In all my time in East Africa I had very little to do with Africans, apart from truck drivers, various officials and the occasional drinking companions in roadside bars. This would change in Kipenbula.

The bus driver missed the turnoff, which meant I had a 3-mile walk through the bush, but my curses turned to cheers on arriving at the hostel; a beautiful location set among palm trees, right on the beach. Gunther and Ulli, two Germans, others from various places, two Canadian girls, Irene and Selena. There is a 12' tide, and when it is out, we could walk out to the coral reef, 500 yards out. The milkman comes every morning; someone else takes orders for meat, fruit and veg, a nearby shop sells cigarettes, what else could we need? A walk through the bush to the nearby Whispering Palms hotel which staged a show for the tourists, while we had beers at the bar. Back 'home', at 2am the girls came and said there was a prowler, trying their window and flashing a torch through. I went looking, but whoever it was had gone. Stayed in the girls' room all night. In the morning Selena had an attack of Malaria; I gave her some pills and my sleeping bag, and she stayed in bed all day. Spent the day swimming and finished reading the 'Iliad'. Slept in the girls' room again, but the prowler did not reappear till the second night, at 12.30. Went looking for him with a stick and a knife, but he had gone. A bit of a wrestle with Irene developed further, till about 4am when she went back to her bed and I stayed with the insects, which were devouring me.

More people were arriving, including Peter and Ingrid from Germany, driving a Kombi from Jo'burg, waiting for a ship to Trieste. Eating meals of steak and eggs, Ulli climbing trees to throw down coconuts. Went into town to the ship 'Kampala' to get the 1st officer to sign permission for me to travel 3rd Class. Paid for my ticket, 430/-. Went to immigration, who had given me a Prohibited Immigrant Notice; they did not want to rescind it, saying I could cash in the ticket. I showed them the ticket and forcefully pointed at the paragraph which stated that I could get the ticket refunded, saying that this said I could NOT get a refund. They extended my PIN. Got a Liquor Licence for India, met Ahmed who had mail for me from Australia, but no money. Two Swiss arrived from South Africa in a Land Rover, which they were taking to India on the 'Kampala'. Gunther and Ulli changed their 2nd Class tickets for 3rd Class, saving P22. We all upgraded our meals to European. Irene and Selena to leave next day, talked to them till midnight, then the next 3 hours saying goodbye to Irene. Peter and Ingrid had spent some time with Ahmed and Mohamed. My 2½ weeks in Mombasa was now ending. Went into town with Gunther and Ulli; we spent a night in the Sikh Temple and next day met Mohamed and Ahmed and all the regulars. Went to the beach where we dug up crabs. Promised one of the boys I would send him some ointment for ringworms; he had ordered some from Australia, but it never arrived. It took another 6 months, but I did send it. In town the Swiss guys called me in to a bar; they were getting drunk and spending a lot of money on women. I left them to it.

AT SEA, SEYCHELLES, BOMBAY

July 14th, 1966. Boarded the *'Kampala'* and organized sleeping arrangements in bunk class. 10 bunks to a section, mostly occupied by Indians, and some African students; cramped but clean. We sailed at 3pm and settled in for 10 days. The first couple of meals were none-too plentiful, but after convincing the cooks that we were growing lads, quantities improved. Deck side movies, mainly Hindi musicals, but also *'King Rat'*. Awoken at 6am for morning tea, 10am boat drill, a shambles, but we all survived. Talked politics with a Tanzanian, finished *'Ape & Essence'* by Aldous Huxley, drank beer with the Germans. The Swiss guy is the loudest and crudest I have met in some time, but on his birthday, beers were on him.

After 3 days, we awoke to the news that we were in the Seychelles. Beautiful islands of high green mountains lay around us. On top of one, through clouds, could be seen the white dome of the American Tracking Station. Ashore by launch at 9am, after throwing coins in the sea for local boys to dive for, most of the others headed for the bars. The main feature is an old silver clock tower in the middle of the town, erected in honour of Queen Victoria, and a clock tower modelled on Big Ben, which strikes the hour twice, for those who missed it the first time. Loved the story of how the Seychelles came to be a British colony; the islands were a French colony, but early in WW2 a British warship sailed into the harbour and the waiting islanders promptly lowered the French flag and raised the Union Jack; coup completed.

I got on a bus going I don't know where. It drove around the coast for about 15 miles, then back again. Everywhere there are beautiful white sandy beaches, coconuts growing to the water's edge, bananas, flowers, small streams running into the sea, and pretty girls everywhere. I thought it was paradise. All is not so rosy, however. While wandering around town I struck up conversation with an old man, beneath the huge spiderwebs, who told me of his daughters who had gone to Beirut to work as house maids and was anxious to know what life would be like for them. I did not want to speculate but was anxious on his behalf for their welfare.

The people are very poor, a labourer earns about 6 Pounds a month, and as everything must be imported, life can be expensive. Later in a bar, I met a local aspiring politician, who could not wait for the promised independence in three years, assuring me that the economy would be based on tourists, and everyone would be well off. The tourist part is certainly true, but wealth distribution is another matter. I suggested they might be better off with the British paying for everything. There are 92 islands, half of which are inhabited, a sailing man's paradise, sea clear and blue, beaches everywhere, weather near perfect. Personally, I felt sorry that the coming airport would bring the hordes of tourists and destroy their paradise. They must make a living however, and it is not for me to pontificate on their lives. Time, however, proved that tourism is indeed the main driver of prosperity; in 2016 the GDP was the highest in Africa. The rest of my day in Victoria spent wandering into bars, chatting with locals, resisting offers of girls and drinking whiskey doubles for 1/6.

Life on board settled into a pleasant routine, with mostly calm seas, hardly anyone was seasick, movies on deck, sun baking, reading. Finished 'Crime and Punishment', 'Arabian Sands', 'The White Peacock'. My air mattress now completely riddled with holes. The Germans got caught drinking in the 2nd Class bar and were thrown out. Stood under a trickle of boiling water trying to get clean, this being the 3rd Class shower. Sleeping on deck when no rain was falling, or decks being washed.

INDIA, MAINLY BY TRAIN

Finally, after 6 days, Bombay. Quickly got off after going through Immigration. Was pleased to see the Swiss getting a hard time about their Land Rover, whom Customs rightly decided they were going to sell in India. Walking through the streets, thought there must have been bloody riots, judging by all the blood on the roads, before realizing it was only betel juice being spat out. Changed money at 28 Rupees to Pound, although the official rate was 21, due to a recent devaluation. 29 was the best I could get anywhere. We were now a group of 10, went to the Salvation Army Hostel, no room in the Inn; Rex Hotel for 4 rupees each. I did not like being in such a large group, so Tata and I went off ahead. Back at the hotel, spread bed bug powder on the mattress, killed some cockroaches, and waited for the rest to come back from the whores' district, where they were 'entertained' for 11 Rupees. Rain continued to pour down, tried to find someone in the shoe district to repair my boot, which had split, but they all said it was too complicated; an African in Nairobi had done the job in 10 minutes. Went to the movies, to see *The Sound of Music*. Bought the cheapest tickets, but the usher was horrified; "But Sahib, this is where poor people sit". "I am poor too". I was taken to the best seat in the house, at 3rd class price. Went to the Tourist Office to get information on South India, to the Station to get a ticket to Poona next day.

The few days in Bombay were spent in pouring rain most of the time, so was glad to get away. Got a spot on the train, outside the WC, next to a window. Outside the City, the country was very attractive, with dozens of small waterfalls rushing from hilltops, into rivers and lush rice paddies, while I spent most of the 100-mile trip with my head outside the window. In Poona, now Pune, I had the address of a Hostel in the University, so after a couple of bus trips there, very cheeky student said the hostel was full. While debating my next move, a young boy on a bicycle asked my name, and immediately invited me to come and stay at his home. After a visit to a gym, where he had some boxing lessons, he and I and the boxing instructor went to the boy's home, where I was fascinated to see how his mother would react to her son bringing a stray Australian home to stay. His mother was a doctor and made me welcome. After dropping my bag, Avinash took me for a stroll around town, meeting several of his friends. Back at his home, met his father, who works in the Meteorological Department. He told me they were Middle Class, earning about 5000 Rupees per year. Friend of Avinash, John, a Commerce student from Kenya, came around, wanting me to stay at his place; arranged to do it in a couple of days. Rain still pouring down, but Avinash and I hired bikes next day and rode around town, checked the train to Hyderabad, leaves at 5pm, arrives at 7am. I figured if I got 1 square metre of space I would be lucky. Rode to the College of Agriculture, checking out cattle. Went walking with John, talking about India, Africa, students. He told me he hated Indians, giving good reasons. Avinash's family were exceptions, and he said other Indians could not understand why he associated with them, as they were a different class than most of the other students, who asked me about Australia, and could not understand that there was no class system in Australia. I did not mention that our class system was just subtler.

The hospitality of Avinash and his family, John and his friends continued. Avinash and his father, Mr Lamay took me around the City, to the 300-year-old fort, which had been home to a Prince of the State, and a dam which in 1961 had collapsed and flooded the city and was now overflowing. Met a friend, Mr Apte, an accountant where we had a special dinner, this being a Hindu feast day, preceded by beers and followed by Pan and talk about cricket. Next day Mr Lamay took me to his office, met everyone, got some addresses in Mysore and Bangalore, stopping on the way home to inspect some ancient cave temples, only half completed. Mr Apte arrived to take me to the National Defence Academy, about 13 miles outside the city, where he was friends with the Commanding Officer, and was selling some cricket gear. A splendid dinner in luxurious surroundings was had, disturbed at one stage by a soldier coming in and whispering to the Officer, who then explained that a training plane had crashed, and "The pilot was our best leg spin bowler". The Academy has about 5000 students from all branches of the military, all catered for in very spacious, modern and quite luxurious facilities. We were given the 'Grand Tour', more tea and biscuits and conversations about cricket before back to John's place for dinner, this time with two daughters of the building's owner; promised to see them next day; slept in John's bed while he slept on the floor. One of the daughters next day introduced me to her father, an accountant, who after a tour of a factory, the College of Commerce, put his Mercedes and driver at my disposal for the afternoon. Spent time with Avinash and his parents, before taking off for the station where I bought my ticket to Hyderabad, 400 miles for Rps.8.20. Avinash met a friend, a doctor, also on the same train, who got two seats for us in 3rd Class, no mean feat. Between Avinash and his parents, John, Mr Apte, the CO of the Defence Academy, and all the other people I met, I felt like I was the King of Poona. Avinash arranged for photos I had taken to be delivered to a holy man he knew in Rameswaram, where I could collect them.

Settled in with the doctor, and a few Air Force guys for the overnight trip. The doctor and I had long discussions, about Travel, India and Somerset Maughan. He gave me a copy of 'Of Human Bondage', which I swapped for 'The White Peacock'. He recommended 'The Razors Edge', which I found in Bangalore. He wanted me to write some articles for a magazine his sister edits. I refused an offer of a bunk, and consequently spent the whole night sitting up with no sleep, a non-talent I now use on long flights. Early morning arrival in Hyderabad; rickshaw driver found me a hotel for Rps4, private toilet and bath, more luxury for A20c. After recovering with a nap, wandered the streets, which are wide and handsome, full of bicycles, cows, and people either selling or begging. Stopped for a meal, which is served on a banana leaf. My leaf featured a large dollop of bird shit; I pointed this out to the waiter, who without any change of expression took it away, and, who I am sure, merely turned it over before returning, thinking to himself, 'Bloody fussy Australians'.

A day exploring the City, beautiful park, museums, temples, State Legislature before embarking on a battle to change my concession ticket to go direct to Bangalore. At the station I was told to go to the twin city of Secunderabad, but once there, to go back to Hyderabad. Two bus trips repeating this farce before I had a mild temper tantrum, at Secunderabad they told me to go two furlongs straight down the road to Division office. Sure enough, the road split 100 yards down, but eventually found it. Got the form filled out, but then needed it signed. The old Chief doubted my Student Card, the one I had bought for a dollar in Paris and filled out on an American Express typewriter, and my permission to stay in India. It became a battle of wills, and I am a champion at out-fumbling opposition, so after 30 minutes he gave in and signed it. I thought at the time, 'No wonder India is in a mess with people like him running it'. It is said that at Partition, India got the Public Servants, and Pakistan got the Military; not sure who got the best deal.

Spent the rest of the day and evening getting lost and found again wandering the streets of Hyderabad, temples and bazaars in a very attractive city, destined in later years to be the Call Centre Capital of the Western World. A very unmusical group decided to display their non-talents at 1am, making sleep impossible. Next day booked a seat on the evening train to Bangalore Rps.8.75 for the 21-hour journey, before spending another day enjoying the sights, sounds and people of Hyderabad, now 25% Moslem, the rest Hindu, as I was informed by a shopkeeper who bought me an orange drink, which caused me to have a strange feeling when I smoked. Must have been drugged.

Met two ex-Naval officers at the station who told me they were having trouble getting their pensions, one 19 months overdue; one of them asked me to send some vegetable seeds when I returned home, which I promised to do; he had been taught farming by some Italian POWs he had overseen in the War. The train was not very crowded, and I was in a 3rd Class sleeper, which is generally comfortable and clean; a Moslem man told me to sleep in his padded bunk, which was very comfortable. Woke at 7.30, breakfast omelette, toast, jam and coffee brought to the train. I have been in so called 2nd Class trains in Australia not up to that standard.

On the station there are many beggars, with all sorts of deformities, which station signs instructed should not be encouraged, which I did not. The hosts of beggars everywhere would often seem to be 'hunting in packs', which meant that any pittance I was occasionally inclined to give would mean continual badgering until escape. This station however, featured India's other beggars; Monkeys. One of them created a stir by going into a carriage, running from one end to the other, accompanied by screams of female occupants, before escaping through the carriage door and squatting on the roof above, with an aggrieved expression, while the men on the platform brandished umbrellas at him. I was fascinated by the resemblance of his facial expressions and glances to that of an old man deep in thought. The umbrellas, however continued to threaten him, and one got too close. The monkey took a swipe and grabbed the umbrella, retreated to the carriage roof, before wandering off with his prize. What a monkey would do with an umbrella? I have visions of him promenading with his mates, swinging the umbrella with the air of a conquering hero. The train continued, and later in the afternoon I awoke from a nap, in Bangalore. I gave the Moslem man my copy of 'Surprised by Joy', by C S Lewis. He was very religious but interested in the book. An hour's walk through the streets finally got an hotel, Rps.7, with bath, but later found the bed full of bugs, so I tossed the mattress on the floor and slept on the boards.

Bangalore streets as lively as any; two magicians had a boy wrapped in blankets lying on the ground, and every now and again he would rise to more than head height. I could not see any support to enable this to occur, so put it down, or up, to levitation. Snake charmers had 3 cobras and a python, and occasionally woke up a mongoose, who would open one eye and go back to sleep. Decided to do a day tour to Mysore for the incredibly huge sum, for me, of Rps.12. Caught a bus to Lal Bagh, the city Garden; walked back to the hotel, and as is common for me, was lost and did not know where I was until I got there. On the way stopped to chat with an Indian Catholic, who advised me not to eat Indian food; too late, and also advice I would never accept. Next day, stroll down Mahatma Gandhi Avenue, listening to some girls singing. Later that night, outside my hotel, some buskers, of the Indian variety gathered at a chai stall across the road for some late-night singing and playing. When they were joined by a young Tabla player, I sat on my balcony entranced by the truly wonderful playing until 1.30.

Next morning a car arrived to take me to the Mysore tour. A fast bus trip, to the once Capitol of Mysore, then the Tippu's palace. He who had ruled Mysore until defeated by the British in 1857. An Indian explained some of the art to me. An American girl on another bus struck up conversation, which we continued whenever our busses met. I was the only non-Indian on our bus, so the beggars made a bee- line for me at every opportunity, but I resisted. Back to Mysore, the Sultan's Palace, the zoo and the Nandi Bull, a large sacred bull carved from very black stone, which must have come somewhere a long way away, as there is nothing like it nearby. A lightning tour of the Museum, then the highlight; a 14 mile drive out of town to the Bandavan, a large dam holding back 3 rivers with a very long wall, below which are gardens. I walked around them with the American girl, then sandwiches before back to the gardens, by now flood-lit. The theme is water; runs, falls and spouts everywhere. Back to Mysore but could not find the American girl's bus. Altogether a busy day, one of which I would not have been able to replicate alone, but I still I do not like group tours and generally avoid them, preferring to find my own way, getting lost or not.

At Madras, now Chennai, a student took me to an hotel, Rps.5 with shower and clean bed. Got collared by a guy, Sami, who took me to buy Whiskey using my Permit, also some Ceylon Rupees at a good rate, if the money is real. Also bought a 45-rpm record of Indian music. Had a drink with some Italian seamen. Decided to leave Madras, as Rupees were getting short. Got a sleeper ticket to Tirrichanapuri, where I arrived next morning and got a ticket to Rameswaram.

In Tirrichanapuri, the weather was very hot, but I spent the morning walking around the Fort, originally built 2000 years ago, but now modernised. The heat made cold drinks a necessity, my most used Hindi phrase 'Thunda Pani', Cold Water; but the variety

---

of temples, old streets, snake charmers, St. Josephs College, the largest Catholic school in South India, the sacred lake in the City centre. Watched women washing themselves, clothes. One kid relieved himself in the lake, but judging from the uproar, this was not acceptable. Green slime notwithstanding, an old man brushed his teeth in it. I sat for a couple of hours observing daily life, conversing with the keepers of the pool in Tamil, before heading to the station, where the train was two hours late. I got a space on the floor for the long slow trip to Rameswaram. When we finally arrived, I had to rush down to the Customs shed, staggered in, presented my Passport and Health Certificate; my Cholera was out of date. No Ceylon ferry for me today. This was Thursday, had to wait till Monday. Someone took me to a doctor who gave me the shot for Rps.3, then to the Pilgrims Home where I got a room.

After an afternoon sleep, went for walk around the town and the famous, huge Rameswaram Temple, with corridors 200 yards long. A baby elephant in the wall will relieve you of money with his trunk. Later found the priest from whom I was supposed to collect my photo from Avinash. He was unfriendly and did not have the photo. In the Pilgrim House, a morning man, Antonio, looked after my breakfast, coffee, and wanted all my clothes. I gave him my torn raincoat. Down to the beach to meet the ferry, met an Englishman who, after trying to get to Australia, was now heading for England with 25 Pounds. He had been around the World and was one of the few people who had driven through Burma from India. I invited him to sleep in my room, rather than the waiting room, where I was kept awake most of the night by dogs barking, donkeys braying, people shouting and him snoring. After two days he finally got a train out. Antonio and I had an arrangement where he would provide meals and I would exchange money with him. A German and a Frenchman arrived and also slept in my room. Finally, Monday morning survived the grilling by the half dozen officials and got aboard for the short trip to Ceylon. Changed black market money with the Station Master. The train was very late, but 3rd Class accommodation 200% on Indian; leather seats, card tables, carriages a gift from China. Arrived in Anuradhapura at 4am, slept in 1st Class waiting room on the floor.

CEYLON, OR, IF YOU LIKE, SRI LANKA

Breakfast, bacon and eggs, stroll to town, the Sacred Area, once the capitol of Ceylon. The largest Stupa, a solid white hemisphere topped by a tower rising to about 76 feet. A banyan tree said to be the oldest historical tree in the World; Buddha is said to have received Divine Revelations beneath it. Watched the women washing clothes in the river, watched monkeys, which had been driven into the town because of drought. A soldier gave us two coconuts, had with a dinner of roast beef, a treat after India. Next morning had to rush for the train and did not have time to buy tickets for Colombo because of the queue. Impressed by the countryside we passed through, lush and fertile, with happy looking people. The ticket collectors wanted us to pay from the ferry to Colombo; we refused, saying we would only pay from where we had got on in Anuradhapura. We decided to go to the Station Master in Colombo, who agreed that we need only pay the correct fare. He suggested we should go to the Youth Hostel, rather than the YMCA, as it was cheaper, and gave us directions. Booked in and went to the Nector Café, as it was reputed to be a meeting place for travellers such as us. Cheap, good food and nice girls.

Next, to the Mission to Seamen, table tennis, magazines and drinks. Back at the Hostel, large rats everywhere. I lay in bed watching them wandering around the window frame before I fell asleep; awoke to see one sitting on my upper arm, his body from shoulder to elbow. We exchanged looks; I said, "Piss Off", he obliged, and sleep was resumed. Next morning met another resident, John Smithies from New Zealand, awaiting an air ticket to arrive for him from Australia. He took us out to Brooke Bond tea packing plant, a very impressive tour, given by the factory manager, of all the tea blenders, packing machinery, printing works, etc. A lot of people working on piecemeal rates, usually making Rps.8-10 per day. Tea earns 60% of Ceylon's Exports, and Brooke Bond handles 2/3 of exports, also owning Australia's Bushels Tea. Back to the YMCA to book in next night; the Youth Hostel too restrictive on late nights. Back at the Seamen's Mission, had to sign the visitors' book; the only ship I could think of was the 'Carpentaria', which was in Trincomalee. The Pastor asked us to vacate the snooker table after a while, as genuine seamen wanted a game. He knew we were imposter seamen but was quite friendly.

Booked into the Y, then down to the Port looking for ships going to Australia. One, the 'Strat Clarence' was first, but as they had an Asian crew were not allowed to take passengers. Agent said they could only take First Class, 185 Pounds to Australia. Tried a few ships, but for various reasons none were possible. Pierre left to go back to India. Peter arrived. A letter arrived saying money had arrived for me the day I left Dar as Salaam. The Germans wrote to say my money would be sent after another year; the English Tax would be paid soon.

A visit to the Museum, to the Metropole Hotel drinking toddy, the sap from the top of coconut trees, fermented, in a filthy bar. It has a strange taste which grows tolerable after a couple of glasses, but very potent. John came next morning to say his ticket had arrived; he was leaving at midday and took my African wood carvings, record and films to be processed in Australia, which I would pick up in Melbourne. He gave me malaria pills; also, his surplus money, Rps.10 each. We went looking for more ships; Udo had heard one could fly from Portuguese Timor to Darwin for 15 pounds. Went to Cooks, who told us this was possible. I decided to go to Calcutta, fly to Bangkok, then get to Darwin, rather than spend money on direct travel. I reckoned the money is much better spent on an interesting trip than on 7 days on sea to Fremantle. Went to the movies to see 'The Dambusters'. The Germans cheered whenever an RAF plane was shot down.

Went down to the Port to meet the 'Fairstar', in from Australia, on the chance that my Aunt Sylvia may be on board, on her way to England, but she wasn't. I felt that the rest of the passengers made me cringe. Mostly Australians, whom I felt were terrible, mainly the girls. I remarked to John, "If this is how things are in Australia now, I am going back to England". The fact that these Australians were heading for England did not ameliorate my disgust with their behaviour, or my recollections on my similar journey some nearly 5 years earlier, such a Goody-Goody am I.

Having got that out of my system, we adjourned to Mount Lavinia for a swim in the ocean near the hotel, which I had last seen, or swum in, on the voyage across; swimming and relaxing with the pineapples and bananas the beach ladies sold. Back to the Metropole for Arak, which tasted nothing like Arak; the waiters tried to charge us double but were not successful. Closed out the day by finishing 'Arabian Sands', by Wilfred Thesiger. Next day Poya Day, the Buddhist Sunday, back to Mount Lavinia. Met a New Zealander who had travelled through Indonesia, and lost all his money, 200 Pounds. Had paid Rps.50 for his horoscope on his life to come, which he found cheered him up, as future predictions were positive. Some Ceylonese bought us some 'Hoppa', very tasty honey. I tell people I am from Austria, sometimes Russia, Sweden. They say we are nicer than English people.

Had to wait two days to get visas from the Indonesian Embassy, as the man was away sick. Enquired at the French Embassy about visas for Cambodia and Laos but was told we did not need any. I forged my Bank Declaration form to indicate that I had more money than was the actuality. Collected Indonesian Visas, enquired about money changing and got some wildly different quotes, also the problems of getting money back on departure without a receipt, which the black market could arrange, for a price. English John and I invited a young French girl to join us on a trip to the Port. A German Navy ship was in, and we were invited aboard for a tour; extremely clean and efficient, as one would expect of Germans. Next, a dirty Norwegian freighter, where the First Officer, who was very drunk, invited us aboard. Gave me a packet of cigarettes, and a can of Norwegian beer, as he staggered around, knocking things over. While we were aboard, the ship moved from a dockside berth to the middle of the harbour, which created problems, especially for the French girl, who had a train to catch. We got her and John on the Pilot boat, leaving me in the tender care of the drunk, who had quickly lost interest after she left. He said he had been Paid Off, and the reason would seem obvious. I got ashore on the barge bringing the labourers aboard; they wanted money, but I said I had just arrived and had no Ceylonese money; they could collect from the 1st Officer next day. Some chance.

Next day decided to buy my ticket from Timor to Darwin, 14 Pounds in black market money. Some 60 years later I enquired of the plane fare from Darwin to Dili, $700. Had to get Portuguese visa, 30/- officially, $1.45 black market. Udo left for Kandy, I took my air mattress to the Seamen's Mission, where I hung it over a bus stop across the road, and watched a succession of people look, and reject. It was gone next morning, probably to be cut up and used to repair shoes. Gunther and I checked out of the Y, went to the Portuguese Embassy where they told me I would have to have a definite date for flying to Darwin before leaving Djakarta, an unlikely event. Got a bus to Koramangala, 60 miles out of the City, passing through very pretty country inhabited by very pretty girls, some the famous coconut sellers, who sell not only coconuts. After lunch, flagged down a car which gave me a lift for about 10 miles; I think he was a taxi, but when I got out I cheerfully shook his hand and he looked reasonably happy. I then took a bus to Sigiriya, where I headed for the Rest House. Left my pack at the Buddhist Temple and went for a walk, but too late in the day to climb the huge rock fortress which towered overhead.

Bright and early next day, set off to climb the mountain, 1250 steps I was told. Built in the 5th Century by a king who had murdered his father – who said Shakespeare had the monopoly on medieval family problems? 18 years later his brother dared him to come down from the mountain, and defeated him in battle, whereby the King committed suicide. He could have safely stayed on top of the hill, but the story says he did not have enough water. Fortunately for posterity, the result is Sigiriya basically intact. Back at the Rest House listened to an American telling the Rest House manager how he would like to see big hotels, and a big propaganda campaign to attract American tourists. Thousands of tourists do come, very few actually complete the climb, and no huge hotel, for which we can be grateful. I felt I could kill people like him; the very things, and people he finds attractive would be wiped out by his compatriots. I left him to run the World, thinking that when he died he should be buried in Disneyland, while I left to sleep in the Temple. Next day, set out for the Rock again; started out in the wrong direction, but eventually got on the right track, and climbed up to the famous fresco paintings of 21 princesses and their slaves. About half are very well preserved, all the bare-breasted girls very beautiful. Steps from the Lion's Paws carved in stone by the ancients, but an iron staircase for the moderns. I spent an hour wandering around the ruins of the fort on top, admiring the view and the remains of the ancient palace.

I left Sigiriya next morning, after another night in the Temple; got a lift with a Frenchman who invited me to come to Kandy. He was 71 years old, and still liked girls, especially Asian girls. He had been a 5000- metre runner, and travelled all over the World, studied Zen Buddhism and runs an engineering business in France. After a pleasant drive through the tea, coffee, coco plantations, stopped to watch some elephants bathing, before arriving in Kandy, the Queens Hotel, where he bought me a beer. Left my pack at the Police Station and went walking. My timing was perfect; this was the August Full Moon, thousands of people here for the Perahera, the Exposition of the Buddha Tooth. I found a place to stand on the street, and shortly Udo and another German came along. The relic is kept in the Temple of the Tooth, and at 9pm the procession began; 80 elephants regaled in robes and lights, accompanied by hundreds of drummers, dancers, singers, chiefs and other VIPs. Flaming torches lit the whole show. The city is a blaze of lights in the streets, temples, on the island in Lake Kandy. The Temple cannon fires the signal to begin and the procession winds its way through the streets, taking about an hour to pass. After the excitement, went to an unexciting carnival, collected my pack and went to the Y with the Germans.

Next day, wandering through the town, especially the Botanical gardens, famous the World over especially for the water flowers. Toured the Temple of the Tooth, home of the most famous of the many tooth relics. The next few days in Kandy, for the Perahera, featuring 82 elephants in full regalia, Karl got dressed up to go to a dance at the Queens Hotel, but when we got there no Ceylonese girl would dance with him; we had the same experience at the Coconut Grove, can't imagine why. A couple of English queers came over to talk and seemed to think we would be better off in the Army, rather than travelling, a very strange outlook on life.

Tens of thousands of people lined the streets for the last night. Myself and a couple of the Germans began pricing items for import to India, such as Milo and Ovaltine, and I bought some Marmite and Ovaltine very cheaply. Everyone started worrying about our Currency Declaration Forms, when the Customs would see no money changed on the form. Buster thought he would play dumb, not hard for him, and say he had changed everything on the black market. At a meal in the East China restaurant, where the waiters were reluctant to serve us because they never got a tip. Buster and Karl carried on a NZ /German slanging match, also abusing locals which I found very objectionable, and said so. Altogether the few days in Kandy were very enjoyable and interesting, although we were probably too much of a pack, as were the rest of the tourists. Time to move on. Last day of festivities, got a spot at the front of the procession and had a brush with one of the Police chiefs, a nasty, surly bastard; my salute as he drove off pleased him not at all.

Bought tickets for Rameswaram; by now I had spent all of my Ceylon money, had to borrow some from Buster. The Monsoon rain was now pouring down, as we were treated to a spectacular ride through the mountain and valleys. Night-time, we had to change trains; sleep was impossible, so I spent the night reading 'Long Live the Victory of the Peoples' War', by Lin Biao, thought to be the successor to Mao, but later to be involved in a plot, supposedly with Mao's wife, to remove Mao. He died soon after in a mysterious plane crash. In Kandy, and various places in Ceylon, the Communist movement was very strong, especially among the young. While I found the whole idea of a world-wide revolution repellent, I engaged in discussion with some firebrand locals whenever possible.

In Anuradhapura, met Bob, an Australian who discovered the gem smuggling business; one brother had a jewellery shop in Colombo, and another brother one in Calcutta. Smuggling Blue & Star Sapphires between them was earning him $75 every two weeks; I, on the other hand, was about to enter the Ovaltine trade to India. We arrived at Talamainapier and went through Customs without a single question about Declaration Forms, which we found to be disappointing, having built up a drama in our minds. A United Nations group, including 4 women from the US Embassy in Delhi were now on board. I lay on the deck to get some sleep, to be awoken by an Australian complaining about how boring travel in Arab countries was. I was too tired to put him straight.

MOTHER INDIA AGAIN

When we arrived in Rameswaram, Antonio my meal man, informed me that because of a cyclone there had been no trains for two days, and offered to buy my Ovaltine for Rps.3. One of the money changing thieves offered 9, but later changed his mind. In the Waiting Room, had a shower, and was told there was no train to Madras that day, but we could take a train launch to the station on the other side, which a few of us did. The sea was very choppy and soon everyone aboard was drenched. We took 45 minutes to cross, everything soaked, just in time to see the train pull out. I walked ashore shin deep, descended on the Waiting Room, which soon resembled a football changing shed. Showered and washed the salt out of our clothes, while waiting for the next reputed train to Madurai, due at 3.30am. A few years earlier, a train had been washed off the bridge by a tidal wave, so now trains only go across when the wind speed is less than 25mph. Some fumbling while reputedly trying to find my non-existent ticket outlasted the ticket collectors efforts; similar tactics at Madurai Station, proclaiming we were headed for Madras. Such antics may now seem arrogant, but at the time the hassles with Indian Rail made it perfectly normal.

After depositing our gear in the Foreign Tourists Waiting Room, headed for the City, mainly to the Meenakshi Amman Temple, one of the most impressive I had seen, 4 large towers covered with 3000 exotic Hindu carvings and paintings, mainly devoted to Lords Krishna and Shiva. The Temple area is about 500 yards Square and contains 8 Temples, including the Temple of 1000 pillars, with many exhibits explaining styles, meanings and periods. I could have spent many hours there, but only had the one day, and at nightfall the Temple was closed. On more mundane matters, sold my Ovaltine for Rps.9, collected washing which

Roger had been watching, and bought a ticket to Madras on a very packed train at 3.30am.

Arrived in Madras, now Chennai, 8am. Booked in at the Y, went looking for a money changer. First offer 15 to Pound, walked out; next 22, walked out; last 29 accepted. I was so tired he screwed me for Rps.20. When I later realized, could do nothing about it and did not tell the others for fear of looking a fool; which I was. An English guy also wanted to change money, an Indian gave us a lift to the Fort area, where a pack of kids, ranging in age from 4 to 8 offered everything from money changing to girls. They took us to a money man, and after the transaction I gave them some money and told them to "Fuck off". The youngest boy asked his sister, in Tamil, what is "Fuck"? to which she gave the direct explanation with two fingers and a thumb. He nodded knowingly. Sex education Indian style. Back at the Y, Roger went to deliver a suitcase he had brought up from Colombo. Retired for a much-needed long sleep.

A long train trip to Calcutta was next. Udo and I booked berths and spent the day passing through pleasant country before arriving at Howrah Station at 4.30am. Left gear at the Cloak Room, after a shower and rest in the First Class Waiting room. Walked over the Howrah Bridge, through the dirty dock area to the main part of the City. Found the address of my contact from Alex Murray in Honda. When I went there, was told he had passed away a few weeks earlier. I resolved to never impose myself on third party introductions again. Went with Roger to the jewellers where he delivered his Ceylon stones, and picked up Indian ones for the return; a very 'Trust me' transaction. The owner was very pleasant, and also able to exchange money at the right rate.

Went to Burma Airlines and booked the flight to Bangkok for the 16th September, today being the 6th. Met Tata, the Japanese boy from Mombasa; he was also booked on that flight, as were Ulli and Gunther. It seemed everyone was heading for Bangkok. Went to the Concession Office to get a ticket to Delhi, told 'today is a religious holiday'; I jokingly said that there are too many holidays in India; how many holidays do you have in Australia? I was asked. I think 14. We in India have only 10. I think if I had said 5, they would have said 4. Our jeweller friend recommended that we should go to the burning Ghats by the river.

Calcutta had a population of 8 million, with 22 million living on the street. Water is provided by many faucets, without which street life would be even more dire. People, rats, dogs, cats and crows pick through the rubbish which lies in the gutters. The streets are also the toilets, people squatting everywhere. The contrast with the parks and imposing buildings such as the Victoria Memorial could not be more extreme. Outside one building, teachers were on strike, a different squat outside the Education Department. We took a tram to the Ghats by the Holy Ganges River. The Ghats are lined up along the river bank. When a Hindu dies, the body must be burned before the following sunset, the body dressed in white and placed on a wooden bed, with the feet painted red. Flowers are strewn over the bier, which is carried in procession through the streets to the Ghats, where there are shallow pits. Different castes use different Ghats. Wood is piled around the body, leaving the head and feet exposed. Fire is lit and soon blazing merrily. Sometimes the fire does not burn well, and legs, head and intestines have to be poked into the flames by attendants. The sight of bright red feet and head sticking out of a blazing bonfire, and the accompanying sickly-sweet smell of burning flesh is not an everyday occurrence I would relish, but 'Such is Life'. When the body is burned, the ashes are taken by attendants to the River and consigned to its Holy waters. Sometimes parts of the body are not completely burned, and if no relatives are present, attendants throw the charred flesh in anyway. A little further down river people are bathing and swimming. One crazy man kept trying to anoint me with burnt bone; other people were also hostile to us foreigners. We had spent most of the afternoon there, most people had now left, except for one man. He was obviously cremating a very small child, daughter or son. No ceremony, or piles of flowers, just a small bier which he attended himself. I watched that man for about half an hour in his grief. Anyone observing him and believing that life in India is cheap must be otherwise convinced.

Back at our jewellers' shop, collected our money, and talked about India, and in particular the Hindu religion, which our Ceylonese friend could not stomach; he pointed out that it is a religion founded entirely on human teachings, with no divine or supernatural inspiration, and many of its teachings were made to suit the Brahmins, and how childish many of its legends are. On later reflection it seems to me, that this criticism could apply to any religion in existence. Later went to the movies 'Lawrence of Arabia', which had been subjected to the usual annoying Indian cuts. On the way back to the Howrah, Roger and I stopped to listen to some music, and were invited in to help celebrate the birthday of a God. We were given sweets while listening to the exuberant beating of drums, clashing of brass cups, and singing. Back at Howrah Station, the Waiting Room was locked up, but we found a comfortable and deserted, except for a cat, Retiring Room where we slept, leaving the rest of the Station to its main occupants, Rats. They swarm everywhere. To quote the Pied Piper of Hamelin, "They fought the dogs, and killed the cats". To further quote the Indian Bard, "You ain't seen nothing yet". Talking to Indians a little later in Agra, I learned that about one third of India's wheat harvest is eaten by rats.

Back at Union of Burma Airlines, checked Udi's receipt from R N Dutt and Son which was identical to my previously bought one. Back to the now open Concession Office for my ticket to Delhi; Roger could not get a student discount, so I took him to the office and got a return concession in my name and collected his ticket to Rameswaram. Said farewell to all and headed to the station for my train to Benares, now Varanasi. While buying my usual copy of 'The Times of India', the old man seller, with a slight smile, whispered, "One for us, Sahib", noting the headline telling of the assassination of Hendrik Verwoerd, Prime Minister of South Africa.

Sharing my 3rd Class sleeper with an Indian couple, arrived next morning at East Benares, and prepared to disembark at Benares. The train headed out into the countryside, is when I was told that East Benares is actually the Benares station. Resisting the impulse to assassinate my too polite Indians, I left the train at the next station, a deserted platform seemingly in the middle of nowhere. Soon after a young guy arrived to tell me that the next train back to Benares would be in 3 hours, and I should come to his village. This seemed an eminently better idea than sitting around in an empty station. While walking back a half mile to the village, he sent a young boy ahead with exciting instructions. My role in the coming time was then explained to me; two brothers in the village had not spoken to each other for years; one was Communist, the other Congress. A public debate was to be held with me as referee.

Arriving in the village, the whole population, about 200-300 people were assembled in a semi-circle. The brothers made an appearance like a couple of boxers; I was introduced to them, and to a great cheer, to the village. Let the saga begin. Brother One, "Please tell that Communist that all his Party does for India is start strikes which damage the economy". I duly passed on this message which prompted a swift reply; "Tell this capitalist loving fool that without workers' actions, all of India would be slaves to Tata and the corrupt politicians in their pockets". Duly passed on to Brother One, to cheers, I think, from the majority of the villagers. Brother One, "If you want India to live under the heels of Russia and China, vote Communist." Brother Two, "India too, could become the Workers' Paradise that Russia is today". And so on, many questions and cheers for both brothers. After about an hour, I declared it a draw and asked if the brothers would shake hands, and, somewhat surprisingly, they did. We all, brothers, me and the entire village adjourned for Tiffin. Later the return train arrived, and I duly arrived in Benares.

Wandered the streets of Benares, bought a brass 20-year calendar, which some years later I gave, to his bemusement, to my High-Tech cousin Bob. By the river, people tried to get me to the Ghats, but I declined; once is enough, so went instead to see two temples, one very old, the other built in 1964.The old temple was over-run with monkeys, one of which had it in for me. The new temple, beautiful white marble with the 'Gita' written in gold around the walls, a small throne of silver and gold stands on the altar. Had to hurry to get to the station for my train. Another Indian day to remember.

Arrived in Agra 6am, had to change trains for Agra Cantonment, left my pack at the station and walked for a couple of hours looking for the Youth Hostel, which turned out not to be a Youth Hostel. Walked a couple of miles through the city before getting a bus to the Taj Mahal; through the garden, at the Gate the classical view of the Taj. In the sunlight, the white marble shone magnificently, a truly breath-taking sight. Some fifty years later I read that the white marble is badly stained and corroded by pollution, another great tragedy of 'progress'. I left my boots outside and spent a couple of hours wandering around the interior mausoleum, spell-bound by the carved marble lacework of windows. Outside, sat on the cool marble, watching the scene down by the river, spending more hours there before heading for the Red Fort. Stopped for a drink on the way where the owner tried to sell me his whole shop. In the Fort, met three Indians, one of whom was a writer; he told me that the educated people in India were miss-using their education by not applying what they have learned to Indian institutions correctly, something that could apply to many other situations in the world. He gave me a copy of 'Bhagavad Gita', and invited me to go to Delhi with them, but they were leaving today, so had to decline. Met Mike, a German, we went around the Fort again and decided next day, to go the abandoned city of Fatehpur Sikri, about 20 miles from Agra.

The City is surrounded by 11 kms of red sandstone walls, entrance through the magnificent Buland Darwaza gate leading to the Tomb of Salim Chisti, a Holy man who had lived in the nearby village. The Moghul ruler Akbar's wife had failed to deliver him a son; the Holy Man transplanted the spirit of his own son to Akbar's barren wife, who then bore him a son. To show his gratitude Akbar built a magnificent city on the site of the village. Included among the Mosques and fabulous buildings is the Pachisi Court, a large chess board on which Akbar played chess, using humans as chess pieces. There is a story that the Sultan of Persia visited and challenged Akbar, the stakes, one grain of rice. Akbar won and accepted the challenge, the stakes doubling after each loss; the result, the Sultan lost the entire rice crop of Persia. What we would now call compound interest.

In a central courtyard is the Tomb of Salim Chisti, in marble with every window different. The central room has walls inlaid with mother of pearl. One of the lattice windows is covered with pieces of wool, left by women who want children. We resisted efforts to take guides, but one young boy was very attentive and full of information; we gave him Rps.50. Further wanderings to an observatory, a princess's pavilion, a bathing pool and a tower offering great views of the Palace and countryside. After 14 years the city was abandoned, due to lack of water, and Akbar left for Agra; an outcome I felt that had a very Indian feel of, "It is God's Will". We stayed till sunset, entranced by and immersed in the physicality and spiritualty of this fabulous place. Many years later I read 'The Enchantress of Florence' by Salman Rushdie, largely invoking myths and legends about Akbar and Sikri, provoking renewed interest in this fascinating City.

Back to Agra by bus, collected bags and took a rickshaw to Cantonment Station. Our rickshaw wallah had to stop halfway with exhaustion and get another to complete the journey. At Cantonment, had a meal and Mike left for Benares. He exchanged his steel bracelet with a Sikh; they both preferred each other's bracelets. Went into the 1st Class Waiting room waiting for the 2.30am train. All the benches around the central table were occupied by sleeping Indians, so I settled down to read and write. A large rat appeared at the doorway, surveyed the scene and took off, leaping from sleeping shoulder to sleeping shoulder, leaving a rippling tide of awakening Indians in his, or her, wake. Having done a complete circuit of the room, with a last glance at the disturbed bodies, Rat gave a smirk of satisfaction and strolled off into the night. Controlling my laughter, I continued reading.

Delhi in the morning, trying unsuccessfully to get a bed in either a YMCA or Temple, finally got a spot in the Sikh Temple, along with a large tribe of travelers, including Chas, whom I knew in Mombasa. He seemed to have gone to pieces; no shoes, raving on incoherently about nothing. Took him for a coffee in an expensive shop in Connaught Place, met Bernard and Pierre, stranded in Delhi until the revolution in Syria was over, as they were flying back to Paris on Syrian Airlines. Back at the Temple, Chas did not appear. Went to the Australian Embassy, met an Australian oil man, who had spent 3 years in Afghanistan, 8 in India. He gave me a copy of the *Gospel*. Added it to the *Gita*. Back to Connaught Place to book a sleeper to Calcutta, a pleasant overnight trip with a young Indian couple.

Last few days in Calcutta, collected my Burma Visa and airline ticket to Bangkok, via Rangoon, using my forged money changing receipt, which meant the fare was less than half price. Back in the Salvos Hostel, met an American, just out of High School who was going to make his fortune by playing markets around the World; he and an Indian friend introduced me to Indian Rummy, and over the next couple of nights relieved me of a couple of Pounds, typical of my gambling prowess. Next day, Mike was interested in the stone carrying business, so I took him to the man. Met Tom Tracy, an American, who had friends in Burma he was trying to get out; he gave me some letters to post in Rangoon, as any mail coming from outside Burma would be censored. He also gave me his Burmese and Thai, money, about $20 worth, for $5. Next morning at Union of Burma Airlines, I was the only European on board the plane, a Viscount. On the flight read *'The Last Days of the British Raj'*; not deliberate timing. I have later been to India First Class, with many other wonderful experiences, but Third Class is where, I feel, that India offers the most. I am always telling people that, in India, one cannot wait to get out, but once out, going back is a must.

LEAVING INDIA

In Rangoon, left my pack at the airport and took a bus into town; soldiers everywhere. Got a room at the YMCA, official rate $2, my rate, 35c. Posted Tom's letters. Took a bus up to the Shwedagon Pagoda, the immense complex dominating the City. The gold-plated stupa rises some 344' and is the center of a complex of temples and religious shrines. The Stupa is covered in gold plate, which during WW2, was removed and hidden from the invading Japanese, to be replaced at the end of the War. Spent most of the morning in the Temple complex; heavy rain, this being Monsoon, fell most of the day, at one place causing me to slip and land on my backside, much to the amusement of some locals. In the evening went looking for a reasonably priced meal, which was not easy.

By 8pm, met a couple of Indian Burmese who invited us to eat and drink with them. We went by rickshaw to a club at the harbor. They told us how everyone hated the Government and would like to see it thrown out; the military would make that very difficult however. They had come to Burma from India, one was still in school and I asked what he would do after school. They said they would go into the only business worth the effort, the black market. Everything here is run on the black market. The Peoples Shops, which are supposed to sell basic goods at fair prices, are usually out of stock, and things must be bought on the black, at inflated prices. I was surprised to read in the local paper next day a letter criticizing the stores severely. Most of the news was straight Wire Service, without leaning either way. Next afternoon, rain bucketing down still, got the Airport bus, handed in the Currency Declaration, with nothing to declare. The Customs people just smiled. Met Ellis, an American, who has just come in from East Pakistan, on the same flight to Bangkok. Ellis, a Jewish man of twenty-five from New York, was heading to Sydney where he hoped to work as a film director for the ABC.

BANGKOK TO BALI

In Bangkok Airport, seemingly hosting many USAAF planes, even an Australian Dakota, we went quickly through Customs. Ellis and I caught a bus to the Thai Song Greet Hotel. Took a room with a shower with Ellis, only one bed, tossed for it; I slept on the floor. A popular spot for the hitch-hiking community this was, met several 'companions of the road', including John Meadows from Sydney. John and Ellis were important companions to my near future life. Meadows was installed in the Hotel with his Thai girlfriend, Thom Pit. He later named his cat after her. We discovered a mutual taste for Mekong whiskey, at 50c a bottle. Whiskey and Coke became the staple, and one night nearly brought us undone. A late-night mock wrestle, and suddenly the night patrol, which was an old man with a big sword, was making it plain, that this was not good. Mama, the hotel owner leapt down the stairs, grabbing a meat cleaver on the way, and proceeded to wave it very close to the man's throat. He and the crowd of interested onlookers dispersed, and John and I resumed our Mekong whiskey, without any wrestling.

Bangkok seemed to be obsessed with air-conditioning; every shop had blasts of icy air assaulting passing pedestrians. I quickly succumbed, catching a bad cold after only a couple of days. All interest in Chiang Mai, Vientiane, Angkor Watt and other exotic Pearls of the Orient took second place, and I spent a few days mainly in the hotel, reading, but after a while went to the hospital for a blood check, before selling a pint for $10. As soon as they finished the extraction, I was quickly hustled out, and blacked out for a few seconds; they then put me on a bed for 20 minutes. I had previously sold blood in Kuwait and Beirut, always for the same price, $10, but Bangkok was certainly the roughest. Stretchers with plenty of blood spatters. There is an unending supply of girls available for 40 Bhat, but I never felt inclined. 70%

of them have some type of STD, of which there are supposed to be 250 in Bangkok. Even school girls of 14 are lined up every day at the hospital for their Penicillin shot. I have the impression that everything in Thailand is commercial, blessed with some of the World's most beautiful women.

The constant stream of Americans on R&R from Viet Nam was also a major factor in Thailand's economy, if culturally not so much so. I was walking down a back street one night behind a group of Thai girls, who were obviously referring to me in not flattering terms, 'American' being the disdainful expletive. I assured them I was not American, but Australian, which changed their tone. They explained to me, with explicit gestures, that an American's main attribute was his "hip pocket". While I was there, the English language paper 'The Bangkok Post', headlined a quote, "Thailand, the Land of the Cheshire Cats," which upset the Thais, but essentially it is true; people are always smiling, for no apparent reason.

My cold kept me mostly confined to barracks. Ian, an Aussie, got a job teaching English to the daughters of a local business man; Ian was not too good at English himself, so I gave him a few lesson outlines he could start with, and maybe build on. Another American got himself into hot water for thumping a Thai, who had picked his pocket. The pocket picking did not matter so much as the Thai's loss of face. The Police made the victim pay $50. John had a constant stream of girls, one of whom gave me a welcome massage. He said he would like to get to Australia via Indonesia, as others were, but most were having a lot of trouble with visas. Ellis went to Cambodia; a Swiss fellow had his monkey Passport stolen.

Ellis came back, and we decided to get a boat to Songkhla, near the Malay Border. I changed my remaining Travelers Cheques, 40 Pounds, for cash Dollars. We had to get a boat out to the ship, moored in the river; I climbed down off the wharf, pack and all onto the dingy; the dingy started to move away, with me and my 40lb pack hanging on by a toe nail. A swift drop to the bottom of the river seemed the only outcome, but I managed to haul myself back. Having got the boat in midstream, we then discovered that it had engine trouble, and would not be sailing for two days, so, back to the Thai Song Greet, bought tickets on the Express for $12, spent the trip drinking whiskey with Thai soldiers and two Indians.

Morning arrival at the Malaysian Border, where Customs were doubtful of my financial status, with good reason, but were happy when I showed them my air ticket from Timor to Darwin. Arrived at Prai in the evening and got the ferry across to Penang. The rickshaw man wanted too much to take us to the YMCA, so we caught busses and got the last two beds, beating two Americans. I offered them my tent, and put it up for them, but one had a fever, so they decided to go to an hotel. Went to the city, in the main street had an expensive meal, and cruised the prosperous streets, mainly Chinese, but also many Australians from the Butterworth Air Base; but mainly the most beautiful girls in the world, who seemed to combine the best of Malaya, Thailand and China. Back at the Y talked to an Australian who had been rolled in Singapore, and a Canadian who was riding his Ducati to India.

After a couple of days in beautiful Penang, Ellis and I took off for KL. Getting lifts together was nearly impossible, so we split up. I got a lift in a truck for about 50 miles, Ellis passed me in a Mini. Lifts to Ipoh, then a tin mining engineer picked me up and said he would take me to KL after he finished work. I waited in a coffee shop till 4 pm when he turned up, and we drove through the never-ending rubber plantations, and tin mines, both large and small. He dropped me in the center of the City, and I was wandering around wondering where the Y was, when a Young Indian invited me to stay in his flat. There were 14 student teachers living there, and I was made welcome. After a meal, they took my shorts and shirt and washed them. The next morning the original boy took me out to the Batu Caves. The main cave is a Hindu Temple, while the roof of the cave has fallen in, creating a large sunlit amphitheater. Spent a couple of hours exploring the cave, which contained several Temples, and was told much was still unexplored; some people had disappeared in the attempt. A five-legged cow wandering around provided a photo opportunity. My friends then took me to see the National Monument, the Parliament building, the Museum, the National Mosque, the main Stadium, all very modern and impressive. After another meal, back to the flat where we had long discussions on Malaya; the three main races here are Malay, Chinese and Indian. Indians are way down on the totem pole, politically and economically. I learned some Malay while they wanted to give me clothes, but I settled for scissors and a dictionary while I told them of my travels, of which they seemed quite envious.

Next day, lifts and a bus took me to Johore Bahru, then a bus across the Causeway to Singapore. The Chinese YMCA was full and spent a couple of hours with a rickshaw driver trying to find a hotel, finally got a room in the New Asia Hotel for $4, near Raffles Place. Back at the hotel, met an American who had his Passport taken by Immigration because he did not have a ticket out; my half-price ticket to Darwin once again proving a good transaction. Went to JAL, bought a ticket to Djakarta for $57, which was nearly all the money I now had in the world. Talked to an American while going down on the JAL lift, who was reading the local newspaper headlining the Djakarta anniversary of the Communist coup of 30th September 1965, in which several Indonesian Generals had been shoved into crocodile holes. Students had attacked the National Monument in Merdeka Square and were beaten back by bayonet wielding soldiers; 65 were injured and one killed. I asked the American what he thought about flying into Djakarta today; his advice, just keep your head down. The flight took off at 6pm and we were soon in Djakarta.

Arriving in Djakarta with only $21 to my name was giving me some concern, but no-one in Immigration asked, only where I was staying. Everyone in front of me said Hotel Indonesia, cheapest room $35. Eyebrows were raise when I said YMCA but got through to the pack of waiting taxi drivers. When I got a cab and said, YMCA, the driver told me that the YMCA was next door to the President's Palace and was taken over by the Army. He took me to a few hotels, but all were full. The Taxi driver, Alphonso, then took me to his home, where I stayed for two days; I am sure there are not many taxi passengers who have been taken home by their driver. Alphonse's home was in a Kampong, and the Kampong chief came to see me and register me, as everyone who stays in a private home must be registered with the chief. We talked for a while about the demonstrations, and the trial of Doctor Subandrio, the main instigator of the attempted Communist Coup, which had just begun. Because of students' action, there had been only one month's work done all year. Next day I went to the President's Palace and walked through the guarding soldiers, exchanging greetings.

After a couple of days with Alphonse and the Kampong chief, I was down to my last $10. Getting the best rate was the game, so at a bar, lined up the prospective dealers, held an auction, sealing the deal with a cold bottle of Bintang beer. Went to the Australian Embassy to borrow $10. Mr. Shannon, the Consul, told me that at the official Embassy rate, I would get 100 Rupia. Come back tomorrow and he would send his "boy". Next day he presented me with 1530, and begged me not to tell anyone, as if the word got around he would have a queue of people every day asking. He gave me his bank details in Canberra, and I made sure that the first thing I did when I returned to Australia was pay him, which I did.

Met Ellis by the National Monument, scene of the big student demonstration earlier. There were troops everywhere, soldiers who were reputed to be great thieves, but considering that they were paid only 200 Rupia a month, they had to do something to support their families. Ellis had a ticket from Djakarta to Sydney, but I persuaded him to cash it in and join me on the trip to Timor, turning a few hour's flight into an odyssey of several weeks; I am sure he was grateful!

Exploring Djakarta; electricity serves the city center, but the outskirts have none, roads and footpaths barely exist; no-one can live on one job alone, most people have two or three, doing none of them effectively. Most public servants appear at 9am, then go off to their other jobs. Back to the Y, where Ellis had got a berth, met a German who had all his money and camera stolen in the Hotel Serakies in Surabaya; the key to his room fitted another five doors, another trap for young players. I, in the meantime, had met a couple of Australians at the Embassy who invited me to their home for dinner. After dark travel in Djakarta is not recommended, but I got a bus out to their home. On the way, standing next to a very tall local who had his hand poised above my jean's front pocket, after my wallet. While looking directly at him I grabbed his hand and squeezed hard; he did not blink and at the next stop left without a backwards glance. Further on I was not so lucky; my shoulder bag with Passport, camera and sundries was caught between pressing bodies and before I realized it, the camera was gone. The crowd assured me that a man who had just got off the bus was the culprit, and I fell for it; got off the bus and had to watch the bus full of laughing thieves wave me off. One up, one down.

Adjourned to the German Club, where we were followed by an Indian, who introduced himself as Sham Muhtani, UN agent, ex Indian Army Captain, businessman, friend of Lauren Bacall, Bing Crosby and LBJ. He kept us amused for a couple of hours before inviting us to his home next day for lunch. Ellis, the German and I went to find the money changer, who bought us all coffee and bananas. Ellis and I head for the Y, were met by Muhtani on the way, who took us to what he said was one of his restaurants, where he bought us beers and cigarettes, later to a Chinese restaurant for a meal. The German, Ellis and I went to the German Club for dinner, met another German who had been 40 years in Indonesia, first as a boxing instructor. Today the Chief of the Indonesian Navy was killed in a helicopter crash, and all flags were at half-mast. Next day met Muhtani and were taken to his home for beer and snacks before dinner, including frogs' legs, which I enjoyed.

Muhtani wanted to make a film of a book called 'William John', and wanted Ellis as Director, having previously learned of Ellis' occupation. He said he had a studio, and had co-produced 'Guide', the most popular Indian film at the time. A friend called in and produced a card showing him to be a movie man; after lunch and a few beers we caught a taxi and went around Djakarta looking for 'character actors' who would play in this movie. After a few 'not at homes', adjourned to a Chinese man's home, who quickly produced beers and prawn biscuits, which we happily consumed while Muhtani raved on. The Chinese man had nothing to do with films, being in insurance, so after Muhtani had invited himself to a party at the man's home, and having consumed all his beer, we took off again, our hero grabbing the last of the prawn biscuits. Back in the city, Muhtani took us to one of his shops, collecting money from the till, to show us he owned it. More beers at his restaurant, then back to the Y before returning to the German Club for a meal. Met a German who had been here a couple of years and had tried to take out a woman that night, but his old car had broken down three times; she was not there when he finally arrived. Back at the Y, I spent an hour reading the October 'Newsweek' before I realized it was the 1962's, this now being 1966. And so, ends a Djakarta day.

Next morning, to the bus station and got a truck to Bandung, enjoyable ride a little spoiled by rain getting in through the back door, which would not close. Passed through Bogor, the President's Summer Palace with hundreds of deer grazing on the lawns, on to Bandung late afternoon; booked early morning ticket for Jogjakarta, managing to get them at the official price, rather than from the scalpers, who buy up tickets for trains, theatre etc. and re-sell at hugely inflated prices; just like in Australia really. Found the Losmen recommended by the German, walked into town and found a shop owned by Muhtani's brother, who told us that half the things he had told us were false, as suspected. He did have photos of him with Nehru and Sukarno however.

Met 2 economics students, one of whom was bargaining for a text book at 100 Rupia but could only afford 50; in a rash moment I paid the difference. He showed us a cheap Indonesian restaurant, but Ellis did not like the food. Back at the Losmen a woman wanted to offer her services, but we declined. Reading by candle-light meant an early night. Next morning got the train to Jogja, 3rd Class, very cheap and comfortable. After checking in to a Losmen, went for a walk and met two girls, Claire from Melbourne and Ellie Seeahaan, an Indonesian broadcaster on Radio Australia, who it seems, is known by everyone in Indonesia. She called us Nomads as we went shopping with them; they were travelling by bus to Surabaya and staying in a hotel in nearby Solo, also on their way to Bali. Saw them off at the Station, then another early night.

Up at 4am to catch the train and get our seats. I got off to have a coffee, keeping an eye on what I thought was our train; fatal mistake. Finished coffee and discovered MY train had gone, with Ellis and my luggage. I didn't have enough money to catch a bus, so went back to the Losmen, reclaimed my bed from the hotel boys, and slept till midday, had a meal and went to the station to catch the Express. In Surabaya, caught a betcha to the Serakies Hotel, where we were going to stay, but it was full. A note from Ellis, they had gone to LMS Hotel with the girls. A note here told me where everyone was. Ellie and I talked until the other two returned from a walk, then had some Vita Weet and Vegemite, papaya and Milo for tea. Ellis not too keen on Vegemite, but then he is American. Stayed the next day, although the hotel was expensive; got washing done, a rare treat. Booked bus seats to a town near the ferry to Bali for next day. Met a doctor friend of Ellis, who told us that we would never get there that way; best get a bus straight from Surabaya to Denpasar, Bali, which we did.

The bus was running late, so we got away at 5.30am. Stopped for a break in a small village, breakfast of pineapple and bananas. Driving down the very attractive coast, through fishing villages; one whitewashed wall adorned with a large "Radio Peking Go to Hell". Sign of the times. Communists are universally unpopular in Indonesia now. Between October '65 and June '66, there were about 300,000 people killed in Java in fighting between Moslems and Communists. Everyone is now anxious to state their hatred of Communists. After an hour's delay fixing the bus's jammed brakes, we were on the ferry to Bali, an old WW11 landing barge. A drive through the classic Balinese terraced rice paddies; they make the growing of rice an artistic experiment in landscape gardening, enhanced by the famous bare-breasted Balinese women working and walking in the villages. Sukarno was trying to get them to cover up, saying they were harming Bali's image; he could not be more wrong.

Arrived in Denpasar 4pm, the girls went to the not yet opened Bali Beach Hotel, Ellis and I to Losmen Pure. We had arranged to meet the girls in the hotel, where I had a hot shower, the first since leaving Africa; could not believe watching my suntan going down the drain. Getting to the Bali Beach Hotel became a daily excursion; the boys who worked there brought mini buses in the town every half-hour, and whatever we would like in fruit or vegetable they would gladly give. The hotel had 290 rooms, and 1200 people working; at the time there were 36 guests, half of whom were Southern Evangelists intent on converting the unimpressed Bali Hindus. There were 12 people working a bar, with no patrons, except us. A Frenchman introduced himself as the Catering Director for Intercontinental Hotels, who own Bali Beach; he told us how difficult it was to train Indonesians to run the place, and how it would never work while they had to rely on Garuda Airlines to bring customers; the International Airport was not yet open. One Garuda plane was 1½ hours late and made a further 2 hours late by the pilot, who refused to take off until he had lunch. If only he could see Bali now!

We could not help noticing the shoddy building work, water leaking through the ceiling, broken tiles, non- fitting wood work etc. The Bali Beach was the only building allowed to be over the height of palm trees in Bali, and it burned down in 1993. After room service steaks and showers, back to our Losmen, where the bed bugs bit furiously until plenty of powder on the mattresses made sleep possible.

Over the next days we spent a lot of time at Garuda trying to get a flight to Kupang, but the military had priority and there were never any seats available; at one stage the Garuda manager said, "come back in two months", so that idea died. Life in Bali, however was anything but dull. The Bar Restaurant became our home away from home. Apart from the beautiful waitress, beefsteak with all the trimmings for 10c was more than enough compensation for being stuck in Bali. Changed our Losmen to Suranadi, bed bug free, checked possibility of a ship to Kupang, no such thing. By now we were regular 'guests' at the Bali Beach, using the pool, cheap drinks; swapped my towel, which had come all the way from Kondinin in WA for a Beach towel; Ellis swapped his Hampstead Baths towel for same. Shopping with the girls, bought some Batik for 150 R. A Legong dance in a nearby village, the gamelan percussion providing exotic music. On the way back a puppet shadow dancing show, altogether a thoroughly enjoyable introduction to Balinese music and dance. Next evening at the Bali Beach, got dressed in our finest for the Big Show, a Tari Kecak dance, story from the Epics about a war fought between the Monkey Gods, Vishnu and Garuda, performed by 150 men, with no music, only singing and chanting the story; a most impressive performance.

Next day the girls left for Djakarta, Ellie to go back to Australia, Claire to do more travelling. Ellis and I to Sanur for a Temple Festival. Women carrying their offerings, men who wished to punish themselves pushing Kris' into their shoulders, but not drawing blood. They all looked emotionally disturbed. The priests then did a dance, and they must have represented the forces of evil, because members of the audience charged and forced them into the Temple, pretending to be petrified. A few tourists, including a photographer with 3 cameras, shooting a picture every 10 seconds, so typical of people who seem to go around seeing the world through a camera lens instead of absorbing the whole atmosphere. On the way back to Denpasar went to a cockfight, held every day under the spreading Banyan tree. The cocks are armed with razor sharp knives attached to one leg; a fight does not last long, and the betting is furious; I think I prefer football.

Next day, hired a taxi with a couple of Canadians for a trip to Kintamani, 450 Rup. For 8 hours. Stopped at many souvenir shops on the way, with ridiculous prices; the village of Mas is supposed to be the center of Balinese art, with many expensive but beautiful carvings and paintings. About 6kms from Kintamani the car got a puncture; while the driver fixed it, we walked to the edge of the old crater; Agung Agung is in the middle, still smoking from recent eruptions. Back in Kintamani the Canadians brought out their trading clothes but could not get any good offers. One sweater was popular, getting an offer of 400 Rupia or a black monkey. Years later, on another trip to Bali, I was staying in a hotel in Kintamani with Linda, watching Agung erupting every 70 seconds, providing a spectacular show; much better than TV, as someone remarked. On the way back, stopped at Sangeh, Bali's most impressive Temple, set out in three layers, with a huge Banyan tree used as the drum platform. Only two Festivals are held each year; hundreds of small snakes live in the banyan and are supposed to come out at night and bite sinners.

Next day went to the shipping line Pelni in a taxi, and instead of paying simply said Thank You, with a smile, which worked quite well over the next few days. At Pelni, there were no ships going to Timor, but one leaving for Bima in Sumbawa in a few days. Later in the evening at another dance met a Balinese man who wanted me to go next morning with him to meet his wife. And so, began my friendship with Wajan Mudara.

Having arranged to meet, I went to Wajan's home next morning, but he had gone to work at the Bali Beach. At the hotel they were preparing for a three-day festival, November 1-3, when Sukarno would officially open the Hotel. Met the German engineer again, stranded in Bali because Garuda flights had been cancelled. Spoke to the Frenchman again, who seemed terribly bored with Bali. Finally got in contact with Wajan when he came around next morning. Went with him to his home, where I met his very attractive wife, Putu, who had been a Temple dancer. After tea and coffee, arranged to come back in the afternoon, where we were invited to his brother's wedding the next day. Feasting on roast pork and 'Toddy'. Arranged with Wajan to send my carvings and batik to Australia, and in return I would send him clothes and other things he may want. Back at Garuda, after the usual lack of help, made my feelings towards them and the Indonesian military plain.

Back at the Losmen, a funeral was about to begin. The Balinese celebrate a death more like a wedding; after a person dies, a funeral bier is made, gaily decorated. People sit around eating and drinking for days; the procession left the Losmen with music accompanying it all the way, with the sealed coffin being carried high on a platform, with 2 kids sitting on it. People came from everywhere to join in the fun; we walked a mile through the town with the happy throng to the cremation ground. The body was taken out of the coffin and placed in a box of green banana logs, dried coconut and other fuel was piled around and on top and kerosene poured on to give it a good start, and soon the old dear was blazing merrily, while the band played on. It seemed a much better way to go out than the drab way us westerners do it.

Wajan had, in the short time I had known him, become a friend for many years. He confided in me that he was originally friendly with me because I was not American; he did not like Americans. Over time, when I was back in Australia, we exchanged letters and gifts. He sent me Balinese carvings and batik, I sent him books and clothes. I also sent Australian friends who were visiting Bali. After a few of these he once wrote to me wondering why nearly everyone I sent, had at some stage a problem; lost Passport, stolen money. I must have been sending the wrong people. He also told me he had named one of his children after me; Petu Geda Jaja Moloney. On another visit to Bali I went looking for him, and enquired in one of the hotels, "Oh yes, Mudara, he is around ", I was told. He was certainly well known. He was a very energetic and ambitious man; after a few years he started growing vanilla beans and had set up an export business to the States. He told me he had made a trip to Australia and came to my address in Neutral Bay in Sydney, waited all day, but did not know my phone number and left. We were keen to set up a regular trading business with Balinese artifacts, but never got to be in any volume. Some years later I sent my golf playing friend to Bali, and Gabe came back with the news that his family were very welcoming, but Wajan had been murdered by an uncle, who became jealous of his success with his business, and stabbed him multiple times. I have never been back to Bali since.

LEAVING BALI

Having given up on any prospect of getting a plane to Timor, Pelni had a ship going to Bima in Sumbawa next day. Packed our gear, paid the bill, had our last meal at our favorite place, said sad farewells to our beautiful waitress, and went to the Pelni man's home for Japanese whiskey and coffee, Ellis tea. Next morning, taken to the ship in Benoa; the ship was already crowded, so found a piece of free deck for our sleeping bags. 'Denara' sailed at 4am, Ellis was seasick by 4.30. We arrived at Ampenan, Lombok 2.30pm, where we would stay till next day. Booked into a Losman, asked the owner if there was any dancing in Lombok? Yes of course. He arranged to take us that evening. His car was a 1948 Nash and going over the rough roads was too much for the front right wheel, which sagged at 45% as the axle jumped off its mounting. A crowd quickly gathered to help, and with two jacks, a hammer and some wire, put it back together, and we proceeded to dance number one, fortified with local whiskey and orange juice. The dance is called Djoged Bambung; one girl, accompanied by a bamboo orchestra, dances alone and flings her fan to a member of the crowd, who dances with her and pays a few Rupia for the privilege; naturally Ellis and I performed as best we could. Soon we left for another dance, where this time I was first up, to the huge amusement of the local crowd, but I am not sure If our efforts at Lombok dancing were really appreciated by the audience. The girl's smile and more swigs of local whiskey eased too many doubts.

Back at the ship, met some people from Sumbawa, one of whom was a violin maker, who drew a sketch of me as we talked for a couple of hours. Found Ellis on the bridge talking to crew; no-one has asked us for money, so we bid not volunteer. We sailed at midday, and by now Ellis had his sea legs. Freddy, the Captain and the Chief Engineer made us welcome and comfortable. We had coffee and a meal, I taught Ellis how to play Patience for money, and proceeded to win Rupias off him. We did this nearly every day for the whole trip to Timor. In the evening, while sitting on the deck, watching the sunset across the islands, with a smoking Mount Agung in Bali, a truly magical experience; I conceived the idea of cruise ships operating out of Sydney and Darwin around the islands. Given a couple of million dollars I think I could make a good success of it.

The ship stopped at Sumbawa Besar, where Fernandez, the Engineer and his wife left the ship. Took a truck to the nearest town, 11kms away. Ellis attracted a crowd, taking his shirt off to have it mended. A young boy took us through the back streets to his house, where he showed us a bird, which I think he wanted us to buy. Ellis thought about going back to Djakarta on a Panamanian ship in port; travelling rough is not really his line but he stayed on. Back on board, after a meal, once again sitting on deck watching the islands in the magical sunsets; something worth travelling for. Next morning arrived at Bima at 6am. Freddy offered us 200 Rupia to help us on our way, but we declined with thanks; we had a free trip with food, coffee, tea and a comfortable place to sleep.

Went quickly through Customs and caught a bus to Sape, from where we were told sailing boats left every day for Flores. A two-hour trip over a range of hills, on rocky roads, before a small village where we picked up a load of people taking their rice harvest to Sape. No-one spoke English, and we were not asked to pay, so did not volunteer. In Sape, surrounded by kids, we met someone who said the price for a boat to Timor was 1000 Rupia, ridiculous. We offered two old shirts and a pair of shorts, still too much. On the way to the port, a policeman appeared and said we had to go back to Bima to register with immigration. We refused point blank, much to the amazement of the villagers. We suggested this could be done by telephone, but Bima would not agree. After much wrangling, the Policeman left for Bima with our Passports to register us.

A teacher who had been interpreting, offered us a bed. After a meal in the only eating place in the village, went for a walk with half the village population, and at the Police Station met the Chief, Francis Hory, who was very helpful, being able to speak a little English. He said we could get a boat next day, and after a bath, shared some coffee and Geneva Gin, before we went back to the teacher's house. There we met other people; two of them had asthma, and I promised to send them inhalers when I got home, which I did, hoping they would survive the sticky fingers in Indonesian Customs. Another boy had water on the brain, which leaked out through two holes in his nose. I could do nothing for him. The nearest doctor is in Bima, and he never visits Sape. Medicine is very expensive and almost impossible to get, and the doctor is very expensive. Having failed to solve many of the town's medical problems, we retired to our mats on the floor. Next morning the teacher left, needing to take an exam in Lombok. Some Police and Immigration officials arrived with our Passports, all legal again. We went to the port, refusing to ride in a cart pulled by a horse which looked as if it would not make 100 meters, typical of much of the mistreatment of Asian animals; we let him carry our packs though. At the Port we discovered that the promised boat was not to be, the next on Saturday, this being Wednesday. The Customs chief invited us to stay in his home.

The Custom man's house was halfway to the port; half his house was not in use, although he has 11 children; the room was cleared out for us. After a meal, we went to his half of the house. He could not speak much English, but his eldest daughter could get by quite well. His garden was surrounded by a wall, at which every night we sat drinking coffee and joining in singing with the daughters. A crowd hung over the wall listening in. Abbas, a teacher living next door, brought his guitar and we sang songs. The girls made a very attractive choir singing Indonesian songs, while we sang rounds of Brother John, and anything else that come to mind. Over the next few nights we learned some words, one song has stayed with me all of 50 years; 'Karolina muka manas, sigantung hate sur'. But apart from Karolina, I have no idea what it means. Our nightly sing-songs usually finished about 9.30, and were enjoyed by all, singers and audience, most of whom were girls done up in their finest. I was able to finish a book Wajan had given me in Bali, 'The Rainbow'. On our last day, went into town with the eldest daughter to do some shopping; cigarettes and bananas. Francis came out for lunch and last dinner. Had a short sing song where I gave my rendition of Karolina, then set out for the mile and a half walk to the boat, picking up kids every 50 yards, finishing up with about 200. The sailing prau was due to sail at 4am for the 3-day trip to Bari in Flores. We went to the prau with Johannes and the teacher; the crew went ashore to their families and we settled in to the boat. A couple of kids came out trying for our bananas, but I was still awake. On the pier a group of people sat singing to us for a couple of hours.

M/V cygnes,
Cannes, 1966

Isabella,
Cannes, 1966

Elfrieda and the
Messerschmitt 3 wheeler
Bavaria, 1966

Workers in the Bavarian Forest, Germany

Steve, Me, Norman,
Tucker and John in
Forstamt Tiergarten, Germany

217

Ukranian grandmother
telling of wartime hardships

Tony, Tom and Geoff,
Kassala, Sudan, 1969

Tina and me, 1972

Top of Ayres Rock, Uluhru, 1970

My brother Brian,
Army Sergeant
1st RAR
Service Corps
c.1970

'Ten Past Eleven'
Cricket Team, early 2000s

Bucks Party, Undercliff Street, Neutral Bay, 1970
Me as Aunty Jack

Brian's Bar
Atherton,
QLD

Julie and Me, Phillipines, 1980s
at the *Apocalypse Now* film site

Mum, Carol and Me, 1989

Mum (on right), my sister Carol and a friend at the Music Hall, Neutral Bay

Dianne and me at the Teacher's Ball

My Father, Harold, Martin Place, Sydney, 1943

With love, Harold

Spanish beauties and me, Malagrat de Mar, Spain 1966

Ricarda washing, camping at Rufert, Spain

FLORES

4.30am, the crew arrived, and we set sail, or at least that was the theory. The boat was about 26', single mast, mainsail and jib, not built for speed. The 'cabin' was a raised hatch over the open hold, just room for two. By 8am we had sailed into a bay where we were to take on water and firewood, and wait the whole day, as there was no breeze in the daytime. Got a couple of coconuts to supplement our meal of rice boiled in seawater and a small piece of dried fish; two plates per day. Not a brilliant diet. Sunburned shoulders rounded off the day's cruise. A stiff breeze during the night and sailing well when I retired to my palatial cabin. Next morning, we were becalmed on a glassy sea; Ellis seasick nonetheless. Picked up a breeze in the evening, the captain headed for the sea, but for some reason returned to where we had started from, where we spent the night. When I awoke, discovered we had covered about half a mile overnight, even though a slight breeze had been blowing during the night. Beginning to think our captain is not up to the job. About 10am, picked up a good strong breeze, and were sailing well. We had to go between two islands, about 300 yards apart. A strong breeze on our Port kept pushing the boat to the south of the gap, but the captain persisted in attacking the gap in a direct line, rather than what I thought, that a series of tacks would have got us through. Anyway, as darkness fell we retreated to the shelter of the south island, dropping anchor for the night, while I took advantage of the ship's toilet facilities, i.e. the bowsprit in an idyllic calm. Ellis in the meantime, had hardly eaten anything, but next day brought out his emergency rations, dehydrated bacon, then, as we were becalmed again, suddenly jumped stark naked into the glassy water. The crew became a bit agitated and with urgent actions got him back on board. Later in Australia I found a National Geographic article about this part of the World's oceans, how it is home to the deadliest sea snakes in the World, which I forwarded on to Ellis. Luckily for him they must have been somewhere else that morning.

We arrived in Bari at 12.45, starting time for the Melbourne Cup, went ashore in a dugout canoe, all correspondence with the crew conducted in sign language. Arrived in a village and met people from the Red Cross; spent the afternoon eating fried eggs, coconut and bananas, pure bliss after our diet of rice and dried fish. After some tea, went for a walk through the coconut palms. After a mile or so came to a small river in which several women and girls were bathing. I stripped down to underpants and joined them; young girls were delighted but the older women soon left. Ellis sat on the bank. Back in the village with the village chief, who told us we were the only travellers to pass through in years. Later we had another meal with the Red Cross, and a man from Djakarta, who was on his way to Australia, not sure how. Back to our 'prau', where he and his wife and two children joined us aboard. We sailed at 10.30 for Reo. I offered his wife my bunk in the 'cabin', but she preferred to stay on deck. Our slight breeze took us steadily along the coast, before arriving at 4pm at the mouth of the Reo River, crocodile infested during the rainy months, December and January. This being November, hopefully no crocs. Went ashore onto mud flats, which had plenty of crocodile prints, but no animals, walked through swamp for 2½ hours, led by our captain.

In Reo, the Police took us to the Mission, where we met two German priests, from outlying stations. They did not speak English, but my German was adequate. They told me that 75% of the population of 1.2 million was Catholic, the rest Moslem. Flores is all mountains, and most of the people live inland. The Moslems live mainly on the coast; 40 years ago they came from Sumba and Sumbawa, and took slaves from the coastal villages, so the people retreated inland, where the climate is much better. Only now are they going back to the coast in small numbers. The Missions, now 400 strong, have been in Flores since 1914, and they are the virtual government, doing most of the education and social work. The Army is not strongly represented, but there are plenty of Police. The Police arrived to tell us we has to go and be registered. The senior priest told us that this is about all the Police have to do.

Any foreigners have 3 sets of finger prints taken. No records are kept of Births, Deaths and Marriages or statistics. Only murders count with the local police. I sat down and talked to a young soldier for a couple of hours, with an interpreter; quite a comedian and we got along famously.

The Police next day spent a lot of time going over our travels, getting some particulars wrong, before we were on a truck for Ruteng, some 40 kms away, a rugged road up in the mountains. An Australian team, based in Ende, is building roads, under the Colombo Plan, but has not yet made it to Reo. First stop to the Police, who were satisfied, then to the tin roofed Cathedral, where we met a Dutch priest, who took us to our rooms; soft beds, blankets, writing table and electricity, pure luxury. At lunch, met the other priests and brothers, German, Dutch, Czech, Polish, Austrian and Indonesian, most of whom have been here many years. There are two secondary schools, primary school and seminary. Nuns teach girls home science, dressmaking etc. They have Friesian cows for milk, pigs for meat; a saw mill supplies the town with lumber, cabinet makers build the town's furniture and a German Brother runs the electricity generating plant. Horses are kept for transport, essential for most of the outlying stations. The nuns have a new automatic washing machine. A 25-piece school orchestra provides music. Went to town to buy matches. Everything is very expensive compared to Bali. A ball point pen cost 50 to 100 Rupia, a truck driver makes 200 per month. Back at the Mission for dinner, which included bread and butter, and peanut butter.

Today should have been the day my Visa expired, but I extended it by 10 days by placing a 1 in front of the 4 on my date of arrival. Another 50 kms to Borong, up into mountains, on rough roads, this time with 25 passengers. Much beautiful scenery to admire, mountains covered in thick rain forest, the valleys dotted with rice paddy. Sat talking with the priest of the difficulties of trying to break old customs and teach new methods. Brides are still bought here; a recent one cost 30 horses, 25 buffalo and 30,000 Rupia. Agriculture is very primitive, people do not seek medical attention, but rely on the village medicine man.

Consequently, half of them die before 30, mainly from Malaria and TB. They also carry on family feuds, and fight with Parangs, which helps to keep the population down.

We drove steadily down to the coast, reaching Borong 3pm. The Polish priest introduced us to the priest at the Mission, a Czech, who told us all about his Mission, while I translated his German for Ellis. He had been in Indonesia 16 years, 5 at this station. His church was built in concrete, with imitation stained-glass windows, the figures painted and black lines representing the lead. The house was too small for three people, so the priest went to a great deal of trouble fixing up a room in the church, with mosquito nets, water basin, soap, towels and an air mattress, to which I laid no claim, leaving it to Ellis. Later in the evening, a tour of the town. The school, one of 42 in his district; the Government has 11 schools in the whole of Mangarai. Many palms, from which 90-100 coconuts are got annually, also copra and palm oil. People live mainly on bananas and corn, rice only for feasts. Heard on the radio that night that Australian rice farmers are claiming a World Record for rice production, 4½ tons per acre, enough rice to feed each of the 1600 people in the town with 1lb of rice each per day for a year. That night listened to music, also the radio news from Radio Australia. Russia, Japan, China, BBC, ABC, and VOA all beam Indonesian language broadcasts every night.

Next morning Ellis borrowed a typewriter to type a letter home, as he says his writing is illegible. I did not ask what he told the folks in New York of his travels, but I am sure he would have persuaded them that going on an adventure with a crazy Australian should be avoided. The truck to Ende expected at noon, the priest came bearing gifts, a steel mirror, note book, woven leaf pouches, pens. He also wanted us to take some of his tinned bread, but we refused; we had already eaten 3 of his tins. He told us how the Government had refused offers of assistance for Flores by Germany, preferring the offered schools to be in Java. The Government's concept of Indonesia is Java, Sumatra and Bali, the other 3497 islands belonging to another world. The central government is very touchy about anything they think smacks of colonialism. The Mission started a radio station, but it was banned on those grounds. We talked of the October Revolution; 106 Communist leaders were killed in Flores, with others being 're-educated'. The plan was for all foreigners to be killed on a signal from Doctor Subandrio, but it misfired. Communists had banned all work on roads, bridges, schools, churches etc, saying that the Government would do all for the people, no taxes.

The mission jeep arrived to take us to Badjawa, 90 kms through very attractive mountain scenery, including a perfectly conical high volcano; the first I had ever seen. Down the coast to Aimere then up into the mountains again. Twice the clutch cable broke, and the driver made quick repairs. A jeep in front of us had lost its headlights, so we swallowed its dust while our light showed the way.

In Badjawa we were taken to the priest's home and shown to a comfortable room. After a sumptuous dinner, talked to the two priests, one Dutchman who had been here 20 years, and a young Filipino, 4 years. Next morning awoken by the sound of Hymn singing; Flores people are very musical and have fine voices. The sound of 500 of them singing together is a fine way to start the day. We both went to Mass, and Jewish Ellis decided on a new cultural experience by joining the throngs of locals for Communion. In the Franciscan Convent, coffee and cakes with two Nuns, one Dutch, who had been in Indonesia 30 years, including 3 in a concentration Camp during the War, and an Irish Nun, 30 years away from Ireland. Their Covent was a fine concrete building, with light fittings, basins & taps, but no electricity or water. The children in the Kindergarten classes sang and recited for us, their 3 and 4-year-old voices upholding the fine Flores tradition.

The jeep for Ende left at midday; I extended Ellis' visa by 10 days with a stroke. Stopped at Mataloko on the way, met Father Popp, an American, 20 years in Flores, at the Seminary, with 200 students; having graduated 160 as priests since 1926. They have a film projector but have not been able to get any film since USIS was burned down in Djakarta. We asked if they needed anything, mainly what they want are books as teaching aids, books such as Popular Mechanics, Popular Science; we promised to try to send some. The Nuns had prepared a meal for us and the driver, and we then took off for Ende. At the top of a large plateau, a large volcano was still smoking, with a river of lava flowing down its side; another spectacular backdrop to the lush Flores landscape. Women walking on the road carry large bamboo pipes, in which they carry water, while spinning cotton thread from the buds as they walk along. Multi-Tasking any Boss would be happy with. Back on the coast to Ende, where at the Mission they had no room, so a hotel, where Ellis discovered some bed bugs, but powder kept them down. Travelling through Flores, from Mission to Mission, enjoying their hospitality; we were told that only three foreigners had been through this year, none last year.

Life in Ende settled down to a series of trucks promised, but not arriving. Met the Chief Engineer of the Colombo Plan, Mr Sam Porsiano and his Portuguese wife, who took us in. A boat was supposed to leave for Kupang next day but had not arrived. The Mission boat was due to go from Maumare to Atapupu in 11 days, taking two Australian engineers back to Djakarta, then Australia. Heard of two Australians just arrived from Kupang, met them at the harbour; they told us that getting from Kupang to Atatpupu overland was impossible, due to collapsed bridges. A Fair was in town, featuring mainly food stalls and gambling booths and dancing. I was not impressed, standing watching a man lay down, have concrete slabs placed on his chest while another man used a sledge hammer on the slabs. Yawn! Then he stood up and revealed the bed of long sharp spikes he had been laying on. Then I was impressed.

Much of Ellis' and my leisure time, of which there was a lot, we spent playing Patience for money. I was some 1280 Rps ahead, which meant that since leaving Denpasar on October 21st, I had spent nothing, but Ellis staged a comeback, and over the next weeks I was finally reduced to nothing, having to borrow off Ellis. Reading also occupied plenty of 'down time'. 'The Rainbow' by D.H. Lawrence, and 'The Life of Oscar Wilde', 'The Night of the Generals' also enjoyable. Ellis got from somewhere 'Evolution in Action' by Huxley. Ellis heard of a jeep leaving on Saturday; we declined other offers as being too expensive. When it arrived, they wanted 2500 Rps to go the 146 Kms. We laughed and told them to forget it; we do not have that much between us. Went to see the two Australian engineers, who were recovering from a bout of Malaria. Arranged to go to Maumare with them on Wednesday, in four days. While walking around the town, decided to get a coffee, called in at a shop and ordered, which was delivered by a young girl. Soon realised that I had ordered coffee from a private home, and when I offered to pay, they declined with many smiles. The girl's mother held a Dutch Passport, and the father had done 9 years in the Dutch Army and is the chief of the prison: they were trying to emigrate to Holland.

The jeep arrived to take us and a few others, including the engineers, a priest and the girl from the PWD office. We climbed steadily to a ridge overlooking very spectacular rivers running between high cliffs, a waterfall dropping into a deep gorge. On the way we diverted to see the lakes of Kelimutu. The three craters are filled with water of different colours, red, blue and green, which can change, depending on volcanic gasses, weather. Flores was once a Portuguese colony, but when the Dutch saw the colours of the lakes, which are close to the Dutch flag, they bought Flores from the Portuguese for one million Guilders.

We stopped at most of the bridges built or being built by the engineers to say goodbye to the workers. At one bridge the concrete bases were in the shape of boats, the idea of one of the local foreman. On one of his inspections the engineer had said, "these are foundations, not boats. Boats have anchors". Next trip there were two anchors worked into the concrete 'boats'. Sam Poisiano shot some birds, very blue birds, about half the size of a chicken, which we had for dinner; meat brown, but very tasty; he arranged to put us up in the PWD boarding house. Next day to Police for registration, my expired visa not noticed, then to see the Mission ship. Spent my last 25Rps on cigarettes. With time on my hands, had been contemplating my future prospects and ambitions, also writing a long letter to the family which I intended to post in Darwin. My immediate aim is repaying debts, mainly to my father, also writing to the many friends I had met around the World. I also waxed lyrical, sort of.

Oh to be in Aussie, now that Summer's here,
There's cricket matches, girls galore, and gallons of
good beer. The sunny beach, the Christmas scene,
blurred in a beery haze, Oh why am I in Flores?
In Sydney town there's much to do, in these golden days.

Now Flores Island's pretty nice, as tropic islands go, There's
mountains high and valleys low, and life is pretty slow.

But what to do in Paradise, apart from sit and think,

In Aussie now it is the time for a good strong Christmas drink.

I sat and thought the other day, of Sydney and its sights, While
here in Flores, while its very nice, they haven't any lights.

So good old Sydney, here, I'll come to share the fun, But most of
all, I'll come to see
Carol, Brian, Dad and Mum.

Went to the boat, the 'Ratu Rosari', to buy tickets. The Captain
was strict about only carrying the allowed number of passengers,
92. Many later disasters in Asian waters could have been averted
by similar attention by greedy operators overloading ferries from
Malaysia to Philippines. The boat was donated by the German
Government and was modern, clean and well run. Goodbyes
were said, photos taken, last meals had, and we went to the boat.
Finally leaving Flores on 18th November, having spent 19 days on
the island. Later, Flores has been attracting tourists, who seem to
remain mainly around the beaches near Ende, then to Komodo for
the dragons, but I think the main attraction is the interior and the
people. Not sure of the remaining influence of the Missions, but
their contribution is, I hope still appreciated.

On board, settled in to a spot on the top bridge, Ellis paid for
my ticket, 136 Rupia, and we ate with the First-Class passengers
and chatted with the Bishop, who was returning to Maumare.
Talked with a young, 19-year-old, Englishman, Tony, who had

come from England in three months; had his money stolen in Delhi and was travelling 'around the world'. Stopped next morning in Ranantuka, which reminded me of the Seychelles, high green mountains capped with clouds, beautiful sea and a neat little town along the bay. Next morning arrived in Maumare. Made ourselves comfortable by the beach, under a shady tree. Organized a young boy to climb for a coconut, had a swim, cut my foot on coral, and talked to an Indonesian woman, educated in Egypt while her father was Cultural Attaché there. While we were on the beach, news came over the radio that students in Djakarta, led by her father, had demonstrated against the National Monument, demanding that the 85lb of gold on the flame, worth about $48,000, be removed and used more constructively. She was not at all perturbed that her father had led the demonstration. We talked about Asian women marrying foreigners and Arabs, which she did not like, citing problems of adjusting to new customs etc.

Later Tony and I went up to the Bishop's house, as he had invited us to do so. We walked up to the front door to be greeted by a Portuguese Nun, who told us the Bishop was not in. Tony, then, to my horror, started gesturing that he wanted food. I grabbed him and pushed him back down the path, apologizing to the bemused Nun in my best Spanish. Having been the grateful recipient of hospitality around the world, often from very poor people, I have never once asked for anything. So, having arrived in Indonesia on 4th October 1966, finally left 22nd November, 49 days.

FAREWELL INDONESIA, HELLO TIMOR

Back to the ship for the last leg to Atapupu, where we arrived next morning. I went first to the Customs, where the official was most unpleasant. He took us into his office one by one to search our bags; me first. I took out a few things then told him to do it himself. He said I would have to go to Atambua to register with Police and Immigration. I told him I did not have any more money and gave him my wallet to search. He said that if I did not go to Atambua I would have to go back to Flores, but I said that was also impossible with no money. The problem was left unsolved. Tony was next and refused to open his bag, which made the Customs man shout. Tony took much longer than me. Ellis was next, and by this time Customs man was in a rare mood. Ellis told him to open the bag himself; he refused, Ellis then opened the bag and started throwing clothes around the room, while the Customs man called him a "F'ing Bastard". He then decided that Ellis was a Communist, as he had a camera which was made in East Germany, and had got his Visa in Cambodia. He wrote USSR in his Passport. We finally got out after 2 hours.

Getting the final 22 kms to Atambua turned into a daylong exercise; waiting at the police Station, annoying the Customs man, going back to the ship for some pineapples, meeting a truck driver who said he would take us on his return in the afternoon. When he finally returned, we all stood at the back, holding on to each other and nearly falling off at every turn. Arriving at night, went to Police Station, told to come back tomorrow; Tony found a hostel, which did not have any beds, but we could sleep on the floor and have a meal for 15Rps, which was comfortable. In the morning back to Police and Immigration to register again. While waiting for a truck, played volleyball with some Police, but had left my shoulder bag open underneath the Police Chief's office, and just as the truck arrived I grabbed it and discovered someone had taken two packets of cigarettes. Left Atambua showering abuse on Indonesian Police, one of whom, carrying his sub machine gun looked bemused, and of course innocent. Not a good move by a tobacco deprived idiot. The truck took us to within 12 kms of the Border. Ellis had 500 Rupia left and we bargained with 3 locals to carry our bags, settling on 50 Rupia each; as they earn 5 Rupia a day working for the Government they were happy. About three k's from the Border they decided they had had enough and handed over to 2 others. At the Border, two Police hurriedly got up from bed, dressed, had a quick look at our Passports and waved us out of Indonesia.

Walked into Portuguese Timor, headed for a beach, swam, ate coconuts, and were told to wait by 3 natives armed with spears, bow and arrows and a parang, who wanted to carry our bags but would not accept Rupias. Started walking towards Balibo. Walked about 4k's; Ellis had fallen behind and stopped a Unimog, carrying water pipes. We clung to the sloping pipes for the 10 kms steep uphill drive in the dark. The Police Chief found us a place to sleep, a house which many years later was the last refuge of the Balibo Five, the Australian journalists who were murdered by the invading Indonesian Army; a crime which has remained unpunished, indeed has been rewarded by Indonesia. A meal and a beer with some local Chinese was most welcome after a grueling day's travel. Santos, the Police Chief was very casual about documentation, which was just as well, as I was the only one who had a plane ticket and visa. Next morning, he conducted a very loud and aggressive phone conversation with Dili about our visas, before stamping our Passports and joining us for breakfast.

The same truck as we had the previous day again took us to Maliama, from where we could catch a plane for the 20-minute flight to Dili. A truck trip through the mountains would take all day; the rainy season rains had made many rivers uncrossable and would cost the same, $3. Stayed the night with the Administrator and two young Portuguese soldiers who were there for a murder trial next day. They showed me the murder weapon, a large, blood-stained rock. A bottle of Hennessey Cognac lubricated a lively night. The flight through the mountains, with villages on one wing seeming to be within touching distance, while valleys thousands of feet deep dropped beneath the Port wing, was enlivened by a local Chinese family and their live chickens. Timor Airlines had two Doves, two Austers and charters a Fokker Friendship from TAA for the Darwin flight, my final leg.

In Dili, the International Police Chief gave us visas for 8 days, and suggested we go to the Mimosa restaurant where we might find a place to sleep. There we met the Chinese owner who told us the price, $1; too much. Further investigations in other places were fruitless; back at the Mimosa, met another brother of the owner. After some bargaining by Ellis, where at each offered price he looked at me, and at each I said No. When we got down to zero, the brother then gave us camp beds in his stables, complete with mosquito coils. Met some Czech Australian tourists who invited us for dinner, and lots of drinks; altogether a great day's work. Tony next morning left for Bacau, Ellis and I booked seats on a truck next day. Walked in heavy rain up to the Australian Embassy where Ellis got his Visa extended.

Back at the Mimosa, a Swiss guy recognized me from the Thai Song Greet hotel in Bangkok. He was a journalist doing a story on Timor, working for a Spanish paper. Spent the afternoon drinking with him, a Czech and a Portuguese soldier who told us what he knew of the Battle of De Cussa a couple of weeks earlier; some Indonesian soldiers had marched into a Portuguese coffee plantation and announced that it was Indonesian. They were shot for their trouble. Troops were sent up from Kupang and some houses were burned. A Company of soldiers was sent down from Dili and threw them out, killing maybe 6. The soldier had not been there but knew all about it from his friends, explaining to us in French, Spanish and English. He bought us a meal and took us over to the Casa de Timor hotel, where there were lots of soldiers and their wives socializing.

Next morning a 2km walk to the bus station, where we got the best seats in a comfortable bus and enjoyed the 130 kms drive along the coast to Bacau. The town is surrounded by cliffs on three sides, which drop away to the sea on the fourth side. We took our bags to a Club but could not sleep there; the hotel charges $7 a day. The boss, Maria, a huge Portuguese woman, returned and told us Tony had arrived the previous day and was sleeping in a shed at the Army swimming pool. Went there and found a beautiful pool surrounded by Flame trees, coconut palms and lots of attractive flowers and shrubs. Back at the Hotel met John, Ian and Lyn the Australian tourists, had beers with them. Australian tourists, it seemed, came to Timor mainly for the cock fights. Heard that Tony had been drinking at the soldiers' camp all day, and was now sleeping off the whiskey and champagne, while we listened to the Election results from Australia. Ellis found a cheap place to eat, chow mien now our main source of sustenance.

Spent a relaxed four days by the pool, swimming and relaxing, reading 'Dubliners' and 'Finnigan's Wake', playing cards with the Australians staying in the hotel. Got kids to go up for coconuts when needed. After this welcome sojourn, out to the Airport. John gave me some Escudos for stuff I could take through Customs for him; Kaye gave me $5 to bring a radio through Customs. At the Airport, we had a wait of a couple of hours, during which time Ellis discovered that he could buy US$ from Maria at $4 and sell them to waiting Timorese for $5. He did this with no worries about formalities from Maria and was making money hand over fist. After about an hour I could contain myself no longer. "Ellis, I just have to say it. You are a F'ing Jew". His reply, "It's in the Blood my son". The Fokker arrived from Darwin; a good number of tourists alighted, including a Scot who told me there was plenty of work in Rum Jungle, the uranium mine south of Darwin, and gave me a phone number.

BACK HOME AGAIN

The plane was late taking off, but we arrived in Darwin after 1½ hour flight and a nice meal. Got through Customs and immigration quickly, although they checked one of my books, *'Tristram Shandy'* to see if it was on the Banned List; gave Kaye her radio, and after nearly five years was back "home". Checked the Post Office, but no mail. Went to the Salvation Army Hostel and got a bed for 50c a night. Called the man at Rum Jungle, but it had closed; no job. A Canadian, an Aussie and two Poms were thinking of going through Indonesia and got me to write out information on Asia, India etc. for them. Had trouble sleeping; bed too soft. Ellis at last was on his way to Sydney. He got a bus ticket, via Brisbane and we said farewell a few days later. Some weeks later I got a letter from him asking, "What's wrong with this Country? We got to the turn-off to Brisbane, but road closed because of rain. Took a 'slight' detour, via Adelaide. An extra 4000kms." Welcome to Australia Ellis. After 4 days in Darwin, I had no trouble getting a job, as a kitchen hand in a mine in Tennant Creek, $60 a week, seven days, all found. Tony got a job in the Power House. At the hostel, a group had become established, and I was somehow elected as cook. Managed to knock up some good meals while we discussed the state of the world, particularly Africa, with the South African. Ellis declined to participate, having decided that his superior intellect had mastered all the facts, which sadly was far from the case. He caught his bus and I collected my ticket from TAA and caught the plane to Tennant Creek.

POST TRAVEL
REFLECTIONS

Having been away about five years, a little reflection on some
favorite places:

Scottish Highlands; lonely and desolate. Bavarian forest in the
Fall when the oak leaves turn red and gold, the early morning mist
creating a tiny, silent haven of peace. The wild exuberant beer
festivals of Munich and Bavaria, rough but great fun if one can stay
out of trouble. The Swiss and Austrian Alps, Summer or Winter.
Florence, fabulous city of Art, perhaps even better than Rome,
also wonderful for Art's sake; the Romans however, aren't all they
are cracked up to be. Compared to Londoners they are provincial
and narrow. Spain, one of my first loves; the excitement of bull-
fights, the fiery emotion of Flamenco dance and music, the barren
sweep of the High Sierra, the tranquil beauty of the islands and
coast (the parts the travel agents haven't opened up yet). English
Pubs, a cosy place for companionship or a quiet drink, as you like
it. Notre Dame Cathedral, massive, ugly, my favorite church, just
now burned, but hopefully able to be restored. Delphi, seat of the
Greek Oracle, one of town planning's most brilliant achievements.
Istanbul, crowded, dirty bridge between Europe and Asia, home
of great Mosques, Topkapi Museum. Beirut, gleaming, modern, a
troubled show-place of Middle Eastern diversity, laying beneath
snow-capped mountains by the warm blue Med. The Syrian desert,
vast, barren but not empty. Here live world's most hospitable
people, the Bedouin, tending their goats and sheep, trading
camels, moving their tent villages across the desert in search of
pasture. Damascus, Queen of the Desert, the Souk, the narrow
intimate streets, the trice yearly renovations. Now the scene of
the 21st Century's greatest tragedy. Baghdad, sprawling city of
four million on the Tigris, no longer the city of The Arabian Nights,

friendly, bustling, striving to be modern, hopes dashed by War and tyranny. Fatehpur Sikri, near Agra, built by Emperor Akbar in gratitude to the Holy Man Salim Chisti who spirited a child to his barren wife. Today Indian women leave ribbons in his Temple to hasten a child. The mountains of Eritrea and Ethiopia, massive, wild and full of fascinating life, human and animal.

On reflection, fifty years on, virtually all of the above is ancient history, but very little could be said to be subject to progressive achievement.

TENNANT CREEK

Arrived in Tennant Creek late Sunday afternoon, no-one there to pick me up. Wandered the deserted street till I met up with an Aboriginal family squatting by the road. I joined them for a chat; they informed me that their father was the 'Gun Drover' in the whole Territory. I was duly impressed. Eventually Gerry the Caterer arrived with apologies. The Peko mine produces mainly copper, but also gold and some silver. The Mess feeds 175 men, three times a day, many of whom seemed to be German or Slav; one Yugoslav had 12 eggs for breakfast every day. Talk about keeping up your strength! There were four other kitchen hands, and I have never worked so hard in my life; peeling spuds, onions and throwing stores around, 12 hours a day, continually being told to hurry; not even time for a smoke. Four kitchen hands were sacked for being too slow. One arrived from Melbourne, lasted six days before being sacked.

I was sharing a hut with Mick, a young Irishman from Perth. One day two very blonde and fit girls arrived in a big convertible and set up for business in the next hut; they stayed seven days and would have made pretty good money before the Police decided that was enough and moved them on to no doubt another sex-starved Outback opportunity.

The other center of off-duty entertainment was the 'Wet Canteen', which particularly on Pay Night was the Place To Be. I have seen plenty of miners lose their entire fortnightly pay in a couple of hours playing the card game 'Banker', or Two Up. Outside, a boxing ring occupies a space reserved for the resolution of disputes; fighting not allowed inside. Diamond Drillers are the elite in the work force, and even some of them have been known to be broke after a 'few bets' on Pay Night.

I worked off my plane fare and was on the point of applying for a mine job, reluctantly, as I had developed a hernia which would have made hard physical work very uncomfortable. When I finally got to Sydney and arranged an operation on the hernia, while lying on the operating table the Surgeon asked if I had any other needs; "I have a wart on my knee." When I awoke the surgeon told me that the knee 'bonus' had taken twice as long as the hernia.

Gerry decided to send Mick and myself out to another, smaller mine, Ivanhoe, about 20 miles on the other side of town. There were only 35 miners there, still seven days a week, but not so rushed and strenuous; also, we could make a bit extra by selling cool drinks and cigarettes, so we settled in.

Having settled in to Ivanhoe, I decided to do something about Education, and enrolled in a WA University Mature Age Matriculation course. Gerry was most impressed by this and decided that I needed privacy to study and put me in a hut of my own. Unfortunately, when the time came to leave the mine, with me having completed only about six assignments, other temptations took over and my aspirations, like so many of my plans, died a death.

Ivanhoe mine was mainly copper, with a main shaft about 2000'. The miners were a mixed bunch; one of them, an Italian called Lucky, had met a young female geologist when she was here, and was writing to her. Lucky's English was not that great, so he got me to write his letters, as if he was actually doing the writing; for which he bought me cartons of beer. This arrangement carried on for about four months, while it was actually me writing in First Person, with the letters becoming more me than Lucky. When asked, Lucky was happy as her letters were more and more familiar; she once complimented him on his improving English! I tried to get Lucky to let me tell her that this was not the case, but he let it continue. When I eventually left I hope that his "improving English" was able to keep her interested. Many other letters and cards were sent to people all over the world, especially in Africa and Indonesia thanking them for their help and friendship.

Working as a kitchen hand in a small Outback mine is not the most exciting existence; if rain threatened, the main concern of the Ivanhoe workers was to be on the 'Pub side' of the creek half way to the town. Miners cut off from their work by a 'an Act of Nature' could not be penalized. Visits to town for movies or beers at one of the two pubs were highlights. A more substantial threat was posed by mice. Far away in Victoria mice had started breeding in the Wimmera, in their millions; they were heading North, devouring anything that grew in their way. One suggestion was that the Air Force should bomb them with Napalm, no doubt inspired by the nightly TV reports from Vietnam. This did not happen and by the time the remnants of the plague reached Tennant Creek we had stored all food on high shelves.

Miners seem to like, every now and again, to vote out their caterers, and this happened to Gerry. The new caterers were a large firm from Perth in WA. Mick decided to leave, and our new cook, Mario, who had been a chef in one of Perth's nightclubs, no doubt an alimony refugee as were many of the Territory's workers. We got on well, but after a few weeks I became annoyed at the waste, particularly of fresh vegetables. One morning, instead of tossing out the cooked potatoes, carrots etc, I mashed them up and made patties, crisp fried both sides; a classic Aussie dish known as Bubble and Squeak. Mario was scornful, declaring that no-one would eat this. After about three days of roaring popularity I came in to breakfast one morning to find him writing and scratching out on the Menu board, finally asking, "How you spell this Bubble Squeak?"

SYDNEY OR BUST!

I had determined that I had to stay in the Territory six months to qualify for Taxation Zone Allowance, also to sit out a qualifying period for hospital benefits. As soon as this period was reached, decided to head south. Got a lift with John, an English 'Sparky' and, via Alice Springs and Cooper Pedy arrived at Adelaide, where I met up again with Geoff, London flat mate. Also went to a football match between South Australia and West Australia; few days there then off West. While waiting by the road, two girls stopped in front of me, once again I thought they were not playing the game; they were soon picked up, and as their car approached, it stopped, and they told their 'brother' to get in. All forgiven. They were only going to Port Pirie to meet up with some Greek sailors they had met in Sydney. The car took me all the way to Perth, about 2500 kms, sharing petrol costs before dropping me at Guildford, home of the Roches.

Many reunions over the next few weeks, notably Phil Gurrin, Roches, then back on the road again, Sydney next stop. In Norseman, on the edge of the Nullabor I spent a whole day without getting a lift, the first time ever, and in my home State! Next morning however, a Land Rover picked me up, heading to Adelaide, virtually non-stop; although I offered to drive. Pulled in for petrol in Madura, where suddenly I was rushed by two girls, flinging arms arounds my neck; the Greek sailors did not work out. In Adelaide had just time to buy some beer and head to Geoff's for a party, where I danced the night away. Next day got lifts through Victoria to Yass in New South Wales, where the next lift dropped me outside the door of Home, in Sydney, with the parting words from my driver, "if you can't get a root in Sydney, you never will".

Back with the family; Mum was overjoyed. Dad, on returning from work said, "What's that on your face?". Don't think he liked beards. Carol was behaving strangely, and I learned that she had been having Mental Issues, but no-one wanted to tell me while I was away. Brian had joined the Army and was in Vietnam. I settled in to a room in the front of the house. After a while I cut off my beard, at which Mum looked at me and asked, "Have you grown a mustache?"

I had repaid all my debts while in Tennant but was now needing to get a job, any job that paid money. First try, selling encyclopedias door to door. Lasted one week before quitting; my only 'sale' could not afford the $10 Deposit. Next stop A.G.Healing, one of Australia's largest Companies. I soon had a job in the accounts department of Healing Controls, one of their divisions. Healings made and sold everything from toasters to locomotives, but I soon learned they were living on the brink, surviving largely through Australia's tariff protections and Government subsidies. The Creditors' cheques were drawn monthly and held in a large tray. Any request for payment was delayed as much as possible. The Company Director still had a chauffeur-driven Rolls Royce however. After some months the annual audit took place, and Healings recorded the biggest turnaround from Profit to Loss in Australian Corporate history, mainly because the auditors finally valued the stock correctly, instead of the past practice of valuing old and unsaleable stock at full retail value. Healing Controls was trading well, with good products, but the writing was on the wall.

After living 'at home' for a few weeks, I got in touch with John Meadows, who decided that I should be introduced to Sydney life, and met me at Jim Buckley's *Newcastle Hotel* in George Street, near The Rocks in the City. This became a seminal moment in my life. Buckley's was a typical Sydney Pub, large front bar, smaller back, saloon bar. It was part of what was known as *'The Rocks Push'*; the Left, Radical, Arts members of the Sydney Scene. I quickly fell in with 'the Scene', including the female side. Isabelle became my first girlfriend there; she worked for *Time Life*, and on discovering that I liked classical music, would present me with the boxed sets that *Time* was currently selling, some of which I still have. She also presented me with the news that she was pregnant. I told her that what she wanted to do was entirely her decision, and I would support her. Thankfully she chose termination; we split the cost and continued a more careful relationship.

Through friends and others at The Newcastle I was now a party animal. One party I attended in Undercliff Street, Neutral Bay, became a central part of life. I determined while at this party that I wanted to live there, and sought out the principal occupant, Chris Moran, informed him of my desire and moved in next week. Over the next six years Underpants Street lived up to its name. There were usually about five or six occupants, sometimes more, often less. After a while I became 'Big Daddy', organizing rent, food etc. At one stage Chris decided to get married and informed myself and Percy Poulos we would have to leave. We approached the Agent and told them that whatever Chris offered for rent, we would beat it. We stayed, Chris left.

Rent was sometimes a problem for some 'residents'. One time I advertised for tenant; a young English guy came, stayed a few weeks and disappeared, owing me some 4 weeks rent. Sometime later someone told me he had been seen dancing in a Spanish restaurant in the City. I found him on the dance floor with one of his Gay friends, tapped him on the shoulder and soon had my money. Tony, another, took off owing; about a year later I was walking down a street in Perth WA when Tony drove past in his sports car. A dinner was arranged and rent paid.

Six years in Undercliff Street could provide enough material for a dozen Damon Runyon books. Some residents became life-long friends; Percy Poulos, Jack Greenwell, Phil Huby, Dennis Disney, Jeanne and Barry, Chris Phelan; others fade into the 'mists of time'. The house was ideal for parties; two stories, huge backyard, cellar, four bedrooms. The Agent was never a problem. One winter we needed some firewood; the fence separating us from the large boarding house next door was falling down, so became our fuel. When some time later the Agent asked if there was a fence there, he was assured we did not think so.

By this time, I had bought a car, Holden with ominous plate END 006. Most mornings I would have to come out to the street and try to remember where I had left it the previous night. Eventually it fulfilled its destiny and it was traded for a Citroen ID

19, which was a great car until one night, while heading to pick a girl to go to a concert in Kings Cross, on a slippery hill in Double Bay it decided to go for a slide uphill and smash sideways into an oncoming car. When the Police came, the comment was made "Michelin Tyres", obviously the cause as they were no good on wet roads. A taxi to and from the concert, car towed away to a friend's smash repair shop in North Sydney, where it was written off. I had Insurance on monthly payments, but when approached they said the Bank was one payment behind; claim denied. I took this as an injustice and decided to avoid paying the balance owed on the car. One night while leaving home, a man was looking for number 4; I asked who he as after; Daniel Moloney. Sorry mate he has gone, lives somewhere in the City. Another time I was watching TV with a friend, Jacqui; she answered a knock on the door and informed the Process Server that, No, Daniel no longer lives here. That was the last I heard of the matter. Sounds dishonest, but I felt the Insurance Company was the real culprit.

The Citroen did however have its moments. An English friend, Tony decided to get married, an event which inspired his parents to come out from England to join in the fun. I had the only vehicle in the immediate group, and was therefore delegated to provide the wedding chariot, which was fine until in the middle of transporting them to the after-ceremony celebrations the muffler parted from its mountings, and we drove through the City sounding like a squadron of tanks. The bemused parents and wedding guests gathered at the Wentworth Hotel for drinks when it was noticed among us that we had not bought a wedding gift. A quick collection was taken up and Irish Mike was dispatched to find something suitable; he arrived after an hour or so with a goatskin which still featured the bullet hole of its demise. Colonial reputations were no doubt further maligned on the parent's return to Blighty.

Healings was now at the stage of breaking up. The accountant at Controls, Mel, a Scot, decided to leave, and as he was not all that familiar with Australian business, took me along with him to my new job, at*The Strata Hotel* in Cremorne, where I looked after most of the accounting work while he handled the politics. *The*

Strata was a very successful hotel, at one stage being the largest beer selling pub in Sydney. I enjoyed the work, and especially the social opportunities. Brother Brian arrived from Vietnam on leave and the girls in the Strata gave him a serviced apartment for his whole leave, during which big parties were held. Mel made a basic mistake; he opened a restaurant in Manly. When the management found out he had to leave, being deemed as having a conflict of interest. I stayed for a couple of more months before getting my next job, with Parker Hannifin, an American fluid power company in Artarmon, where I spent the next six years.

Life at Parkers, and Undercliff Street was never dull, but out of the blue another opportunity to travel arrived. Sven Paterson from Wisconsin sent a letter inviting me to join a University expedition to study Central American traditional medicine. I was to be the expedition coordinator, i.e. donkey man. Being keen to once again impose myself on the world, I set about organizing myself. First, get a U.S visa. This meant satisfying the Consul that I had money. To solve this, I borrowed money from everyone in the Newcastle, depositing the cash in my Bank account and getting a Certificate of Balance showing my wealth and then returning funds to friends. Then I had to have transport. Air fares across the Pacific at the time were very expensive, so I got a passage with the French cargo line Messagerie Maritime to Los Angeles and a plane fare from New York to London with BOAC. Duly presented myself to the US Consul, Marilyn Meyer, who made it her mission in life to deny me a visa. Having been forced to accept my financial and travel arrangements she demanded that I show my accommodation in the States. I had to produce a letter from Sven about the expedition, but unfortunately, he had also said that if I wanted I could get a job; that was enough for Ms Meyer, I was going to deprive some American of a job; visa denied. Had to reluctantly write to Sven and decline what would have been an interesting time. President Trump would have been proud of her!

'The Newcastle' continued to provide many good times. Sydney underworld was at the time dominated by two men; Abe Saffron, Mr. Sin, and Lennie MacPherson, Mr. Big. Two of Lennie's 'Girls', Gloria and Gwen were regulars and Gwen had taken a shine to me.

One Saturday while drinking with her and some others a pushy guy in tight suit and trilby hat kept trying to join our group, telling us that if ever he had trouble he always had his 'little friend'. I asked if this was a cheque book or gun, as I pulled back his suit lapel. Question answered in the latter. He liked telling everyone he worked for Lennie; Gwen made a quick phone call from the back bar, and soon a very large guy came in and asked, "Gwen, where is the guy who works for Lennie?" He had disappeared, never to be seen again.

Sydney in the Seventies a haven for US servicemen on R & R. A friend, Bob, was a chef and decided to set up a restaurant in Kings Cross. As he was organizing the set-up he was visited by men from Mr. Sin, who informed him he would be buying his supplies, liquor, furniture etc. from certain nominated outlets. Bob changed his aspirations and fitted out a yacht as a Chinese junk on the Harbour and did very well with the R & R trade. In The Newcastle one Saturday we persuaded an American soldier that the immersing of a choko, a nobbly green vegetable, in the beer glass was an old Australian custom, which he partook of.

One of the patrons was a well-known journalist for the evening paper; he one night approached me to ask if I would take out the barmaid, whom he fancied, and he would then come and break in on our date and take over; I told him to get his own women. Another time the employer of my friend Peter Milligan approached me and demanded to know Peter's whereabouts; Peter was with employer's wife, "Tell Milligan I am waiting for him with a shotgun," was the message, passed on and ignored.

'The Newcastle' was never short of 'Interesting Characters', none more so than Paddy Black. A wild Irishman, Paddy was never afraid to go for the Main Chance. At this time, in the 1970's, mining was on everyone's tongue. Poseidon Nickel in Western Australia was in 1970 a small nickel producer, in 1971 their shares at one stage reached $270. They are now .04c. Paddy decided to become a Mining Magnate; he started two Companies, one Blackstone Minerals, and attracted quite a bit of investors' money. At one stage he decided to place Mining Claims on a whole town in New South Wales; first claim on the Masonic Temple, none on the Catholic Church. He arranged flights for some investors to his Claims in WA. Unfortunately, none of Paddy's Claims bore fruit, and many Share Holders, including me, were left with Share Scrip with which to decorate kitchen walls.

Back in Sydney, Paddy pursued other ventures; at one stage he tried to find capital to make an electric waffle iron, but he was ahead of his time. One 'venture' was to have a physical altercation with a policeman at the El Alamein Fountain in Kings Cross, which resulted in a spell in Long Bay Jail. Never letting a chance go by, Paddy managed to have his complete set of teeth replaced, courtesy of the Jail. The last time I saw Paddy, in the Strawberry Hills Pub, he lifted me up and carried me around the bar, shortly before his death.

Apart from regular work, other opportunities sometimes arose. One was setting up an airline. An English man I knew, Clive, was a pilot. He had a club foot, but otherwise very fit. He wanted to set up an amphibious airline servicing islands in the Pacific which were without landing strips, such us Cook Islands, some Fiji islands, Samoa. He had the permission of the King of Tonga to base it in Tonga; he recruited me for my accounting 'skills'. We set about organizing planes; Grumman Gooses from the US, finance through a Sydney man with 'contacts', Peter Barbarich. Things were going well until we were informed that the funds would be coming from the US 'Family', and our stake would be 1% of the Company. Time to bail out; being tied up with the Mafia was not recommended. We got our seed money back and left the idea with the 'Family'.

Undercliff Street life became somewhat more settled as time went on. Relationships that lasted anywhere from one night to a couple of weeks changed when I met Fay. Fay was a nurse from New Zealand, and had been, in South Africa, the Theatre Sister for Doctor Christian Barnard who performed the World's first heart transplant. Fay moved in and was my first real adult love. After some time, she decided to go and work in a Central Australian Mission, and to drive there in her Fiat 500, what I called a Toy Car. She told me later that if I had asked her not to go she would have stayed. Another potential life changing moment missed. Fay later went back to South Africa and married an Aide-de-Camp to the South African President.

Tina became my 'steady' next. She was ready to believe in Extra Terrestrials, and at a party one night told me to watch closely a well-dressed man; his suit she said, had no seams, proof that it was welded, and he was from Outer Space. Linda, an English nurse, moved in until she departed with John, a ship's captain whom she later married. John later moved to Canada and married a Canadian; years later I stayed with them in Vancouver Island, where I was often introduced as "the boyfriend of the girl I married".

THE OUTBACK BY AIR

Travel was still very much in my blood, and an opportunity arose at which I gladly leapt. A friend, Lyn, signed up for a trip around Australia by plane, and asked if I would like to join. Yes, of course. Three four- seater Cessnas, twelve people. We set out from Griffith in New South Wales, starting with Leigh Creek in South Australia. Apart from the three pilots, most of my fellow travelers were English. My pilot, Stewart Savage, owned a wine company in Griffith, and generally after he had taken off I would do most of the flying aloft, he of course landing.

Flying North, first stop the town of Fink, where we taxied right up to the pub before setting up camp in the main street; traffic not posing any sort of a problem. Next on to Andado Station, on the edge of the Simpson Desert, where our organizer had arranged a stay. This had to be extended as when taxiing for take-off our propeller hit a marker and broke off a piece. A new propeller had to be flown up from Adelaide, which took a couple of days. In the meantime, the Station owners returned from Adelaide where they had taken some cattle to be sold. After agisting them and getting some weight on they sold them, for the paltry sum of $10 a head. On the way back from the sale bought some Kentucky Chicken for $5.

Alice Springs next stop; camped by the Todd River and explored the nearby canyons and attractions before hiring Mini Moke cars and heading for Ayres Rock, Uluru. Camped out at the foot of the Rock, and next day a few of us climbed to the top. Now, since Uluru has been handed back to the Traditional Owners, climbing the Sacred Rock is not allowed without special permission, but I found it to be a moving experience as myself and the young English couple were the only temporary inhabitants, apart from a circling eagle.

Further North to Katherine, and a cruise on the Katherine Gorge, North to Darwin, at one stage navigating by ground features; Mount Hopeless was not an encouraging beacon. Flying into Derby in Western Australia we found ourselves to be on the same flight path as a local, he being not sure of his altitude had me looking anxiously out the window; when Derby Control came on the air; "Watch him Bert, he's bigger than you". We managed to avoid a collision.

In Broome, the group descended on the Roebuck Bay Pub with lots of local people. I got into conversation with a young Italian, who after a couple of hours announced he had to go. He was married to an Aboriginal girl who had leprosy and was living at the mission run by Nuns near Derby. The others had by now departed for a BBQ on Cable Beach; I was still in the Pub at closing time. Had to get to the camping ground, now the Cable Beach Resort. Stood in the middle of the road and stopped the first car. A couple of young Aboriginals agreed to take me but first had to go to the 'other' pub. After a couple of beers, we headed out of town to the creek bed where a number of Aboriginal men were camped. A couple of more beers and chat; they were carpenters heading for Perth from Darwin, but soon said we had to go as there was a big fight brewing. Got back to camp about 3am, fight avoided. The trip continued to Dampier, Geraldton, Perth; across the Nullabor, Port Augusta, Adelaide home to Griffith, a great month's trip.

Work at Parkers continued, I was the Accountant, Peter Coroneos the Company Secretary. The CEO Alan Hyslop and the Sales Manager Jim Godsell were English friends who had both parachuted into Normandy on D-Day. Alan was also President of the Staff Club, and at an Annual Meeting I was, without my foreknowledge, voted in as President. Very awkward, but he took it well. Being an engineering company, staff BBQs at Undercliff Street now had stainless steel BBQ plates. Again, lifelong friendships were formed, particularly with Tom and Des from Purchasing and Alan and Tony from Sales. I also did my bit for Women's Lib; our favorite after work watering hole was the Longueville Hotel. One evening a dozen or so of us, including three females, were sharing drinks in the Public Bar, when the Manager approached me with a worried expression, asking that we get the women to not drink in the Public Bar. I told him right away that if women could not drink with us, none of the patrons there would be back. Next night we were back, and the No Females in the Public Bar policy was Dead.

After six years, Parkers decided to leave their North Shore premises and move to Castle Hill, which for me was a long drive, so I decided to look for alternatives. I soon had a job in North Sydney with a Real Estate development company owned by Roy. The Company specialized in getting people who would normally have a great deal of trouble getting finance for a home, into brand new project homes, generally in the Western Suburbs. My job, together with Nicole, was keeping track of the various financial transactions involved. Roy's methods of 'arranging' finances were not orthodox, and after some time attracted the attention of the State Consumer Affairs Bureau, which we came to call "Head Office". Nothing illegal but penalties were imposed. I decided to leave.

I had met Dennis Disney while at Parkers, when he was working for our Collection Agent; he was now also a resident of Undercliff Street. One day he got a call from Melbourne from Geoff Bishop, offering him the job of setting up Bishop Collections in Sydney. Soon after I was also working for Bishops, as a Sales Rep. I was fortunate enough to make some good sales, including a wine company, which Dennis informed me was the best sale in the business; this was my first endeavor as a salesperson, but not the last.

Undercliff Street had many memorable residents, probably none more so than Jack Greenwell. Jack was studying to be an Accountant, but his nocturnal social life provided more highlights. One night after a meal in a Greek restaurant, Jack decided he needed the toilet, and descended steps to the street where two bemused plain clothes cops found him hanging onto a light pole tending to his needs. Jack was deposited in the nearby Central Police Station where he was expected to spend the night. Dennis and I negotiated with the Desk Sargent, and after counting out enough money for our taxi fare home, offered the balance as Bail, to which the Sargent said, "Sold", and we three departed.

Jack some time later decided to leave Sydney and go to Perth, looking for adventure. The day of his leaving of course required a suitable all day send off in a number of City Pubs, at one of which our hero managed to down a yard glass of beer. By the time we, Percy Poulos, Peter McDonald and myself managed to get him to the train Jack was in no fit state for a 4000 kms trip across the Continent. Railway Police promptly arrested him, at which Greek Perc declared, "If this is democracy you can kiss my arse". Appeals to Democratic Justice fell on deaf ears, and this time Jack spent the night in a cell. Next morning in Court, Percy was charged with some offence, and when his words were repeated, the Court burst out laughing; "Dismissed". By now sober, Jack was given a lecture and let go. A newspaper article headed 'Jack was on the Wrong Track' is still in my archives.

Jack remained one of my best mates over the next 40 odd years. He worked for oil and mining companies in Australia and Libya. He contracted MS and throat cancer, which he vehemently refused to associate with cigarettes until he passed away in 2015.

The Golden Sheaf Hotel in Double Bay was a favorite venue, and here I met Julie, the central core of my life for many years to come. Julie was a dentist, over from Adelaide in South Australia, working with a dental surgery in the Eastern Suburbs. She was living in Paddington, next door to the home of an old Tivoli girl and her partner, who ran a 'Two Up' school in a shed in his back yard. During breaks in the 'action' she would take plates of cakes and cups of tea for the punters, successful or not, surely the most civilized Two Up school in the country.

Undercliff Street by now had only a couple of residents; Julie moved in and shortly thereafter decided to look for a dental practice of her own, not before having replaced all my upper front teeth with Crowns. Julie quickly found a practice in Glebe, an inner west suburb, and set about completing the transaction with Jack Wainwright. Glebe is on the South side of the Harbour, making Neutral Bay a drive too far in rush hour traffic, so we set about looking for a place to buy in Glebe, soon settling on a townhouse, into which we moved; Julie of course now the principal earner and therefore the sole owner.

Having now left Bishops, earning a living became a priority. Ever since my travels in Europe I had fancied the idea of owning a restaurant, along with no doubt thousands of other idiots, and set about looking. After checking out about 10, came across a French restaurant called *'Le Zig Zig'* in the main street of Redfern, on the first floor. Redfern, on the edge of the City was dominated by the Aboriginal population in Eveleigh Street and nearby areas, and consequently had acquired a reputation in Sydney for unsocial behavior. Nevertheless, we negotiated with the Bank for the purchase price of around $20,000 and I bought the business from Carla, the American owner.

LE ZIG ZIG

'*Le Zig Zig*' became the centre of my waking life, the day starting in the Fish Markets at 8am and finishing after midnight with the putting out of rubbish. My chef was Trentis, or James, Greek, trained in the Hotel Australia, was an excellent chef; Barbara the main waitress, and a kitchen hand. We seated 65 and opened Tuesday to Saturday lunch and dinner. My Landlord was Greek. I tried to maintain the French atmosphere with taped, mainly French music and the windows painted with French themes. I set about promoting with as many local businesses as I could and set about a changed lifestyle.

Redfern, despite its reputation, was a lively inner-city scene, and because of its near city locale was on the verge of acquiring 'trendy' status. However as is usual for me, my timing was slightly off. While maintaining an excellent menu and good wine list, along with some good media reviews, the reality of restaurant survival in Sydney seems to revolve on a three-month cycle; a good review is followed by a period of excellent patronage, then another restaurant, or others become trendy. We managed to keep just in front of the wolves, and developed a core of regular patrons, together with others attracted either by word of mouth or various promotions. One lunch, for some reason I had the whole American cast of Porgy and Bess arrive. Among my regulars was Father Ted Kennedy, the local Catholic priest. Father Ted was not your normal priest. He held that the Church was there to serve the local people, not the other way around. If some people had no home, he would allow them to sleep in the Church. He was highly unpopular with the Church hierarchy who tried to maneuver him out or install other priests above him, but the community would have nothing of it. Father Ted would often have lunch with us.

Another regular was Mum Shirl Smith. Mum Shirl was a Saint. She was a tireless worker for her Aboriginal community and was awarded an MBE for her efforts. Aboriginal convention places the family as paramount, with sometimes unfortunate consequences. People arriving in the City, usually Redfern, from the country, usually had nowhere to live and arrived on the doorsteps of any relative they could find. Arriving cousins, uncles and aunties tended to create housing problems. Mum Shirl stopped me in the street one day to complain, "Dan, I am always getting pulled out in the middle of the night to translate for some Koori in Long Bay (Jail), but you know, I have been burgled 14 times BY Kooris. It makes me tired". On a lighter note, Father Ted, Mum Shirl, a Nun and Christian Brother were having lunch, and I could not help myself, telling them, "This is the first time I have had Mother, Father, Sister and Brother on the one table".

Another of my regulars was Sir Lennox Hewitt, at the time Head of TNT Transport, previously head of the Prime Ministers Department, later Qantas. He once told he I made the best vodka martini in Sydney. One day he called and asked if I could do a special dinner for a special guest, on a Monday night. James could not work that night, he had another job. Who was the special guest? Gough Whitlam, former Prime Minister of Australia. Sir Lennox had invited Gough and about a dozen others to his favorite restaurant, and I had no chef. Not only that, he wanted a particular wine which I had to search for and find. James said he would prepare the meal. Stuffed shoulder of lamb main course, choice of a couple of entrees and desserts, I would have to cook and present them. Julie was called in as waitress. The party arrived and the 'second team' performed without a hitch. While I was slaving away in the kitchen I was summoned by the Great Man, who had two helpings of the Lamb and pronounced it, "The Best Lamb dish I have ever had, Comrade". I only wish I could have thought to bring a camera; typical of my disastrous record in the photographic world.

Always looking for something to enliven things, I asked Nicole, with whom I had worked in the North Sydney office, and her partner, if they would play and sing on Saturday nights. They did not think the main content of their feminist repertoire would be suitable, but they were popular features of Saturday nights, even inspiring an occasional sing-along from some happy partygoers.

One Christmas, closed for a holiday, Dennis Disney and I took a trip to WA in my Chrysler Galant car. Being a 'Naturalised West Australian' I like to go back every year or so. Dennis does not drive so the deal was when we stopped for the night he would set up camp, pass me beers and cook dinner. We had a great trip, staying in Perth in Phil Gurrin's home while he was way. Coming back across the Nullabor I pulled in for fuel at Cockalbiddy, virtually in the middle of nowhere, where I went into the bar to pay and found myself standing next to Phil, on his way back to Perth. On return to 'Le Zig Zig' discovered that the Indian girl who did the cleaning had turned off the electricity, resulting in a lot of meat in freezers no longer smelling good. I should have warned her.

Dennis and I did another trip, taking a train from Sydney, hiring a car and heading north through Silverton and on to Tibooburra, supposedly the hottest town in New South Wales, also home of the Family Hotel, featuring murals by two of Australia's most famous artists, Donald Friend and Arthur Boyd, who were stationed there during WW2. Further on to Cameron Corner on the border junction of Queensland, New South Wales and South Australia.

Back in Broken Hill, while climbing hills to see some statues noticed how Dennis was laboring. Sometime later I noticed that Brother Brian was similarly restricted and made me once again grateful for having given up smoking, thanks to Julie. One Sunday she introduced me to her friend Les, who, after about 20 minutes under hypnosis had me giving him my cigarettes and lighter, declaring I would not need them again; I have not had a cigarette since, some 30 plus years later. Les, who weighed about 150kgs and smoked like a chimney, made his living from getting people to lose weight and stop smoking.

Restaurant life is not what many dreamers imagine it to be; long hours, hard work and often marginal financial rewards. After two and a half years I decided that I was not to be the Paul Bocuse of Redfern and set about selling 'Le Zig Zig'. One of my main problems was that my Lease was about to expire, and Julie, as

Co-Tenant was understandably reluctant to enter into a new Lease; in effect this meant I was selling with no firm tenancy. So, entered into my life, Theo. After a few people had looked at the restaurant and pulled out, young Theo decided he wanted it. He could not get immediate finance for the total asking price of $22,000 but paid a deposit and Stock with the promise of the balance, Soon! I found myself in a situation with virtually no choice. Theo took over, James left. Theo had a new chef who roller-skated around the kitchen while Theo dreamed of impossible expansions. I called in on him whenever I was in the area to listen to his promises. Theo had taken over the restaurant, but it was still in my name until settlement.

One night at home I got a call from the Redfern police; there had been a fire at the restaurant. This was a Monday night. I immediately called Theo and told him to meet me there. He denied any knowledge, saying whoever had done this must have climbed in by the roof and for some strange reason tried to set fire to the bar area using an accelerant. I fronted the Police, telling them that Theo was actually the manager, no further action was taken. Redfern police must have had bigger fishes to fry.

Theo had his family backing to the extent of keeping him afloat, but not of paying his debts, and Theo now decided he needed not one restaurant but two. He bought a large restaurant in Sydney's South West. Again, I called in on him whenever possible. Theo, for all his ambition was rather naïve about how things worked in Sydney. He told me about his 'dealings' with a prominent Police officer, also a well-known Rugby League player who called every week for protection money. Theo was aghast that such things happened. Not long after Theo went Bankrupt, and I said goodbye to any prospects of getting my money. Years later I got a phone call. Theo had gone into a new career in kitchen supplies but was still bankrupt. He blithely announced that he needed a letter from me saying I had been fully paid. My slamming down of the phone was followed a few minutes later asking if I had cooled down. He never got his letter, but I don't think that really bothered him.

TELECHECK

Time to move on; applied for a job in sales with Telecheck, a US franchise of a cheque verification service, which allowed retailers to accept cheques which Telecheck would guarantee. I think I got the job by saying that if I had this service I would not have needed the "No Cheques" sign on my restaurant. So, began my next six year's life. Credit cards were becoming the dominant payment method in shops, but cheques were still widely used and accepted. I was soon making good sales, and after a couple of years became Sales Manager. Signing up some of the major retail chains helped propel Telecheck Australia to the top performing franchise in the system, with the result that I was chosen to go to the US to receive the accolades. A trip to Amelia Island resort in Florida was arranged.

The prospect of spending one week in Florida then returning was not, to me, acceptable; one month travelling in the States was. I arranged to get a one-month Pass on Greyhound buses for $150 and Return Flight from Los Angeles one month hence. Departure from Sydney had a slight problem; airport evacuated because of a bomb scare; an X-rayed suitcase was found to not contain the suspected bomb, but a Bible and a coat hanger. Arrival in Los Angles, via Hawaii where I became aware of the strange habit of some American women of applauding whenever the plane touched down. I assumed they must have been holding their collective breaths the whole trip.

Spent a day in LA; went to a Bank to change a Traveler's Cheque where a young African American teller asked if I would do her a favor and say "G'day", duly obliged. Crocodile Dundee was sweeping America at the time... Long flight to Jacksonville via Augusta, picked up by hotel car, then I sat in Reception for some time before I was informed that the Front Desk manager was checking me out; she liked Australians and gave me a seal of approval. Over the next week I was there Corrine and I became something of an item, probably not the normal hotel guests' welcome, but delightful nevertheless.

A week of Telecheck seminars, meetings, socials punctuated with outings with Corrine to nearby villages and bars. Billy Joel was staying at Amelia Island and playing in nearby Jacksonville and one night sang a few songs in our late-night bar. One night one of the Telecheck girls told me I had to sing Waltzing Matilda for the couple of hundred assembled guests. Backed by the local country band, whom I asked to pick up the tune from my none too wonderful voice. Did my best until I got to the last verse where I forgot the words; "big finish guys" and retreated from my one and only public recital.

The week in Amelia Island ended; I was supposed to carry the large trophy awarded as Australia's prize home, but as I was going to be travelling made sure they sent it home by air. Set out by Greyhound starting in Orlando. On the way we picked up four guys who seemed very happy to be aboard. The driver quickly made sure they knew the rules; late on board you get left and no smoking 'funny' tobacco. One of them, a young black guy with muscles on muscles was sitting next to me and I asked where they were coming from. "The Penn, Man". Enough information. Spent a couple of days in Orlando, home of Epcot, or Disneyland, then south to New Orleans.

I spent a few days in New Orleans, going on a river boat cruise to battlegrounds, all the usual things, a French Quarter Jazz Festival, soaking up the City and loving it. Found myself in the front row for a concert in Lafayette Square, Doctor John arrived by helicopter and someone passed me a cold beer; great way to spend a day. French Quarter Jazz Festival featuring Wallace Davenport, plenty of exploring. Loved the atmosphere in New Orleans. On a bus one day a large African American woman got on declaring, "I'm short a Dime, anyone got a Dime", and was nearly knocked down in the rush to give.

On to the bus, to Memphis, did not get to Graceland. St Louis all the sights including the Arch; while eating meal in a restaurant overheard a couple at the next table. Son to Father, "I want to go to Australia and start a new life". Father to Son, " You don't want to go there, everyone is a drunk and spend their lives falling out of bars". I could not resist, and in my best 'Educated Australian' accent asked if they knew if Paul Hogan had won an Oscar for Crocodile Dundee. Next Washington DC. Stayed in a motel in a seedy part of town, walked through the streets without any troubles. Toured the US Senate building, Vietnam memorial, Smithsonian Museum, various bars, Lincoln Memorial, as usual mainly wandering around getting half lost but enjoying it all.

My highlight of the trip, New York. The bus landed me in the Port Authority Terminal, found a hotel on the phone, the Iroquois in 44th Street, where I booked in for three days. Walked around the back of Times Square that night, did not get mugged, decided New York's reputation was undeserved. Spent days in places such as the New York Library, up the Empire State Building, Washington Square, Little Italy, Soho, Central Park. A night in the Blue Note Jazz Club featuring Brazilian singer Tania Maria, with me perched on window sill. Every day going down to Reception and adding 'one more day' to the eventual total of twelve. Met up with one of the Telecheck girls and spent a day with her as she did some cold calling around the dock area; one very attractive woman to whom she was talking took it all in but only wanted to know what I thought. I thought more time with her would make New York even more attractive, but time said NO.

The Iroquois was the sister hotel to the famous Algonquin, in the same street and I made my drinking home its front bar, where conversations were always lively and enjoyable. My favorite tipple was Jack Daniels and Dry, introduced to me by Corrine in Amelia Island. One night, for a change I asked for a 'Jack and Coke'; the barman, an ex-Marine drawled, "You know, most people who ask for that have a ponytail"; I switched back to Dry.

Another day with Telecheck, bought a couple of slices of pizza and was asked on leaving, "what about a tip". My reply "I'll give you a tip, make a better pizza", was probably not greatly appreciated, but I make no apologies; I have always hated the American purchase prices followed by 'Plus Tax, Plus Tip', and think (a) that their computers should be at least the equal of Australia's and include Taxes in the price, and (b), US employers should pay their staff proper wages. But I am never going to win.

My last Sunday, and my New York highlight. Eggs Benedict breakfast on 5th Avenue, Guggenheim Modern Art Museum, Metropolitan Art Gallery, stroll through Central Park to Strawberry Fields and in the evening a concert in Carnegie Hall by a young Greek pianist Dimitri Toufexis. I have always aspired to a concert in Carnegie Hall since I bought my record of Benny Goodman's 1938 Concert. The evening finished by a night cap in an 'English' Pub.

Next stop Kansas City, Kansas, where on arrival it was discovered that my suitcase was not on the bus, had to spend a couple of days daily checking before discovering it had been sent to Dallas, Texas. It eventually got back to Kansas. One of the Telecheck guys took me out for steak dinner and later a Chinese lunch where I stunned everyone, including the Chinese owner, by asking for chopsticks.

A 24-hour trip to Denver via Cheyenne through lots of snow. In Denver I got directions to Boulder, Telecheck headquarters. A guy had set up a tent in the bus station to give information, for free, to travelers; he had spent time on the road and wanted to help any other lost souls. I got the nominated bus, made a phone call and was picked up by Telecheck girls I knew from Florida. They promptly bought me a bucket sized margarita, followed by another, booked me into a motel and took me to Telecheck where I was feted. A few days over Easter, awoke to find Denver under a foot of snow, but had to catch my next bus to San Francisco.

While having a drink in a downtown bar with a bunch of journalists, fell into conversation with the partner of one who suggested she and I should leave and she would show me the town. Nob Hill hotels for dancing, Chinatown for eating and finishing at her home; where she asked when I would be back in town. My stupid honesty confessed that I did not know, so we said goodnight. Next day when wandering saw a sign advertising all day tour of City and highlights for $8. This was the sort of price one might expect in India; was picked up from my hotel by limousine next morning and taken on an amazing tour of City, Haight Ashbury, Fisherman's' Wharf, Sausalito, Redwood Forest and a boat cruise around Alcatraz, best $8 I have spent in years. San Fran is also home to the best dressed beggars in the world, one of whom followed me nearly all day without success.

Final stop, a quick flight to Los Angeles for a day. A bus to downtown, as usual sitting in the back where I was the only white face, which did not seem to meet with approval from some more front of bus patrons. Sat next to a young girl who was getting grief from some of her fellow passengers; when she left the bus, she made it clear to her protagonists that when her boyfriend gets 'out', they would be in trouble. Spent the day wandering, also looking for a public toilet, which did not seem to be around. Wandered into a bar where my accent was identified by a Swede as 'Aussie''. Later caught what I thought was the Airport bus, which dropped me in a seemingly deserted South LA barrio. Could not find a human, much less a taxi. Walked to the LAX Freeway, where I managed to hail a cab, who declared that he would dine out for weeks telling of the crazy Aussie hailing cabs on the Freeway. And so back to Sydney.

Working for Telecheck over the next five years was generally enjoyable and successful and Julie and I also managed to fit in travel, to the Philippines, Bali, Norfolk Island, New Zealand and Fiji. On one earlier trip to Bali with Linda, we were laying on the beach at Kuta, with Indonesian Army helicopters flying in with body bags slung underneath. The Pan Am plane had hit Mount Agung, with no survivors. One trip with Julie and Margaret, her mother, to the Cook Islands and New Zealand with Air New Zealand was cancelled by Air New Zealand because of a strike. When told, I contacted Air NZ and objected, saying that the Cook Islands section was gone, but they had to re-instate the New Zealand portion, which they did. As usual, we looked after ourselves with no hitches except for one hire car, a Holden, giving trouble in some place in the South Island, which provoked comments by some locals of "Aussie Crap", reinforcing my general impression that the south was much less friendly than the north.

On my previous visit some years earlier, I had arrived in the South Island late in the day and set out to hitch to the west of the country; had to go through the Buller Gorge, which had recently been hit by earthquakes and was practically deserted. I walked without getting any lifts, found a deserted farm house by the road and thought I may as well sleep there, but was soon surrounded by thousands of possums, which made sleep impossible. Kept walking in the dark, by now through hilly country with no sign of humans, except for the occasional car which drove past without stopping. Could hear water in the gullies below, but any attempt to go down in the dark would be most unwise. Rolled out my sleeping bag and slept by the road. Next morning walked on to where two Policemen leaning on their car gave me a slow handclap. My not friendly greeting and enquiry revealed that two escaped murderers were in the Gorge and I was set up as bait; all motorists were told not to pick me up. Welcome to the South Island.

Another happier occasion, waiting for a lift to Wellington, a white sports car holding a very attractive blond stopped, and to my amazement invited me aboard. While chatting I asked what was the best restaurant in Wellington, and that night took her there; not the usual hitch-hikers response, and Lesley made the remaining time in Wellington most enjoyable.

THE NEXT SIX YEARS

Six years at Telecheck seemed to be about my limit to be in one job; I was 'headhunted' by an opposition company, Chequecard, from Perth. Telecheck could not match the offer and I somewhat guiltily made the move. Chequecard had a different operation, in which they gave members a card which enabled them to present the card with their cheque to have it approved. The card was free for the first year, and it did not take long to realize the fundamental flaw in this; the Company had no cash flow for twelve months and a considerable exposure to 'bad' cheques, not to mention staff, offices, and general expenses in Sydney and Perth. My first week there I was sent to Perth to meet the owners, Nick, a gold prospector, Laurie Connell and Steve, whom I knew in Sydney, and had been the reason I was offered the job. Chequecard also sponsored the Perth Wildcats basketball team at considerable expense. The rise of credit cards over cheques in retail made both Companies existence less relevant. Back in Sydney we ploughed on for 6 months, but the curtain was finally drawn.

About this time my father, who had become increasingly more ill, entered a Nursing Home, where after a few months he passed away. He had had a hard life, made more difficult by being barred from the Law. Several jobs and futile business ventures left him depressed and I believe happy to depart. One of the last things he said to me was, "I guess I will soon find out if there is such a thing as an afterlife", to which I had no answer. The Australian flag draped his coffin.

Not many years later, Mum had battled on, working in hospitals to nearly 76 years of age. I managed, together with Brian, to see that she was reasonably comfortable, until one day two Police arrived at my flat. Mum had collapsed in her shower and must have died instantly. She was 82, universally acknowledged by all who knew her as a wonderful woman.

THIS SPORTING LIFE AND INDIA

My active sporting life was confined to occasional social cricket, tennis and swimming. One night a dinner invitation changed that; Julie and I met Greg Aitken for a dinner with a publisher of an 'adult' magazine and a 'Madam Lash'. During a lively and enjoyable evening Greg mentioned that he was in a group starting a Cricket Club, and I leapt aboard. The 'Ten Past Eleven' players were a mixture of actors, writers, film directors and occasional others like me. In one of my first games I hit 3 sixers in one over, but as usual did not go on to a great score. I bowled with occasional success but was not the star I had aspired to be in my youth. Saturday afternoons in Summer were accounted for, for years to come.

The TPE, as we became, lasted 21 years, which for a Suburban cricket club, is no mean achievement. We never actually won a competition, but were always competitive, competing in the level of what would be about 7th Grade in Sydney Cricket. My playing career commenced at age about 40, hardly my peak, and finished when I decided that my bowling was becoming embarrassing. I was elected President later, keeping me involved with a great bunch of men and boys, mainly Stephen Wallace, Greg Aitken, Ned Manning.

Travel was always uppermost in my ambitions and led to my great idea; a cricket trip to India. I set about promoting this and formed the Half Moon Bay Cricket Club for the purpose. A dozen or so players from the TPE and other clubs signed up, and I approached Air India. They arranged for Bob Simpson, the former Australian Cricket Captain to organize an itinerary, which he did. A great trip was set out, starting in Mumbai, Pune, Goa, Agra, Varanasi, Delhi and places in between. One by one our cricketers dropped out, leaving Julie and me as the sole members of the Half Moon Bay Cricket Club. Wherever we went Indians were anxious to meet the cricketers.

In Delhi, with a free week on our hands I arranged to get a bus up to Nanital in the Himalayan foothills. An overnight bus trip landed us at the town entrance early morning. The town is set out around a sacred lake; no cars are allowed beyond the town's entrance. The hotel in town was closed for the Winter but re-opened for just us. After 2 days, arranged for a taxi to take us further; accompanied by a young Sikh couple on their Honeymoon. We spent the whole time with them, but after a couple of days were asked if we could eat at separate tables, as they were vegetarian, and we were eating meat. I immediately said we would eat vegetarian and we continued to eat together. One village high up was the site of 'Gandhi's Ashram', where we spent a night sleeping on grass mats on the floor, which did not thrill Julie, but she survived.

For the whole trip we had drivers and arranged accommodation, much different from my earlier Indian experience. In Agra I asked if our driver could join us for a meal, but he had to decline and sleep in the car. In Ajmer, Rajasthan, while waiting for our elephant ride up to the Palace, an Indian man, when told we were from Australia, said, "You must know my friend Richard!" "Of course", I said, "very tall man". "Yes, was here making a film". I do know him, Richard Walker from Sydney, had been in India making a documentary. I wondered how many people he had asked before hitting the jackpot.

Julie and I were one day in the maim Mumbai Market; Julie went shopping, disappearing into the interior. I waited outside and was approached by a Hindu Pilgrim. Many men decide, after a time in normal life, to go 'on the road', with just a begging bowl, asking for nothing but food, spending their time in prayer and meditation. While talking to him we were joined by a young woman with a baby on her hip, who in language I could not understand, began berating the pilgrim as a fake, saying any charity should go to people like her, rather than him. A crowd gathered to take sides in the discussion, all in good humor, but I had to leave them to it as Julie re-emerged from the market; another illustration of Indian street life. In later years, India has rejected the Congress Party of the Nehrus and Gandhis and Hindu Nationalism has arisen again, which I believe is the road to disaster, in line with all Religion in Politics.

India continued to impress, from Udaipur Palace, Ellora and Ajanta, Agra and the Taj, and once again in Fatehpur Sikri then back to Mumbai. Our driver picked us up and drove to the airport for the flight home and asked for our tickets. Problem; they were in his office in the City. He made calls and managed to get us past Customs and Immigration while our tickets wended their way through early morning traffic. They made it just in time.

LIVING ALONE

By now we had moved out of the Glebe townhouse, and Julie bought a house in Arcadia Road, one of Glebe's best streets. We lived there for a few years before Julie fell out of love with me, and I made way for Peter, with whom Julie had a daughter, Georgia. I moved out into a flat in Glebe Point Road, and began a series of sales jobs, none of which were very successful. Eventually I got a job with a Queensland Angus Cattle stud, selling investments in cattle embryos, this time with a company car. The obvious main targets for this type of investment were professionals and investors, but there was a saying in Sydney circles, "If it has four legs and eats hay, don't buy". I managed some sales to Dentists, but not enough to sustain a living, so back to the drawing board, but keeping the car.

Stayed with cattle about 8 months; David N, originally from Iran, from where he said he left because of the rule of the Mullahs, had a Company which acted as business brokers, and my job, to sell businesses which we listed. I quickly became aware of the truism that buyers should be well aware of sellers' rosy projections of their business; sales, however were made, ranging from corner cafes to large wholesalers. At one stage I enlisted my great friend John Dengate to write ads for the listed businesses. John was one of Australia's best known, and loved, singers and composers of folk songs, often with Left political themes, but mainly traditional Australian stories. John was known as The Bard of Glebe. We had become friends soon after I had moved to Glebe and stayed so until his untimely death, aged only 74. John's wife Dale, sons Lachlan and Sean, remain great friends.

Julie had a very successful Dental Practice in Glebe, where she was known as the Dentist to the Stars; actors, writers, TV and film personalities. Judges and Lawyers were prominent patients, and Julie was a high-powered personality dentist; sometimes some of her staff could not keep up the pace, which is where I re-enter the scene. David wanted me to move to Brisbane to open a branch of his business, which I was not keen on, and at the same time Julie asked if I would take over the Receptionist position in the Surgery. Male receptionists were not a common sight, but I said yes. So, commenced my latest, and last career move. Practice Manager sounds more macho, but receptionist is the reality.

Two years after becoming Julie's receptionist, everyone was shocked to learn that Julie had been diagnosed with breast cancer. She quickly had an operation, which was successful, but decided that enough was enough; she would retire, which meant selling the practice. Julie interviewed a few prospective people, with her principal concern that the new dentist would be the one her patients would relate to; after a short time, she decided on David Nguyen.

David was a young Vietnamese man, who had come to Australia, via Malaysia and various boat trips at the age of four. He came with excellent references and proved to be the ideal choice. He also retained me as receptionist, which without blowing my own trumpet, was also an excellent choice. Receptionists in a dental surgery are, apart from keeping things running, principally the PR of the practice. I modestly think I do that well.

David quickly settled in making a success of the practice over the next 9 years that I was there. One day he announced that I should go to a seminar in Hoi An in Vietnam, quickly accepted. The seminar was for only one week, but as is usual for me, I decided that one week is a waste, so asked if I could take my annual leave and extend it out for a month; No Trouble. To cover my job, I asked my friend Arthur Crutchfield and took off for Saigon.

A MONTH IN VIETNAM

A week in the resort in Hoi An was not hard to take in the company of about twenty other Dental workers, but still doing my usual tricks. Got on a motor bike and forgot the exhaust is close and hot, result a nice burn. The next three weeks promised more exotic adventures, so got to Danang, Marble Mountains from where the Viet Cong used to bombard the USAF base in Danang, some of the results still evident.

Next a train to Hue, where I stayed a few days wandering and hiring tuk guides to the Citadel and City, site of some of the bloodiest fighting of the 'American War'. Some 5000 American casualties made it the costliest battle. As usual, got caught by one scammer, offered a ride and beer, finished up donating some money to 'brother' in Brisbane for a wedding present of a bottle of scotch. Major destination, Hanoi, where I went to the hotel of the sister of Danang hotel owner. One day while sitting by the famous Hoan Kiem Lake, casually accepted an invitation from 'Kim', which led to her shadowing my every move. The owner of my hotel said she was a liar and thief, and my attraction was just 'Lust', which was not really true. Kim would wait outside the hotel waiting for me to appear, and to be fair, she did introduce me to some of Hanoi's attractions, including the famous water puppets.

Meanwhile in the hotel, met the other guests, including Clive and Luna from Melbourne, meals shared, and friendship carried on back in Australia. One night the hotel owner, after what must have been quite a few beers, insisted that we should try a local delicacy, and proceeded to produce cuts of dog in various sauces. I have no desire to repeat this culinary fare, but while it was not exactly pleasant, also not unpleasant. Dogs, and other animals continue to be treated atrociously in Asia; and dogs continue to feature in diets throughout. Hopefully there are signs that changing attitudes are evolving. Did the pilgrimage to 'Uncle Ho's Mausoleum'; after a hot day's walking in Hanoi, he was looking better than me.

Hanoi is an attractive city, particularly the 'French Quarter'; organized through our hotel a day on Ha Long Bay, beautiful but the large city being built on an overlooking mountain did not bode well for its future attraction. Moving on, I had wanted to go to Dien Bien Phu, but instead took a bus up the mountains to Sa Pa, where I spent a few days, cruising to nearby mountain valleys and villages on the back of a bike, based in the usual cheap, comfortable hotel looking over the view to Laos and China.

Time to start back, another hair-raising trip down the mountain to Hanoi, Kim still lying in wait. Soon after, when I found her looking through my wallet, left her in tears and her dream of me paying her air fare back home to The Delta in tatters. Caught a plane to Saigon, only a few days before returning to Sydney. Altogether a great trip, leaving me with the desire to return some day.

BROTHER BRIAN, SISTER CAROL

Brother Brian "Blue" was now a well-known personality in North Queensland; a Vietnam Vet, he became the President of the RSL Club in Atherton; he was also well known to many 'clients' at the Commonwealth Employment Service in Cairns. One such ritually presented himself for Unemployment payments, wearing filthy clothes, a shaggy beard and long hair. Brian challenged him on his appearance, refusing to authorize payment until he at least looked as if he was looking for work. The 'client' refused to accept this and said he would just go to the next office. He proceeded to try four, heading south, but was told at each, "Blue says you are barred". He turned up back at Cairns cleaned up, shaved and wearing clean clothes. I visited Brian a few times over the years, and wherever we went he was known, respected and well liked.

Brian suffered from Emphysema, and one day I got a call from the woman who did his housework to say he was dying. I immediately arranged for Arthur to again cover for me and flew to Cairns, where I was met and taken to Atherton. Brian was in hospital and only lasted a couple of days. Yet another victim of cigarettes. His funeral, as an ex service-man was organized through the RSL, and I spent a week seeing to his affairs before driving his new car back to Sydney. He had left all to me and I shared some with sister Carol.

Carol, some years earlier, had had a child. Because the 'Department' had decided that Carol was not up to the task of bringing her son up, he was fostered out. Many years later I received a letter from a woman who had been fostered with Carol's son, and had done extensive work in tracing the Moloney and Singleton families. I made contact and learned many things about my ancestors, particularly my namesake and Grandfather.

ENOUGH OF WORKING, LIFE AS A "GREY NOMAD"

Back in Glebe, working for David; he bought the adjoining property and transferred the surgery from Julie's house, which she subsequently sold. David was an excellent Boss, apart from sending me to Vietnam, and I believe we made a good team for the next 9 years. I continued a sporting life with the Marrickville Golf Club, with an occasional win but no great distinction. Music and theatre, mainly at the Opera House, Membership of Sydney Swans AFL team, highlighted by seeing them win the Premiership in 2005, beating West Coast at the MCG in Melbourne. Active social life with plenty of goods friends, but time was marching on, and at the grand old age of 67 I decided to retire.

The prospect of retiring in Sydney was not enticing; my somewhat haphazard financial history meant I could not contemplate buying or even renting decent accommodation in the Sydney market, and so set about making alternative plans. I decided that a life 'on the road' had appeal, and so commenced my 'Grey Nomad' phase. My friends James and Merle Everard lived in Wangi Wangi on the North Central Coast. They had a caravan which I borrowed. I bought a 1996 Mazda Bravo utility, dual fuel and with some 230,000 kms on the clock. A few lessons on how to tow, reverse and generally handle a caravan and I took off for 3 month's cruising around New South Wales and Victoria without too many dramas.

Back at Wangi, the Everard's set off for a cruise, I house sat for them while looking for a van to buy. Found a 17-foot van with all I needed, particularly a double bed. Fitted electric brakes and paid $22,600 for my new life. While travelling, stayed mainly in caravan parks, with an occasional 'bush camp'. My general approach was to book into a town for three days and decide then to either stay longer or move on.

House sitting for friends around the country gave a break from van parks; friends in Perth, Melbourne, New South Wales south coast, Sydney, all go on holidays and leave their homes in my care, with occasional dogs and cats. The next nine months travelling in New South Wales and Victoria, mainly country towns and villages until friend Norma asked if I would like to join her on a cruise. She had a two for one deal with a Russian cruise company; given a choice I nominated a river cruise in the Ukraine, organized visas, paid air fares etc. I had worked and travelled in Western Europe at the times when Eastern Europe was extremely difficult and expensive, now was time to make up.

UKRAINE, EASTERN EUROPE AND S/E ASIA

With no definite plans for the rest of my life, typical really, travelling in Australia and occasionally overseas became life. I found that I could live and travel on a budget of about $500-$600 per week. After Ukraine, Eastern Europe, SE Asia, Canada, US, Ireland, England, China, all had highs and occasional lows. Odessa and the Black Sea to Yalta, Sebastopol, up Dnieper River to Kiev; victim of scam in Kiev, fake policeman got EU80 from me, EU100 from Norma. We were scammed by a policeman and his mate, and soon realized that the 'policeman' was one of the many ex-police; when they leave the police they retain their warrant cards, uniform and guns. Ukraine is a very corrupt country, politicians, police all on the 'take' in various ways. One major problem, very many Russians, which was exploited by Putin in the annexation of Crimea. Many statues of Lenin, all pointing to Moscow, none remaining of Stalin.

We were friendly with Alvin and Donna from Oregon. Alvin had Ukrainian ancestors and one day in Kiev decided to find them, and asked Norma and me to join him; hired a taxi and took off on a 100 kms plus trip to his ancestral village. Could not find a relative, but the village administrator introduced him to a family who had known them. They invited us for lunch, and turned on a real feast, which probably cost them a week's income. Hardly any English spoken, but the oldest Grandmother, with the help of a young girl who spoke some English, became very emotional telling me of the times they had endured during the War. A very moving day, and a real highlight of my time in Ukraine.

Altogether a worthwhile trip, finishing in Lviv before flying out to Warsaw, where I 'hit the road' for Lithuania, Estonia, Latvia, Czech Republic, Hungary, Austria. Maintaining lifelong habits, staying in Youth Hostels, where the advantages are not only financial, but the company of generally young people much more fun than the older inhabitants of hotels. In Olomouc in Czech I was presented with a coffee by a couple of Canadians, and in reply to my query was told, "You are my hero, I just want to be doing what you are doing when I am your age", at the time 70.

My hitch hiking days well gone, travelling by bus and train, mostly comfortable and cheap. On one bus from Krakow to Prague, the Czech student seated next to me tried to have the Chipmunk movie changed; the driver said he would have to have a vote, and the Chipmunk movie won by one vote. Democracy in action. Loved the Franks Hostel in Riga, greeted with a beer, near all night pub crawl with bunch of Scots going to a football match somewhere, led by a crazy local girl with a Cockney accent, all that remained of her English marriage. Next day found me standing within touching distance of Angela Merkel, who was about to be given a tour of the Museum of Nazi Occupation.

In Krakow in time for big celebrations of the 600th anniversary of the defeat of the Swedes and Teutonic Knights, also 1910 Independence and 100th birthday of pianist and composer Paderewski. Lots of dressing up in medieval costumes, jousts; found myself in the front row following the bouncing ball on the big screen and singing in Polish. Many highlights, including Krakow Salt mines, where a Danish guy fed me at least 6 large swigs of vodka. Young guy in my hostel tells me how he saves nearly all his money to buy medieval costumes. Joined various walking tours in Prague, Warsaw, Budapest, river cruise in Prague, Chopin concert in Krakow, 100 crosses in Klaipaida, erected and replaced every time Russians destroyed them. Tallinn hostel, older 'hippy' owner, I found to be an ex-Russian General, who smuggled people out of Russia and Estonia during occupation. My many discussions with local people in smaller East Europe countries such as Estonia, Lithuania and Latvia, reveal some anxiety about the numbers of

Russians who remain, often comprising a major portion of the local populations.

I had seen posters advertising the Poets Corner Hostel in Olomouc, in the Czech Republic, so headed there. It was run by an Australian and his Czech wife. I was introduced to Frank Dvorak, caretaker of Museum archives, including Napoleon's Well, in a cave underneath a church, where Napoleon is said to have drunk during one of his campaigns. The Town square has a medieval clock tower featuring the customary jousting figures; during occupation the Soviets had them replaced with Working Class Heroes, where they remain; the originals are kept in storage, to remind people of the Occupation. Frank had worked in Sydney and asked if I could send him a photo of his Sydney home, which I did on return. A concert in the church with a 1000 pipe organ was spectacular.

Last stop Budapest, five days in Aboriginal Hostel; the owner had been to Australia. Lots to see and do, Terror House, films of Nagy and Gabor's trials, Budapest Jazz Club, Buda Citadel, German anti-aircraft museum, night in Ruin Bar, where any unoccupied building can be taken over as a bar. Last days in East Europe, bus to Vienna, hostel near WestBahnhof, some cruising with Chas, who was road manager for rapper Snoop Dog, now cruising Austria looking for gigs. Went into Bank to change various left-over cash, was told "zu wenig", too little. "Great service", says I; "Where are you from?" "Australia", at which the transactions were completed. Train to the Airport For the flight to Bangkok.

Silom Road Hostel, major errors of judgement; got sucked in by shil for Unseen Travel, decided to let Ida organize my month in SE Asia. Ida organized trips which turned out to be a disaster, starting with the bus trip to Vientiane, overnight. Full bus, had an Israeli girl occupying three seats in front of me, refusing to make a slight adjustment to give my seat a little more room. Unfortunately, she was typical of a lot of Israelis, very arrogant. In Vientiane found the Hotel Chendamay, after 24 hour bus trip, needed a beer, down to bars by the Mekong River. One girl offered 1 hour, 500 Baht; intrigued by the possibility that she was Boy Girl but declined. Teamed up with Ahn, who was my girl in Laos.

Met American John and his daughter. John had declined his countries invitation to partake of the Vietnam War, and has lived in Laos, Thailand ever since; he talked of how Laos is being destroyed by illegal timber cutting. After a few days in Vientiane, caught bus to Luhan Praban, the famous World Heritage listed town. Off the bus, tuk tuk driver tried to tell me he did not know Thomsit guest house, told him to take me to Police, whereby he found someone to give directions. Walked up to the night markets and found myself standing shoulder to shoulder with Clive and Luna from Melbourne, first met in Hanoi.

After a few days enjoying the sights, back to Vientiane and Ahn for a couple of days, then bus to Hanoi, 7 hours wait on Border, arrived late in Hanoi bus station, taxi drivers not helpful, even hostile. A Viet girl tried to help but was threatened by taxi drivers. Eventually got a taxi to Lake View Hotel, which was the wrong hotel, but booked in for the night. Typical stuff up by Unseen Travel, whose itinerary showed a day in Hanoi, which turned out to be less than 12 hours at night. Flew from Hanoi to Saigon, Thang Lien hotel, once again the wrong one, changed to Hong Loi Hotel, met Mr. Pat, travel agent who told me he had heard of Unseen Travel's stuff ups, and would no longer deal with them. He took me on his bike for a day trip to Chu Chi tunnels, and I also did an all-day trip on back of a bike around Saigon, Museum of War Remembrances, Giant Buddha, markets. Agreed price 500,000 Dong, on arrival my driver tried for 1,000,000 but told him a deal is a deal, which he accepted. A river trip on the Delta rounded out Saigon, now called Ho Chi Min City but only, as a guide informed us, by Embassies and Airlines.

Next bus trip to Siem Reap and the 'No Problem Hotel'. A 3 Day pass to Ankor Wat $60, plus tuk tuk $20, money and time well spent. Girl selling books, "I give you credit". Nightlife with Karen, German tennis pro, Swiss guy very keen to know Karen better but settled for a night of cheap cocktails. Policeman offered to sell me his badge for $20, "I get another one". A few days in Ankor Wat then bus back to Bangkok and the HQ Hostel to collect my suitcase and resume 'discussions' with Unseen (Useless) Travel. Although they had basically booked buses and hotels, often the wrong ones, and vastly over-priced, I was inclined to complain to the Tourist Police, but that would also have been a waste of time. Let anyone travelling to Bangkok beware of Unseen Travel.

Last stop an indulgence, a week in Surat Thani Resort, fairly basic but comfortable. Another couple, Canadian, also victims of Unseen Travel. Anna gives massages in garage, the lady selling petrol to bike riders also sells beers and her and Anna and some local girls are pleasant company. One young girl asks me to find her an older man, "All Thai boys are interested in is drinking in bars".

OZ AGAIN

Settling back in Oz now revolved around caravan travel, house sitting for friends, mainly Bette in Ballan in Victoria where I am practically a resident, even joining the Golf Club, later with Andy and Anne in Sydney before hitching up again and heading West, stopping off at Wilpena Pound in the Flinders Ranges. Picked up two Germans in South Australia who were members of the Carpenters Guild and had to spend one year away from Germany working in their trade, not allowed any contact with home; they were heading for a job in Port Lincoln and I wondered how Australian apprentices would handle that.

Back In WA, dropped in to the Norseman pub for a beer with Maryanne and her crew of mine workers. They had just struck a good vein of gold and were celebrating that, "everyone will get paid this week". From Kalgoorlie down to Esperance, where instead of heading West went East along the wonderful coast, beaches and capes such as Cape le Grande, Hellfire Bay, Thistle Cove and the Pink Lake in Esperance before heading for Perth via the South West, visiting Phil and Jen in Busselton and staying with Phil Gurrin in Perth.

ELEVEN MONTHS AROUND AUSTRALIA

Having made several repairs to caravan and car I was ready for a long trip across the North and back down to Sydney. Set out on the day a mini tornado hit Perth, fortunately in a nearby suburb. Geraldton first stop to see my 'twin' Frank Roche, on to Kalbarri, Hutt River Province for a chat with Prince Leonard of Hutt, who had seceded from Australia some thirty years earlier over Wheat Board controls and has a certificate on a wall saying he does not have to pay Australian Tax. Not sure how that works. Prince Leonard died in 2019, with the status of the Province still unclear.

Shark Bay and Monkey Mia, Hamelin Pool and Stromatolites, the source of life on Earth billions of years ago. Carnarvon's Mile Long Jetty, and the old whaling station. The guide was telling her customers that it had been closed in 1960, but I told her that I had seen whales being processed there in 1962. On to Ningaloo Reef, some diving looking for Blue Whales, but none seen. Onslow, explored Cape Range National Park, Old Onslow, and the huge piles of salt being loaded for export. Monkey Mia, supposed to have dolphins coming up to be fed fish on the beach by tourists; the day I was there, rain, two people standing in the water with fish, no dolphins.

Port Hedland is the export port for the huge iron ore mines. Got talking with an owner of a local museum who had two children qualified to work in the mines, but she says mines will not hire locals, who seem to be only able to get work in service stations, supermarkets. A few years later, when the mining boom busted, they seem to be changing their minds, but the North West is still predominantly Fi Fo - Fly In Fly Out.

Further north to Marble Bar, reputed hottest town in Australia, then Broome, most expensive tourist venue in WA, Derby where

I took a 4-wheel drive trip to Windjana Gorge and Tunnel Creek, in the King Leopold Ranges, site of Jandamara's rebellion. He led what was nearly a civil war against the WA Government in the 19th Century and was finally killed in Tunnel Creek after being betrayed by women in his group, but gave the Government a big scare in the meantime. Fitzroy Crossing booked into a van park on the River and did the Geikie Gorge walk and river cruise. Had a beer in the bar, and an old Aboriginal man, Arthur, asked if I would buy him a beer, which I did, low alcohol, and was surprised an hour or so later when he bought one for me. The bar was run by a young Canadian woman who kept strict control of the local patrons, who sometimes gave the feeling that this may be necessary.

Mabel Downs Station, where I took another 4-wheel drive tour, this time to the Bungle Bungle Ranges; I have finally realized that paying $50 for an all-day tour is much more sensible than bashing over bush tracks in my 12-year-old Mazda. In Kununurra, an all day cruise on Lake Argyle visiting the sandalwood factory. Large plantations of sandalwood are proving to be one of Lake Argyle's big successes .

Anunfortunate incident in Kununurra illustrates some of the social problems of some indigenous communities. While I was sitting outside a store, a young woman with a baby was pushing a full shopping trolley when she lost control and it spilled the contents. As I was sitting nearby I picked up the groceries and repacked it; she did not seem to know what had happened, and soon knocked over the trolley again. A group of youths just looked and laughed, while I repeated the packing; not sure what that says about Race Relations, but simple kindness certainly did not get a look in.

Katherine, where I stayed for about a week, cruise the Katherine Gorge again, after fifty years. Very friendly group in the van park, disturbed by a young Kiwi girl who set up her tent behind me and went to the camp kitchen where she proceeded to racially abuse some German tourists, telling them to leave the country. She was so out of control that someone called the Police. By the time they arrived she had calmed down and knew she was wrong but said she could not control herself. The Police were gentle but firm and took her away.

A week in Darwin for some needed repairs to the van before heading back to my old work place Tennant Creek; now no longer a mining town, all but one mine having closed down years ago. It is now very much an Aboriginal centre, museums and art galleries seem to be thriving. Went out to the site of what was the main Peko Mine, now a museum of mining, met Rhonda who was also a former worker in the mines as we stood on top of what was once the main shaft.

Now into Queensland, a week in Mount Isa, Cloncurry, John Flynn of the Outback museum and the Qantas First Hanger where I spent the day. It also rained for the first time since I left Perth three months earlier, so I gave the car and van a bath, knowing that in another couple of days my efforts would go unnoticed. On to Winton, where Banjo Paterson composed that great Australian ballad 'Waltzing Matilda', and the town has the Waltzing Matilda Centre, which a few years later was burned down and replaced. My timing was good; Winton Races, spent the day and a few dollars on horses still running. Ted Egan, a great friend of the Dengates, was performing there and I told him of John Dengate's ill health. The other great attraction is 'The Age of Dinosaurs' outside in the country which has a very impressive collection of fossils and artifacts. There are supposed to be imprints of a dinosaurs' stampede, but some people say they are just cattle imprints. I could not tell.

Longreach, home of Qantas and the resting place of the first 707 plane; spent the day in the Qantas Museum, then the Stockman's Hall of Fame. Tourism seems to be doing very well in this part of the Outback. On to Barcaldine, where the Australian Labor Party had its origins under the Tree of Knowledge, a large tree in the middle of town which has now rotted down to a stump inside a cement reproduction. A cutting has been taken and is growing as "Son Of". Very impressive Workers' Heritage Park displays a fine collection of Trade Union history. Little town Tambo, site of the first and only Qantas plane crash.

Chatted with a local who told me of a scam about 'stolen' cattle. A local reported 869 cattle stolen from a Station somewhere in Queensland where there was no evidence of any such number but got paid insurance. Sounds like he should be working for one of our 'Financial Institutions' where his talents could be put to good use.

Through Charleville, Roma, Dalby, home of Australia's 'Flying Saucer', which once was supposed to fly for a few minutes. While leaving the van park here I was stopped by an attractive young Aboriginal girl asking if I would give her a lift home, a few streets away. She was in the car only few minutes before placing her hand on my knee, and having it gently removed. She then asked for $10, also refused. I took her home and she asked my name, hers Jenna. I only hope she later managed to avoid the consequences of offering $10 sex to passing tourists. Passing through Pomona, visiting friends Roy and Norma, Phil and Yvonne in Buderim, then back to Sydney and Bathurst after an eleven month trip around North Australia, particularly the fabulous Kimberleys, highly recommended.

The New Year, 2013, Bette once again off on a cruise, Africa and beyond, I am house sitting again, fitting in trips to Melbourne, Ballarat, becoming a regular Victorian, subscription to Melbourne Symphony, Art Gallery, then start arranging trip to Canada in June.

CANADA, AMERICA AND IRELAND

Arrive in Vancouver, settle in to Samsun Hostel downtown, before calling John Phillips on Vancouver Island, where I spent a week, being enlisted as BBQ cook for John's birthday party. Learning things Canadian; Vancouver Island has nine distinct Police Forces, which to me sounds like democracy gone overboard. Back in Vancouver, Stanley Park, City attractions. Another thing happened which I had never experienced in many years of staying in hostels around the World; someone stole a voice recorder, but more bizarrely, took my foot orthotics; hope they fitted their new owner.

Spoke to a young girl begging in the street who did not seem to know how she got there or why; must have been partying hard, but the number of young beggars setting up semi-permanent camps in main streets was not a good look. Bought a phone and told the sellers that as I would be in Canada for only six weeks, I would need to get it unlocked. Big mistake! Phones cannot be unlocked in North America, which I think has now changed, but that caused me more disasters later on.

The Rockies were the chief reason for being in Vancouver, so set about checking out the Mountaineer train, which I found would cost about $1000 a day for a four day trip. Back at the hostel, joined a group of backpackers for a four day bus trip for $400. Eight of us, mostly female, Irish, Dutch, Spanish, staying mainly in Eco Hostels, kayaking, walking, Bridal Veil Falls, Kanoola, Lake Louise, Banff, Jasper, Silver City, Bluff Knoll, Lake Moraine, glacier walk. At one mountain we learned it was the object of a World War 11 offer. Seems in Scotland the people had, as a gesture of gratitude, decided to name a hill in Dwight Eisenhower's honor. Canadians thought they could go one better and decided to name a mountain after him. A great ceremony was arranged, but Dwight could not make it; a golf date had taken precedence. There is no mountain in Canada named Eisenhower. Altogether the four days with a great group was a lot more fun than I would have had on a tourist train trip. In Calgary flew to Chicago, where I had a tube of Vegemite confiscated by Customs, "You Australians like this stuff". I refrained from comment on American Sweet Tooth to the heavily overweight Customs Lady.

Arriving in Chicago late at night, the taxi driver who got me to and into the Greektown Hostel in South Chicago earned his $10 Tip. Chicago in a 40 degree heatwave, was made more uncomfortable by me getting Gout in a big toe, needing to borrow a walking stick for a day. Getting baked dandelion leaves tea from the hostel helped, enabling me to spend a few days exploring Chicago skyscrapers, canals, galleries, local bars and restaurants in relative comfort. A room-mate in the hostel was a Russian, who never seemed to do anything but spend time on his phone, probably setting up 'hits'. He reminded me of a young Dutch guy in a Bangkok hostel who sat on his bunk for five days watching movies on his phone.

Would have loved to spend more time in Chicago, but back to Canada on the overnight bus via Cleveland, Indiana, Ohio, Des Plaines to Toronto where I got a room in the university summer hostel. Another first; a room all to myself for four days. Naturally the highlight, a bus trip to Niagara Falls and 'Maid of the Mist' trip, sitting with a young Polish girl who was always anxious about something I could not fathom. Looking across to America, glad to be experiencing Niagara from the Canadian side. Montreal beckoned, so another bus overnight, then a long walk to the Auberge Bishop, a very classy building once the home of a wealthy businessman; a large stained glass portrait of his beautiful wife overlooked the stairs. Few beers in the nearby Irish Pub with an English ex Royal Marine rounded out the day. Five days in Montreal, admiring the Old City buildings, Old Port, but particularly the Beau Arts museum. Montreal Comedy Festival on, supposed to be one day French, one day English, but in typical Gallic style, all the English seemed to be French. Had my first steak in the Habibi Restaurant since leaving Sydney, surrounded by Hubble Bubble smokers.

Another bus, 17 hours, $69 later, arrived in Boston. The bus driver must have been new, did not know how to find the bus station, but fortunately some of the passengers were able to assist. A taxi to the Backpackers Hostel in Everett, South Boston, home for the next week, but I could quite happily have made that two or three. Into the City, to get my Charlie Card, for discounts on public transport. To anyone old enough to remember the Kingston Trio song about Charlie, who was trapped on the Boston subway because he did not have the 10c exit, Charlie has now been immortalized. While waiting fell into conversation with John, who was moving back to Boston, and he decided to show me the town. We spent most of the day exploring Boston Common, Paul Revere's house, Bunker Hill Museum and Monument among other sights. A much appreciated Welcome to Boston.

Over the next days, Salem, USS Constitution, redline Freedom Trail, House of Seven Gables, Harvard University, where I spent a couple of hours in the Natural Science Museum, Boston Museum of Fine Arts; the first room had paintings by Monet, Gauguin, Picasso and others worth millions of dollars. Wandering the city, Cheers Pub. While waiting for a train in Everett, overheard a conversation with a couple with a friend; "Heard you had some excitement yesterday", "Yes a young guy here shot two people, don't know why, then the Cops arrived and shot him". Just another day in Paradise.

At the same time Boston was avidly following the story of local lad James "Whitey" Bulger. He was the Number One Wanted Man by the FBI and had just been captured in California. James was in his 70s and had been on the loose for years. When captured he had been convicted of 32 murders, on contract. When asked Why? He simply said, "It was my job". He was also an FBI informant against the rival South Boston Irish gangs. A search of his house in Santa Monica revealed over $800,000 in cash, so he had a well-paid job, but now will spend the rest of his life in goal. Whitey's 'rest of life' however was cut short in October 2018 when he was murdered in goal by a cell-mate. Johnny Depp played him in the 2015 film Black Mass.

A Whitey postscript; seems Whitey wrote to a juror on his trial for 11 murders where he describes how he was a participant in a CIA experiment with LSD. According to the CIA's chief chemist, he was offered reduced time to take part In research on schizophrenia, which ultimately caused him, and others, to become not responsible for his violent actions. We will never know.

Time in Boston ending, tried to unlock my Virgin phone, no can do in North America. Chris from the Hostel gave me a tee shirt and hoped we could meet again, maybe in Vegas. In my regular Brazilian restaurant on the last night Kevin, ex-US Marine Corp, and his family, plied me with cocktails, and next day another bus, this time to New York.

Port Authority Terminal where I had arrived on my previous visit some years before. Walked to the Big Apple Hostel on 45th Street, $94 for three nights sharing with Philip, an English wine maker on his way to the Napa Valley. I had three main objectives, walk the Brooklyn Bridge, catch the Staten Island ferry and visit the 911 Monument, all accomplished. In Times Square an attempt on a World Record was in progress; the biggest number of people in their underwear, target 2600; don't know if they made it but it was without me. On my last stay in New York, my regular watering hole was the front bar in the Algonquin Hotel. Front bar no longer there, but a couple of beers for old times' sake. Philip and I did some wandering around Wall Street, Central Park, 5th Avenue, another visit to the fabulous New York Public Library; Deli's for food, Bars for beers. Still love New York.

Booked Aer Lingus from JFK to Shannon in Ireland, one of my better decisions. Arrived after night flight, Customs guy said nothing to see in Shannon, bus to nearby Ennis, booked into hostel; Grace in reception tried to get me away from snoring Pom, earplugs useless. Plenty of music in local pubs, day trips to Cliffs of Moher, the Burren, 30,000 acres of shale. Loved the story of Red Mary, an Irish rebel who led a band of merry Irish against the British. An Army company had her baled up in a small one turret castle; Mary decided to negotiate, seduced the Army Officer who married her and joined the rebels. Make Love not War. Walked the Cliffs, found the Moloney Family Crest, 17 families still in the County, chat with a carpenter in pub about the number of vacant new houses, priced around EU150,000; locals cannot afford them because of Ireland's economic problems. 3 nights in Cork, went on Ring of Kerry bus tour; this being Ireland it rained all day, but being joined by Sarah from San Francisco made the rain unnoticed.

I had enquired about renting a car for my Ireland adventure, but when disclosed my age, over 70, the prices became double, so buses and trains were transport, but all without any problems. Bus to Sligo via Galway, where I booked into the Harbor Side Hostel. I quickly discovered the Swagman Pub, where Mick and Mick became regular drinking companions. They had a band and mowed lawns in the day time. On Sunday Mick was anxious to show me the local district but unfortunately phone numbers got waylaid so I had to do my own exploring of the WB Yeats museum and other local attractions. After one long session with Mick and Mick I decided to walk back to the Hostel at 1.30am, got lost. Eventually found someone at 3am, asked if he knew where the hostel was, "Sure it's just there, 50 yards away".

Dublin by train, had booked the hostel in College Street, opposite Trinity College for one week. I had thoughts of seeing the Book of Kells at Trinity, but the queues hundreds of yards long put me off that idea, as I am sure that the viewing would be cursory at best. Spent more time in Dublin Castle, O'Connell Street Post Office, walking along the Liffey, exploring the City, the Oscar Wilde Memorial, a train trip to Howth, north of Dublin, where I spent a day. Heard of the death of my best mate John Dengate in Sydney. Doyles Pub near the hostel became a regular spot; met a young guy from Uzbekistan for a few beers; he has a Jewish mother and a Moslem father; if only there were more like that. A week in Dublin comes to an end, booked the ferry to Holyhead EU69, got a taxi to the ferry cost nearly as much EU39.

Arrive in England horrified to discover the train from Holyhead to Cardiff, 87 Pounds, should have gone on internet to get my English Rail discount card. More disaster, had to change trains in Crewe, got off with my case and discovered I had the wrong one, identical to mine; scrambled aboard as the train took off for London. Had to explain that this stupid old Colonial had stuffed up. Trip to London, back to Cardiff where I had booked into a hostel in the shadow of Cardiff Arms Park, Rugby sacred ground, but to me Cardiff is more interesting as the home of Doctor Who. Wandering the City, Cardiff Castle, the city seemed to be overrun with Manchester City football fans. Back at the hostel watched a great game with Cardiff actually beating Manchester, probably for the first time ever. Three Aussie boys from Kununurra in WA got me into a drinking game where they were confident of drinking me 'under the table', but I reversed their anticipated outcome.

STOPOVER IN HERTFORDSHIRE

My mate Doug Jenner lives in a small village in Hertfordshire, Kimpton, my next destination. Doug picked me up from the Harpenden Station. Doug is a great folk musician and has been instrumental in establishing the Kimpton Folk Festival as one of the premier Folk Festivals in England. A great week with Doug, Julie, their children Max and Polly; I had previously been to St Albans and was impressed with the St Albans Cathedral. Nearby George Bernard Shaw's home, still as he left it, and the Roman ruins of Verulamium, the second largest Roman settlement in England. Country Pubs where Doug tried once again to convert me to Real Ale; I like the taste but now find English Ales quickly fill my stomach; must be getting old.

Next stop Oxford. At the hostel met a freelance journalist, also a part time speech writer for a Conservative politician. This is September 2013, Syria becoming more disastrous by the minute. The journalist, on his way back from New Zealand, and I watching the Commons debate on whether Britain should become involved. He was adamant that Britain should not. From the very beginning of the situation I have believed that Syria would become the greatest disaster on the Century, but as I told my friend, England now would only become involved if it was directly affected. Another instance of Little England rather than Great Britain, backed up by the Obama tentative approach, leaving Syria to Russia and Iran. The resulting flood of refugees heading for Europe unleashed a Right Wing xenophobic, even racist, backlash against the largely Moslem exodus, in Slovenia, Hungary, Czech Republic, Poland, Greece and Italy, while Germany despite the Alt Deutschland movement has largely accepted and welcomed the refugees. Britain and America largely unaffected by their role in the initial crisis.

My week in Oxford, Trinity College, Balliol Library, University colleges, walks and local pubs. Got a bad cold and decided to go to a doctor; was delighted and surprised to be told 'no charge', also at the chemist; "You are Australian". Donald would be horrified.

London; stayed at Generator Hostel near Kings Cross, share with French guys over for a concert, Belgian girls for shopping. Tower of London, Horse Guards Museum, Churchill's War Cabinet, things I never got to do while living in London for a year. Another photo disaster; somehow lost a lot of camera photos on England and Wales. Met up with Moira Jack, sister of my friend Margaret in Sydney, an Indian meal went well. Went to my Pub in Warwick Road, the Warwick Castle, it had not changed in 50 years. A photo of Ken the then publican posted on the wall. I bought train ticket to Bari in Italy, 277 Pounds.

WHERE THINGS BECOME UNSTUCK

Train trip to Paris, changed at Gare du Nord for Gare Lyon, one station on the Metro, surrounded by Gypsies or Arabs on a crowded train, my front jeans pocket, normally tight, but from being well worn was now quite loose. Did not realize the wallet was gone till halfway to Bologna. Fortunately, the stolen wallet was the travelling one, which contained EU110, but also my Bank Credit Cards and Cash Passport. Managed to get the cards cancelled by the Italian train guard, and my main wallet was in the suitcase; however, could not have the cards loaded again until my bank in Australia could get a new card to me, which would take over a week, leaving me with about EU400 on my spare Cash card and my American Express card, from which I could not get cash.

In Bari, walked to the Olive Tree Hostel in the Old City, many helpful locals finding the way, but also many not knowing Corte Altini, where hosts Aussie Dave and his wife Valentina were very helpful on computer and phone trying to solve my banking problems. I had not been to Bari since 1966, but it seemed to have not changed much; prefer Bari as Port for Greece to Brindisi, even though I still get lost in the Old City. Finally got the ferry ticket on Amex and departed for Patra.

Welcome to Greece! Trying to get a bus from Patra to Athens seemed to be something that the ferry staff did not want to know about. Myself, New Zealand couple and two German girls had to wait 4 hours, and the ferry staff would not even acknowledge our existence; one of the staff women got very upset when I took a photo of her. Just in time to miss the 11am bus from Patra to Athens, had to get a taxi to the Zeus Hostel, which at EU8 per night was the cheapest I had ever had. Basic but OK, roof top bar, easy walk to the Plaka where I found a restaurant that would take Amex.

Walking around Athens was a sobering experience; whole streets of shops closed down, graffiti everywhere, but the Plaka area seemed to be thriving with plenty of tourists. The Greek Financial Crisis very real on the streets. Walked up to the new Acropolis museum, very impressive, wandering through Roman Agora, Hadrian's Library; an old Coptic Church where the smoke stained walls and interior were being restored by students. In the hostel, I shared a room with four others, including an Italian girl who when climbing out of her upper bunk let her loose fitting underwear display all her attractions.

A week in Athens with virtually no money was not solving my problems. I had booked flights to China before returning to Sydney through Malaysian Airlines, who I discovered after searching, did not have an office in Athens. Flight Centre in Sydney were able to cancel the China flights and get me a direct flight to Sydney. A fight with travel insurance on return got me a refund of the $753 cost. With stop-overs Athens to Sydney 42 hours.

Back in Sydney sorting out the aftermath; the Paris pickpockets had got away with over $2500, which ANZ and ING both paid to me with minimum fuss. Paris Police sent a letter saying they had found my Driver's License. Back on the road again, van again 'principal place of residence', via Ballan in Victoria, across the Nullabor, in Kalgoorlie power steering pump gone, replaced for $550, on to Perth, met Sonia Gurrin whose father, my old mate Phil, had just died. After 6 weeks in Perth, back across the Nullabor to Ballan for more house sitting for Bette, off on another cruise. Peter and Julie arrive from Perth, took them on tour of Ballarat, Bendigo, Hanging Rock and Clunes. Back to Sydney, house sitting for Andy and Anne.

Cousin Bob, recovering from a hip injury, started a University course at age 62, while I spent the three months between Sydney and Bathurst, golf, sailing, movies, bought a second hand iPad and generally enjoyed life. House sitting for Robin and Graham in Terrigal. Diane and Carol came calling; Diane has been diagnosed with bowel cancer.

GERMANY, BUT NOT A GREAT HOLIDAY

Diane's tumors getting worse, she decides to go to Germany for treatment, and as she does not speak German and is not a great traveler, asks me to go with her; her Amex points paying for most of the expenses. Booked to fly to Frankfurt. Stayed in an hotel in the city before a week in an Air BnB apartment. Diane commences treatment with Professor Vogel at Frankfurt University, who is highly regarded and seems very impressive. Diane is in constant pain, which Vogel says is normal and part of the treatment. I take her out for dinner on her birthday and we go to an opera, Hansel and Gretel in the new Opera House.

Eventually to Martin and Ute's, who will be our hosts in the main apartment when we return from the next phase of treatment with Doctor Herzog in Badsalzhausen, a spa town about 60kms from Frankfurt. Diane was booked into clinic accommodation which she did not like, and so booked into the Hotel Weisnau with me. While Diane had daily treatment, I was wandering around the nearby towns and villages, also using the mixed Sauna. Nearby village of Nidde to the 11th Century Tower Jewish Memorial for locals killed in WW11. Two weeks in Badsalzhausen, very pleasant for me but not for Diane; she was very unhappy with the treatment from Doctor Herzog.

Back to Frankfurt where we settled in to the apartment of Martin and Ute. We were made to feel like family rather than paying guests. Ute is a dentist who was trying to persuade Martin to spend more time travelling and less renovating houses; Martin more intent on working for a good retirement income. We had a spacious apartment in an older building, with kitchen, TV, two bedrooms and bathrooms; luxury. I checked out the TV for news, only BBC and CNN, both crap. BBC had lots of ads and repeats,

CNN mainly American local news.

Diane had a friend in England who wants to visit; she can have my room while I go to visit Doug in England. Check Ryan Air, fare EU53. Their Hahn airport is halfway to Luxembourg. Martin drives me to the City to get a bus at 2.30 am. At the Airport, because I did not read the instructions in German, I am told I do not have a Boarding Pass, must go to another counter, where I am confronted by a 'Blond Bitch' who says the flight is booked out, and closes the desk. With steam coming out of my ears I return to Counter One where things were sorted, and I got a Boarding Pass, EU70, Flight 53. Resolve never to fly Ryan Air again. Arrive in Stansted, should have booked bus for Luton, not Victoria, had to waste another EU15 on bus, where Doug was waiting.

A great week in Kimpton; Julie is working on the Collectible Fair in Blenheim Palace where we spend a day, seeing Churchill's birth bed; closing the circle, as I had also been to his funeral. Stayed in Hotel in Woodstock while visiting Blenheim. Once again visiting St Albans Cathedral, my photo memories doomed again, losing another lot of computer photos. Flight back to Frankfurt on BA, paid for with Diane's Amex points. Martin takes us to Fleckenboher, a local drug rehab co-op started from scratch, now with 200 people. Train trip to Bad Holmberg, a day wandering markets, Romer Platz. Martin meets up with his friend Rolf and his 92 year old mother, also Manfred whom he has not seen in 50 years. Many visits to Markets, including Pink Market in Palmgarten, also back to Goethe Tower where Martin's friend Hans Klaus explains Ute's and Martin's relationships, both still married to other partners; seems I know other such 'couples' in Oz. Christmas is approaching and many festive outings are arranged by Martin, including a Roast Goose dinner in a Frankfurt restaurant.

Time in Germany is running out, Diane's treatment seems not very successful; she is in constant pain. I spend a whole day in the galleries in Shaumainkai before Martin drives us to the Airport. Diane loses her temper with Customs staff as her medicines are in her hand luggage. I am amazed that the Duty Free guy knows about Philip Hughes, the Australian cricketer killed a few days earlier in a Sydney match.

AUSTRALIA AGAIN

Back to Bathurst, shortly after the Martin Place siege. To Mt Eliza for Christmas, Jack is getting worse, has a fall in the kitchen and giving Pauline a lot of grief. Jack is trying hard and has more falls, but manages to stay cheerful for Christmas. I head back to Terrigal for Robin's 60th Birthday and New Year, then Robin and Graham off to ski in Japan and I assume control of Reg the dog and the two cats. While there Frank lets me know Mrs. Roche has died, aged 93. Shortly after Jack also passes away; back to Mt Eliza for the funeral. Perc and I both share some of Jack's exploits.

For the next three months, spent travelling between Sydney, Bathurst and Victoria, repairing car and van, then once again to Ballan while Bette goes off on another cruise. Seems everyone but me is travelling, but then I see an ad in the paper for a tour of China for $3000. I figure China, although I had to miss it because of my Paris 'intervention', a tour is probably a reasonable way to go. Booked for October. Meantime life in Ballan goes on. A wasp plague makes life interesting; they invade the house interior, a couple of Tiger snakes are around in the garden, but I am still playing golf twice a week.

On one of the golf days I have a dizzy spell, which lasts for about twenty minutes. After a week I do something really intelligent and go to the doctor. Tests commence, Ballarat for scans and x-rays, all seem good. So, commences years of tests and medications, two exploratory operations, constant monitoring including an implanted monitoring device, but ever since I have had no repeat of the original incident.

Life continues, Melbourne for visits with Pauline, Clive and Luna; Sue, who does volunteering with the Supreme Court has tickets for some interesting events there, including the re-enacting of the Eureka Stockade trial, and of course football at MCG. Bette returns in time for her 80th Birthday, I decide on a trip to Tasmania to see MONA gallery. Booked free flight with Amex, and hire car with Avis, all prepaid. When I got to Avis desk, was asked if I needed insurance. I said I was told insurance included; Oh no, that is only 3rd Party, full insurance is $45 per day. I declined, will just drive carefully. $45 a day would be enough to buy a new car. A hotel in North Hobart completed the deal.

Tasmanian trip was mainly about MONA, where I spent a day with the vast and varied art collection; also drive around to Richmond, Huonville, Mount Wellington, Kelting and Hobart. Enjoyed the week, caught up with Tony Hope for coffee in Salamanca Square; Tony has written books on Hobart history. A dinner in a Turkish restaurant; got into discussion with the owner. She had been a 'Gast Arbeiter' in Germany, her German husband a guest worker in Turkey. When our discussion turned to modern times, and I enquired when Islam would forget about something that happened 1300 years ago to create the Sunni/Shia schism; I'm afraid the discussion did not go much further. Continued on with Hobart galleries and museums, a walk around the foreshore to Bellerive, past the gun emplacements established to repel an invasion, not sure if it was French or Russian. Altogether an enjoyable week in Hobart.

Back in Ballan, my next medical event; started passing blood, extremely painful. Walked up to the local hospital at 2am, they could do nothing but booked me into St John of God Hospital in Ballarat. Next morning Bette, who had just returned from her cruise, drove me there where I booked in. Tests over two days determined that an operation was necessary. So, commenced my prostate history. Four days in hospital watching the World disasters, Bali executions of the Australian drug mules, Nepal earthquake, Sydney storms, drowning refugees in Europe put my troubles in perspective.

I had made a commitment to house sit for Andy, and although I should have stayed longer in hospital, checked out and with help from neighbor John, got the van hooked up, delayed departure a day, feeling weak. Set off at 7.45am, took a wrong turning to Hume Highway, drove through Yarra Valley, getting to Andy's just in time for them to leave for Tokyo, while I settled in for 6 weeks. To top it all off, my orthodontist, Tony Sved says I need big work, another $1500. More tests in hospital, all OK.

Still having a lot of pain, went to Glebe doctors, had another dizzy spell playing golf with Peter Grislis, doctor says I have a heart condition, but not serious, commenced seeing Professor Latimer, neurologist who had treated John Dengate, whom she said was her favorite patient. By this time, I have decided that my main problem is lack of fitness, and while trying to do more walking and exercise, think I need a disciplinarian, one of those long legged blonde Ukrainians would fit the bill nicely. I seem to have more tests and probes than seem necessary but will leave it to the experts. After three years of constant monitoring I am finally told all is no longer necessary and I am cast back out into the world.

Travelling up to Bathurst on snow covered roads before once again heading to Victoria. While there Jacqui called to say Diane had died. Back in Sydney for her funeral, attended by a large number of her friends and business clients. Driving back and forth to Sydney and Mt Eliza and Ballarat, finally something had to go wrong; approaching Albury, suddenly my clutch ceased working. Called NRMA, towed to nearby Howlong where I spent a couple of days while repairs were made. Howlong is a popular country golf venue and many beers were shared with men from a Melbourne club.

CHINA

Back in Sydney, more tests, more computer problems, Bob tried to do some adjustment on phone, managed to lose about 200 photos, mainly from Canada, US and Ireland. More car repairs and registration, all done before setting out on China tour. Flight to Beijing, met with other 42 members of the group, from all States in Australia. Beijing pollution very thick and I managed to get a chest infection which basically lasted the whole trip; only two days with no pollution when we were in the hills tea plantations. For me the highlights were the ceramic warriors at Xian, the Forbidden City in Beijing, the at least half a million people in Tiananmen Square, a Chinse acrobats show which was truly spectacular, the Great Wall, where I climbed to the highest part and pretty well exhausted myself, stopping to chat with a few locals on the way. I was travelling solo and became the object of envy with regard to hotel accommodation; all hotels were at least four star and I had a room to myself in all, also on the bullet trains, being traveler number one, had front seat with leg room.

Our guides were all knowledgeable. While travelling on the trains I was curious about the number of half- finished apartment buildings. There were literally hundreds of them along the railway lines. One of our guides explained how this is so. Much of the land on which they were built was farm land. The Party decided that the local Party cadres had certain quotas they had to fulfill in the time they were in their district; land cannot be owned, only leased for 70 years. A developer buys the lease on a block of land for, say, $1 million, goes to the Bank where he already has corrupt contacts, borrows, say, $5 million, then erects the 'ghost' buildings for, say, $3 million, splits the remaining $2 million with the Banker and Party cadre and moves on. The Party cadre has an impressive monetary figure to show for his five year appointment as 'development' and does not care what happens next. The buildings, all of which are about 20 stories high, are half finished and will require a lot more capital to complete; not his problem. James, our guide, explained this to the assembled group on a bus. When someone asked if he was taking a risk telling us this on the bus, he smiled and said the bus driver does not speak English.

Two days in the Longxi terraces, no pollution. Guilin, surrounded by limestone hills carved into fantastic shapes, the Reed Flute Cave also impressive. Flight to Shanghai, the Bund, River trip at night; asked our guide May, who has an Israeli boyfriend, if the Government pays for the electricity to power up the lights, big tourist attraction, but must cost a fortune; she says she thinks so.

Visits to Hanhzhou, the Tea Village, and a terrific water show on the water of the WestLake, with a cast of seemingly hundreds with music and costume. Back in Shanghai to the French Quarter, also found the hall where the first meeting of the Chinese Communist Party was held. Our guide May realizes that a group of 43 is too many, but handles everything extremely well, says she will advise the Company to restrict groups to 30. I had no complaints, even though I am not a 'Tour Person'; hotels all very good, altogether an interesting 2 weeks.

CARAVAN'S DEMISE, TRAVEL WITHOUT

Back in Sydney, Bathurst, Terrigal before leaving for Ballan again as Bette is off on another cruise. Arranged to also drive to Perth to house-sit for Peter Jeffery for three months. My Auntie Dot's funeral just before leaving.

Driving to Victoria, suddenly life changed. Near North Albury, driving serenely down the Hume Highway. Large BDouble road trains have been a part of life for the past 9 years, sometimes causing concern as they come up behind, requiring attention. This one caught me; very big, very fast and very close, causing a larger than usual vacuum between truck and van; van starts to sway with increasing intensity; I can do nothing but watch as the van overtakes the car sideways, in the air. All this in a matter of seconds but enacted in slow motion. The van crashes on its side in front of the car in the middle of the road. Fortunately the people in the car behind me could see what was happening and slowed the trailing vehicles to watch the drama. When the dust had settled I found myself still strapped in with no physical damage; climbed out to survey the scene. People appeared from everywhere to see if I needed to go to hospital, which I declined. Soon Police and tow-truck operators appeared and took control of the traffic jam, which eventually cleared in about two hours. I wandered around looking for items spilled from both the van and car, including 12 bottles of red wine which were all unharmed. I asked if the Police wanted to breath test me, clear of course. The tow-truck guys finally got the van upright and towed away with the car and took me to a motel. Called Bette to let her know, she came up next morning. Between trips from the tow-yard to Ballan got started in assembling my possessions, some of which were no longer worth saving. Took Bette to the Airport and settled in for two more months of Victorian summer.

Settled down in Ballan, organized the van and car insurance with no hassles. Total payout about $21,000. Computer problems eventually called for a new one. World dramas; David Bowie dies, Essendon Football Club found guilty of doping, weather hot, 39 degrees in Melbourne, Stock Market Crash, trips to Ballarat for movies and Gallery, Melbourne for cricket, visit Clive and Luna, Pauline and Sue. While waiting I am using Bette's old Commodore car.

Bette returns, I go looking for a new car in Ballarat, after a few days find a Holden Adventra, 2006, $8500. Never heard of the model, but it seems to have everything, including LPG. After a couple of test runs, pay cash. Have a hassle trying to get it registered, but with the dealer's consent leave it in their name until I return from WA. They trust me to not get any tickets while I am away. Without a van, packing is easy, and I am ready for another trip across the Nullarbor. On to Coolgardie where I stop at the Denver City Hotel, the same group of people in the bar as were there when I last called in some five years earlier. A TV movie had been made by a couple of Dutch girls who worked there as bar attendants which did not paint a rosy picture of the customers, but as they were mostly fly in fly out mine workers it would be hard to tarnish current occupants.

On to Kellerberrin, where I spent some years as a very young schoolboy. I arrived on a Sunday morning, so headed for the Catholic Church. Mass had just finished as I arrived, so I approached some of the parishioners for a chat, and noted that the convent school was no longer there, and the Church seemed much smaller than my boyhood memory. One of my companions pointed out a much older lady, who when I mentioned my name immediately mentioned my father; she was 92 and said Dad and her regularly sat together during Mass. Altogether an enjoyable trip down Memory Lane.

Back in Perth, settled in to Peter and Julie's home in inner city Mount Lawley, which is also the suburb I lived in when we first moved to WA after the War. Peter and Julie headed for Victoria for three months, I settled in with their two dogs. Took Sonia to Cottesloe beach for the Sculpture by the Sea; not nearly as big as the Sydney one, but good quality. 24/4/15 got a call from Random House. Some people had mentioned that I should write a book, so the Random House call had me persuaded, so I signed up to the commitment. Can only hope that my literary talents are up the challenge.

Three months in Perth visiting friends Sonia, Phil & Jen in Bussleton, Trevor & Pat in Dunsborough, Geoff Parker; plenty to do, ice hockey game, Fremantle Markets, drives to Hills, Saturday Poetry group, Gallery, dog walking. Jeffery's back from Victoria, having hit a kangaroo near Cockalbiddy. Peter had school reunion in Nedlands to which I accompanied him. Sonia and her son Mitch took me out for my 75th Birthday. Few more days in Perth before heading East again. In the middle of South Australia, Kimba, got a speeding ticket, 10ks over the limit, $417, most expensive ever. Back to car dealer to sort out rego, but still having trouble, have to do it in NSW. Had to drive with no number plates, just a note saying I was legal; fortunately, no Police took any notice.

Back in Sydney. House sitting once again in Terrigal. My cousin Winston, a young married man committed suicide, no-one is sure why. Attended his funeral in Kincumber, Central Coast. Federal Election night; Government returned by one seat. Prime Minister Turnbull makes a disgraceful speech, blaming opposition 'Lies'.

Jenny had called asking if I could house sit for her in Nambucca Heads on the NSW North Coast while she is in Europe. Spent a month at Jenny's house by the beach in Nambucca Heads, lots of beach walks, reading Jenny's book 'The North China Lover' before driving to Coffs Harbour to pick Jenny up on her return from UK. Watched Sydney Swans go down in AFL Grand Final to Western Bulldogs, their first GF win in 62 years. More Card frauds, this time have to cancel Mastercard, two entries from a US 'Health Company' for $931. I think this is the fourth time over the past few years.

With apologies to my Christian, Jewish, Moslem, Hindu friends and others, I feel obliged to rave on a little about the one subject that always seems to have the World in torment. Being brought up a good Catholic boy, who has somewhat strayed from The Path, I find myself often reflecting, and a year or so ago suddenly proclaimed to myself, "IT IS ALL TOO SILLY FOR WORDS".

RELIGION

Our little blue dot of a planet, stuck in the middle of billions of other matter, most of which are billions of light years away, has become the only one that matters; our God, or Gods, have seemingly found our blue dot and set themselves up as the reason we are alive; to worship Them and aspire to gaining Their approval, and hopefully a place in Their spiritual abode. We, however, are the ones who have set these admirable goals. The main trick is to have backed the 'Right Horse', so to speak; a very tricky road to travel, ensuring that at least 90% of us are doomed to be in the wrong stable. From Time Immemorial, whenever the first religion was dreamed up, someone was deciding that they would set up in opposition, and so it has been down the ages, with varying dire consequences for those left in the 'old' belief.

As a young Catholic I was taught that only baptized Catholics could aspire to the Ultimate Reward. Many years later, on National TV, Catholic Cardinal Pell was asked, "Can Atheists get to Heaven?", to which he replied "Yes, if they are good people". The next question was not asked, "So what is the point of being in a religion?". Later, in the Woody Allen movie *Café Society*, a condemned Jewish criminal declared that he was going to become a Christian, because, "They have an After Life, Jews don't". Subsequent investigations reveal this to be true of certain Jewish Sects. A Hindu believes in re-incarnation, everything from a hard place to a rock. Moslems believe Martyrs are entitled to 72 Virgins; what happens when they run out? What do female suicide-bombers get?

In my youth and early life I have accepted the Nuns' teachings that we must simply have Faith, no matter how many doubts we have. This is the corner-stone of all religion; the application of reasoned logic does not get a look in. Catholic Faith demands that we accept the infallibility of the Pope; the current Pope concedes this may not be so. Various Mullahs get up and preach all sorts of violent hate against non- believers; many Indian males decide they can rape women with impunity; Burmese Buddhists rape and murder Moslem villagers just because they are Moslem. The lists go back to the dawn of Time, Crusaders just a fore runner of the myriad slaughters. No religion can claim innocence.

Universal acceptance by all religions of the abhorrence of premarital sex has given countless excuses for murder, mutilation, imprisonment and ritual punishments. Current revelations about priests and other religious, mainly men, exposes the basic hypocrisy of much of the condemnatory preaching. Sex is, after all, in its purest expression, Love, and Love is supposed to be the basis of religion; expect of course where Hate is deemed the Real Truth.

Tolerance for others' religious beliefs is the essential ingredient of humankinds future, and until various leaders, real and imagined, start to believe and practice this the future is indeed bleak. Presidents from America, Russia, Syria, Iran and many other countries need to 'Lift their game', but none of these seem capable or willing to do so. Down the ages, Religious Nationalism has been the root cause of many of history's disasters.

Jesus Christ is obviously a huge historical figure whose philosophy and teachings, if in fact they are directly from Christ, are sound and admirable. I personally hope that I abide by their essence, and admit to occasional feelings of the possibility of spiritual awareness. Atheists can claim immunity from responsibility but are generally bound by the tenets and rules of religion. AND HERE ENDETH MY RAVE. But, what if I have it wrong; as my father said as he neared the end, I suppose I will soon find out if there is an after-life.

THE DREADED 'SETTLE DOWN' PHASE

More motoring disasters! A slight collision in a shopping center parking exit caused $2900 damage. NRMA paid $2300. While driving to house sit for Andy in Forestville, suddenly my transmission ceases to work. Called the NRMA who informed me that as it is a sealed unit it will cost about $5500 to replace, no insurance. Just in time for Christmas. I had to be towed to Brookvale, and would have no car over Christmas, spend the holidays between Forestville and Terrigal.

February 2017, time to collect my belongings from the various places in which they are spread. Decided that Sydney is impossible to find a reasonable place in which to rent. The Central Coast, only an hour from Sydney by train, 2 hours by car, so I start to look around. Real Estate agent Raine & Horne shows me a unit, which after checking out a number of others I decide to rent. Two bedroom unit in small block, $300 per week. Robin and Graham generously provide space in their lock up for the things I cannot fit in the unit. I somewhat foolishly think all I need is a bed and a fridge. Robin thinks otherwise, and before I know it I have all kitchen, bedroom and living room furniture installed from her excess stock. I buy a TV, some bookshelves and start assembling my new life. I have collected some 350 LP records, over 500 CDs; DVDs and books, all of which I should probably cull, but am determined to keep; bought a new turntable and did a numbered catalogue of the records, confirming for some my anal retention nature.

James Everard, whom I have known for 40 years, has developed cancer which quickly ravaged his body. I was able to see him in hospital where he could recognize me but was unable to speak. He died a few weeks later and had a funeral attended by his many friends. In the meantime, Doctor Wong had me booked into Strathfield hospital for my prostate operation, which he said should see me out. On completion he told me to, "Come back when you are 97". Once again medical insurance and Medibank covered most of the cost. Andy and Anne complete the sale of their home in Forestville and purchase of a unit in Neutral Bay in Sydney. Concerts in Gosford with Merle and Margaret, mainly with Goldner Quartet; in Sydney joined the Art Gallery Society after going to an exhibition. My 76th Birthday, bought more furniture; getting too domesticated.

Continuing to enjoy life in the Central Coast, despite the various political and social upheavals which are increasingly making the future look very unpredictable. In no particular order I find myself concerned/alarmed/hopeful; Australian Drought, quickly followed by hugely destructive bushfires; floods in Queensland causing stock losses of over 200,000; school children's Climate Change walkouts inspiring millions, but evidently not politicians who think they should stay in school; can't wait for children to get to voting age; US politics (Trump) goes from bizarre to ridiculous; Trump declares war on ISIS won, territory certainly but US sources say there are some 218,000 jihadists still "under orders"; their leader, Al Baghdadi finally eliminated; much of the world's politics is dominated by Right Wing Strongmen, Putin, Trump, Xi Jinping, Duterte, Bolsonaro, Kim Jong Un, Bashar al Assad, Netanyahu, Al-Sisi in Egypt, plus many in Asia, Middle East and Africa. Think the world needs more females in control.

Meanwhile travel now seems, for me, to be in Australia. I fly to Perth to meet up with friends, Sonia Gurrin with whom I stay, Peter Jeffery, Phil and Jen in Busselton; go on demonstration to support Same Sex Marriage in WA Parliament. Passed in national poll 62%-38%. When I left Perth in 1962 the population was around 500,000, now some 2 million. Perth Airport much larger; when I lived in Perth the Airport bar was the only place to get a drink on a Sunday night. National Parliament resembles a Comic Opera, total of 15 Members now declared dual citizens and either seek re-election or quit. PM Turnbull reluctantly calls Bank Royal Commission, subsequent findings by that Commission show that

Bank and Financial institutions have been behaving very badly to their customers.

Back in Gosford, I meet Lynette, who lives a in a village in nearby Foresters Beach, and shortly after we sign up for a cruise to the Great Barrier Reef. Joined the ship in Brisbane, after driving up. Cruise quite pleasant, stopping in Cairns, Airlie Beach and going out to the middle of the Pacific to watch a weather balloon being released; uncontainable excitement.

Lynette and I have embarked on a number of Australian expeditions firstly to Victoria and Tasmania, from whence Lynette comes, and, as she has stated many times, she has never been "West of Wagga Wagga". Stayed in Victoria with friends Graham and Margit, drove around the countryside introducing Lynette to places she had never been to, then off to Tasmania where I was introduced to places and people from Lynette's life. Altogether an enjoyable eight weeks, despite the fires which had devastated much of the State, but smoke was the main impact for us. Visiting Maria Island and the Wall, a fantastic 200 meter sculpture in Huon Pine some 100 plus kms north of Hobart. A highlight for me was running into former Senator Jacqui Lambie at the Wellenough Pub somewhere in the bush, and later near Hobart where I had a ten minute chat with her.

ANOTHER SALUTORY LESSON

I sometimes wonder how I have got this far in life without some disaster occurring, but I still keep giving disaster a chance. In December 2018 I get a call from a man in Singapore asking if I would like to buy some shares in the Canadian cannabis company Aurora Cannabis. I did as many checks as I could on the Company, Hampton Trading International, very impressive website and no negative information I could find; bought 470 shares at Can$4.30, and watched them climb to as much as $14. transferred Aus$3474 to Bangkok Bank. Then things became complicated – but I am pretty fatalistic and decide it's 'all or nothing'. Phone calls and emails were getting nowhere until I was informed by Harry Robinson, Director, that Hampton had been sold to SAP One in Luxembourg on 31st May, and my 'portfolio' has been transferred to them, and are being properly handled by them. So begins the final chapter.

In the end my Bank counsels me that they think I have been scammed; the Luxembourg regulator, CSSF, issues a warning that SAP One is not known and should be avoided. Too late, but I have put myself in the game, and now the final whistle has been blown. Altogether I have put about $38,000 down the drain. Can only hope that I have learned the lesson.

TRAVELS IN AUSTRALIA

Lynette, who now calls me 'her travelling companion', goes alone to Kangaroo Island, before the devastating fires, and later we travel North and South to visit friends, before I persuade her that "West of Wagga" needs further examination, to which she somewhat dubiously agrees, so we set about planning, this time without caravan, now staying in motels, van park cabins. We set off, calling in on my friend Noel in Nowra, through NSW and Victoria, stopping in Yass and Mildura, to Kimba in South Australia, where, on a previous visit I had copped a Speeding Fine, $471, most expensive ever. Made sure I was legal this time. Stayed in B&B with Christine, long discussions about the possibility of Nuclear Waste being dumped there, which has divided the local community as well as that of the other possible site of Hawker in the Flinders Ranges. Having traditions to uphold, I managed to leave a thermos, map and folders behind. Pick them up on the way back.

Through Ceduna, Streaky Bay, Eucla on the WA Border, again across the Nullabor, I think for me about the sixth time. Driving on LPG, becoming more annoyed that so many service stations no longer stock it; none in Cockalbiddy or Balladonia. At Norseman, turn south to Esperance, staying at a chalet overlooking Twilight Beach, exploring my favorite coast east of Esperance, Cape le Grande, French's Mount and many of the beautiful beaches and coastlines. Back in Esperance to Stonehenge, a full sized replica of the original, but in much better shape, made with local stones. In Albany, another excellent chalet on the coast at Emu Point, visit to the Anzac War Memorial on Mount Clarence; the original Anzacs sailed from Albany in 1915. To the Gap, which now has wooden walkways to stop tourists falling in off the dangerous cliffs. When I first came here when I was working in the Bank, 1960, the signs warned of King Waves, which would sometimes wash over the top of the 90' cliffs. One legend tells of a local, picked up by a King

Wave, deposited on a ledge some 20' from the top, then another wave came, picked him up and put him back on top.

In Denmark, after doing the Valley of the Giants treetop walk, was having coffee in a café when I recognized from the back, Steve and Jenny Pickering from Sydney, whom I had not seen for about 30 years; his hair cut has not changed at all.

On to Perth via Fremantle Markets, where I searched for the Indian curry lady, from whom I was under instructions from Bev in Bathurst to buy her fabulous curry powders; Indian lady gone, but now curries from Sri Lankan lady also excellent. Met up with Peter and Julie, some blues music in the Inglewood Bowling Club, which was now situated in what was in my youth the 'bottom paddock'. Julie is now doing a weekly Blues program on local Community radio and I loaned her some of my Blues CDs, then off to stay with Sonia again.

My right leg has been extremely painful for the whole trip, had X rays and scans done but no time for any treatments. Drove to Busselton to visit Phil and Jen, Lynette visiting friends in Fremantle, before heading East again. Got another speeding ticket in the Darling Ranges, this time only $100, Irish cop says he is more friendly than Kimba cop. Booked into motel in Coolgardie, and of course headed for the Denver City Hotel. Melbourne Cup Day, as we arrived at the bar, a young guy was cheering on his horse on the TV; it came 2nd, he dropped $500. He was a worker in the nearby sandalwood plantation, but later on the night finished $450 in front, and also had a massage from Lynette. I, in the meantime, was getting the Good Oil from Bob, the champion Prospector, who gave me a list of all the companies who have recently struck gold; I have not invested. Dave from Townsville also a great source of local knowledge and laughs. Never had a dull night whenever I have stopped in the Denver City.

On to Kalgoorlie, visit to the Super Pit, big enough to swallow a small city, but said to be closed in 2021; one suggestion is to fill it with water, but not sure where that scarce commodity would come from. At the Pitt head museum, a great documentary on CY O'Conner, the engineer responsible for much of WA's infrastructure, including the Goldfields Pipeline and Fremantle

Harbour. Lynette was anxious to visit the top tourist attraction, La Casa brothel, but it was closed for lunch, or something.

Back across the Nullabor, stopped at Caiguna overnight; went looking for the Caiguna Blowhole, scrub bashing for 20 minutes before I realized it was 100 meters off the highway. Back to South Australia, a day in the Flinders Ranges, particularly Wilpena Pound, Quorn and Hawker, which featured many No Nuclear signs; beer in the Blinman Pub with John, recently returned to take up his 70 hectares holding, on which he is hopeful of finding a vein of a precious metal, the name of which I have forgotten, but he has plenty of experience; hope he finds it.

Through Ceduna again, two days in villa by Lake Boga, home to one of the Catalina bases during the War, now a Museum. Car made some funny noises, took it to local garage in Swan Hill, but after number of tests could not find anything. Drove on and the noise went away. On to Bathurst and Orange, went to Banjo Paterson's birthplace, another Speeding ticket $100, then home. Total 11,500 kms with no car trouble, apart from Swan Hill.

THE STATE OF THINGS, THROUGH MY JAUNDICED EYE

Back in the Central Coast, without any contribution from me, the World, and Australia, lurches from crisis to events. Australia loses another Prime Minister, attempt by Right Wing Dutton fails, and almost by default Morrison is elected, calls election with hardly a policy and, mainly on the anti-Labor leader Shorten vote, is elected with two seat majority.

In the US Trump acts as if all he has to do is sign Executive Orders cancelling anything done by Obama. China continues on its path of World domination through economic pressure and military threats; Trump and Xi Jinping the two most dangerous virtual dictators in the World. Iran and Israel provide plenty of concerns, Iran through the domination of the Mullahs, Israel by threatening to annex large parts of the Jordan Valley. Trump's pulling out of the Iran deal to insult Barack Obama, then to pull out of WHO because of perceived pro China bias is simple childish behavior. Most of the world's populations seem to be disenchanted with politicians, with the result that right wing and extremist groups are coming to power in Europe, Asia, America and Africa.

What is even more disturbing is that most of these right wing populists are elected; Australia has its share but hopefully on the fringes. Trump's inner cabinet of sons, daughters and in-laws seem to hold a lot of power but no solutions, particularly in the Middle East. Britain finally gets its Brexit, but the future still looks vague in economic terms. Who is going to work on their farms and orchards?

Violence continues to flourish throughout the world; massacres in New Zealand, Britain, Sri Lanka the worst of many. In the US, the seeming unending stories of Police shootings suddenly come to a boil, the Black Lives Matter movement erupts around the world, bringing promises, yet to be fulfilled, of major changes, but shootings continue. The BLM movement morphs into an anti-historical-racist movement; statues of virtually anyone not a saint are pulled down and insulted. The most egregious insults are to Captain James Cook, who, because of his brief voyage of discovery on Australia's East coast, has been falsely accused of racism and murder. Winston Churchill, who certainly had racist views, particularly towards Indians, is a prime target, although his only physical acts of violence were against African lions, which he delighted in shooting as a young soldier; I think his leadership against the real racists in Germany outweighs his faults. Having said all that, racist attitudes, politics, religious violence has taken hits through the recent events and hopefully will bring about some real changes in the near future.

The world's biggest crisis hits in early 2020; a virus which originated in the Chinese city of Wuhan's wet meat markets erupts on the world. Coronavirus, Covid19 is suddenly the worst crisis since WW2. Spain and Italy are the worst hit initially, but the rest of the world is quickly affected. People like Trump, Boris Johnson, Bolsonaro in Brazil, try to laugh it off; Boris contracts the virus and spends two weeks in hospital near death. Trump tries to sell the idea of injecting detergent into lungs will be the cure; Bolsonaro laughs it off as 'a little flu', but later contacts it while his country suffers, at over 150,000, the second largest death toll, after the US, in the world. Sweden says 'not to worry, just keep on normally', and has a death rate one of the world's worst. New Zealand and Australia seem to be handling it well, but still with problems. US States, Texas, Florida and Arizona were big deniers, but soon become the hardest hit, after New York got over its initial disastrous infections.

Too many concerns which I am unable to influence, only to have a vocal opinion. The treatment of refugees in Australia, the advice to overseas students when the virus hit, to 'go home', which for many was not possible rankles. While I try, putting these concerns to one side is not possible, and I really must be thankful to be in Australia, which for all its faults remains the best place to be alive in, contrary no doubt to the opinions of millions.

So I have come to some temporary finality, if that is possible. My hope resides in the first phrase I learned in German 'Alles ist Möglich' – Everything is Possible; perhaps not everything.